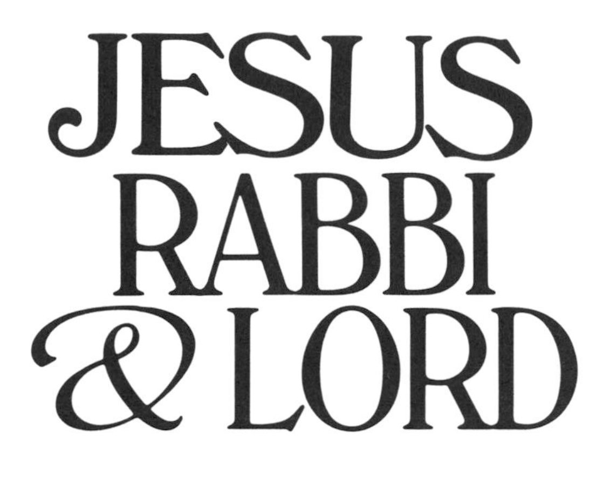

THE HEBREW STORY OF JESUS
BEHIND OUR GOSPELS

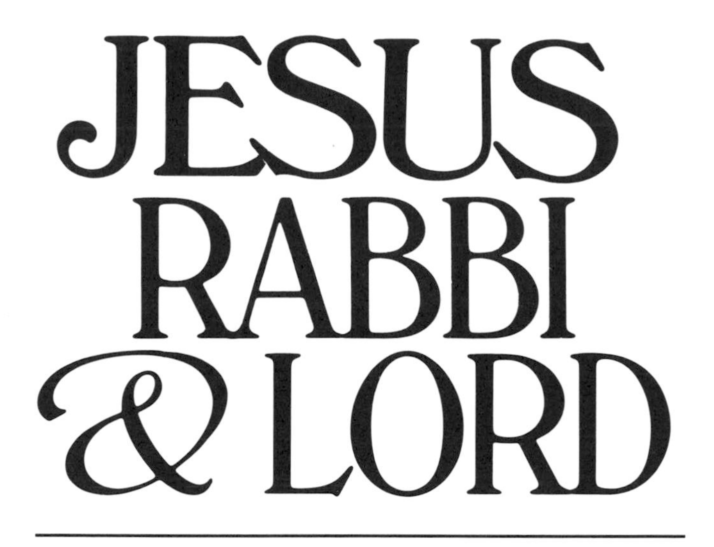

The Hebrew Story of Jesus Behind our Gospels

Robert L. Lindsey

Oak Creek, Wisconsin

Jesus Rabbi & Lord

P.O. Box 311 Oak Creek, WI 53154

Cover Design by Joe Ragont
Cover Photo: Sea of Galilee by David Harris

All Scripture quotations are translations made by the author.

Library of Congress Catalog Card Number 89-062723
ISBN 0-9623950-0-5
CJ-5000

Printed in the United States of America

May 1990 First Edition

Contents

Foreword

Very few Christian scholars have ever even come close to doing what Robert Lisle Lindsey has done: experience almost fifty years of serious engagement with the New Testament text, in the geographic context of its narratives, in dialogue with the person whom some believe to be the world's leading Jewish authority on Jesus and the New Testament.

Robert Lindsey's story has something for all of us. For those who are interested in a personal perspective on events in Israel and Mandatory Palestine before its birth, there is the fascination of this young University of Oklahoma graduate as he encounters Jerusalem prior to World War II, and is a participant in its changes across the years with his growing family.

Biblical scholars will find intrigue in Lindsey's adventure with the documents which give us three biographers' perspectives on Jesus' life: the synoptic Gospels. His "detective" work, tracking clues and investigating the evidence of our earliest texts, led Lindsey to conclusions that challenged the assumptions of the scholarship he had learned to respect. He was not alone in his search for the earliest Gospel text and its meaning. One fellow "investigator" in the examination of the evidence he was confronting, was an orthodox Jew, who became a close colleague, Professor David Flusser.

Lindsey and Flusser for many years carried on a study of the Gospels together at the prestigious Hebrew University of Jerusalem where Flusser taught early Christianity in modern Hebrew. They also met frequently in Flusser's home. Rarely, if ever, have a Baptist and a Jewish scholar been involved together so intensely in scholarly pursuit — and in Jerusalem. They challenged each other, shared their discoveries, and were struck by the conclusions to which they were compellingly drawn.

What were these conclusions? One had to do with the nature of the documents behind our present Gospels: they could not avoid the evidence of an original Hebrew source, no longer extant. They felt they had to reject some widely-held assumptions of New Testament scholarship as to which Gospel was first composed, and propose some fresh ideas to which their research led them.

Lindsey's experience in Israel has not been in an ivory tower. His study and writing have been integrated into a life of service among people. He is convinced that the message of Jesus has continuing relevance, that God's kingdom not only broke into history during Jesus' earthly ministry, but that it may also be experienced in healing and other life-transforming events today.

From the beginning of the almost 12 years I lived in Jerusalem, I had the privilege of numerous associations with Robert and Margaret Lindsey. I learned from them: I was impressed with their integrity, their love for the peoples of today's Israel as well as for the Bible. Their friendship enriched my life. In a seminar led by Dr. Lindsey, with the participation of scholars from Asia and South America, I had a taste of that exciting adventure of research in the Gospels. The book that follows will introduce you to that world in a personal, challenging and thought-provoking way.

Wesley H. Brown
Professor
American Baptist Seminary of the West
Berkeley, California

Author's Preface

This book is an attempt to tell in a simple way why I have come to a number of conclusions about the life and words of Jesus as they have been handed down to us in the Gospels of Matthew, Mark and Luke.

My experience reflects nearly half a century of constant contact with the people of Israel, where I lived with my family in the city of Jerusalem and where people like Professor David Flusser of the Hebrew University gave me the warmth of their friendship and knowledge and studied with me as the relationships of the sources of the life of Jesus became clearer and the person of Jesus more manifest.

My conclusions are not all new and often agree with those scholars of a hundred years ago who approached our Gospels with the conviction that they are reliable, if secondary, reports of the words and deeds of Jesus of Nazareth recorded in the first century of this era. I am thinking of students like Lightfoot, Delitsch, Blass, Dalman, Thayer and Edersheim who laid the foundations of the study of Jesus as a first century Jew whose Jewish and Messianic consciousness lies like a silver coin in a dark pool on every page of our Semitic Gospels.

It has become the fashion to assume that our Gospels originally appeared as little loose-leaf collections of this or that story or teaching of Jesus which had descended orally among Greek-speaking, non-Jewish, Christians and had been collected after much distortion and addition by Hellenistic Christians late in the first century. Some famous modern scholars have maintained that our Gospels retain only a few sentences which can be said to go back to the mouth of Jesus and that a large number of the short narrative incidents in our sources were in fact invented to accompany some aphorism or saying of Jesus dimly remembered by early Greek Christians.

I have told in my book *A Hebrew Translation of the Gospel of Mark* (Dugith, 1973, Baptist House, P. O. Box 154, Jerusalem, Israel) of the way in which I came to doubt this general assumption of modern New Testament scholarship and in the present work I repeat some of the argument there, but hope what I here write will provide many further reasons for asserting that our Gospel materials retain highly authentic pictures of Jesus and his teaching which no Greek community could have produced in the Hebraic and Jewish form they now share in especially the Gospels of Luke and Matthew.

Not only do many of our narrative, teaching and parable units present a Greek text which can be translated *word by word* to Hebrew (something only translated Greek materials usually demonstrate) but the units themselves have been so well preserved that we are even able to join together scattered units which at a pre-canonical period appeared in written Greek texts as *longer* stories.

This would be impossible had our "loose-leaf" stories gone through a process of Greek addition and embellishment of the kind suggested by many New Testament scholars of today.

In short, our Gospels clearly reflect a tradition of *written* records which descended from one principal Greek translation of the Hebrew life of Jesus which as early as 135 A.D. Papias refers to as "the oracles — or things — of Jesus" written by the Apostle Matthew "in Hebrew."

What was this first documentary of the life and sayings of Jesus like? So far as we can tell it was a story written on the plan of the typical Old Testament story of David, or Elijah, or Elisha. Jesus came to the Jordan to be baptized by John, he then went to Capernaum, to Nazareth, to Bethsaida, to Jericho, *etc.* In each of these places he performed a miracle, or met and conversed with a synagogue ruler, or gathered disciples, or taught his followers.

All this is typical Hebrew biography and although our texts have been passed down to us with many signs of rearrangement, the essential story of Jesus and the materials for that story are preserved so well that we can catch hundreds of Hebrew and rabbinic nuances. So certain am I and some of my colleagues in Jerusalem that this is true that more than a dozen Semitic scholars meet regularly there today as "The Jerusalem School for the Study of the Synoptic Gospels" and hope one day to produce a careful commentary on these Gospels.

One Christian theologian once asked me: "Do you believe this Hebrew life of Jesus you talk about was inerrant?"

My answer to such a question is that that Hebrew source — did we have it — would be for many of us truly inerrant, seeing it must have been the work of an eyewitness (compare Luke 1:1-4). Whoever wrote it — and I see no reason to think it was not the Matthew Papias mentions — has written down the words, expressions and stories of a genius. Were it true, as so many scholars suppose, that the "Hellenistic Church" painted the picture of Jesus we have in the Gospels the

"Church" would turn out to be the most amazing inventor of all time, and to all intents and purposes, greater than Jesus.

The evidence is otherwise.

No doubt many will say that my story here is "too popular to be scholarly" and "too scholarly to be popular" and that may well be true. My apology is only that as I neared the famous three-score and ten I decided this book would have to be popular enough to honor my kind friends of yesteryear yet say many things a gracious Providence has allowed me to see about Jesus.

1 WAS THIS JESUS' BOAT?

Early in 1986 a strange, plastic-covered, boat-like object was slowly dragged through the shallow waters of the kibbutz Ginosar on the western shore of the Sea of Galilee. Its destination was a special pool built at the shore of the lake and eventually covered over as a part of the new museum at Ginosar.

Hundreds of Israelis, many of them members of Kibbutz Ginosar, watched the scene with fascination and curiosity. It is not every day that an ancient, wooden ship is unearthed in Israel.

The age of the boat has been determined by Israeli archeologists to be over 1800 years. Somewhere between 100 B.C. and 100 A.D. the ship plied the waters of the Sea of Galilee, a beautiful lake set in the Jordan Valley some 14 miles long and about 7 miles wide.

How was the ship found? Due to the lack of rain for several years before the boat was found the surface of the lake had gone down more than nine feet and since the plain around Ginosar slowly drops into the Sea of Galilee, making a long, slow beach, someone who had walked out to the water saw one day the rough outlines of a wooden boat lying full of clay only a few feet below the lake's surface.

The kibbutz members of Ginosar were alerted. They called in Israeli archeologists and experts who came to check into this unusual find. Parts of the exposed, wooden sides were examined under microscope and found to be ancient. Eventually the date between 100 B.C. and 100 A.D. was determined.

Someone said, "Maybe this was the boat Jesus used when he sailed with his twelve disciples from village to village around the shore of the Sea of Galilee in the time of the "Second Temple," as the first century is called in Israel. The newspapers picked up the story and soon everyone in Israel had heard that "the boat perhaps used by Jesus and his disciples" had been found. Since then many Israelis speak of the ancient craft as "the Jesus boat."

Most of the Israelis around the lake know very little about Jesus but some of them have read the first books in the New Testament — the Gospels of Matthew, Mark, Luke and John — which tell about the life of Jesus. A few of these have read widely and studied the words and teaching of Jesus and marked on maps the various places mentioned in the Gospels where Jesus healed and taught its Jewish inhabitants so long ago.

They call the Sea of Galilee by the ancient name of *Kinnereth*, or *Kinneret*, which may itself be derived from the word for harp *(kinnor)* in Hebrew. This famous lake does indeed bear the shape of the harps of antiquity. On the northwest edge of the Sea is a dusty tel or ruin thought to be the remains of a town known in biblical times as *Kinnereth*.

In the days of Jesus, roughly between 4 B.C. and 30 A.D., the Sea of Galilee bustled with activity. Nine towns lined its shores and in some of these the sound of ax and hammer rose above the marketplaces as ships of many sizes were constructed. Fishing boats searched the edges of the lakes by day and night and so many fish were taken that one town was named Tarichaea (from *tarichei*, Greek for fish) because in it thousands of tons of fish were salted down or dried and sent to Jerusalem and abroad each year.

It is not surprising that Herod Antipas, one of the sons of Herod the Great, was given control of Perea (a strip down the Jordan River on its east side) and of the province of Galilee and moved his provincial headquarters from Sepphoris in Galilee to Tiberias, which he founded in about 18 A.D. He was the ruler of Galilee and Perea when Jesus went healing and teaching and gathering disciples around the lake in about 26 A.D.

Although Jews in this period avoided Tiberias because certain heaps of bones had been found by Herod when he began to build the city, they later settled it in large numbers after the destruction of Jerusalem by the Romans in 70 A.D. In fact it became a large center of rabbinic learning between 200 and 500 A.D. and famous rabbis like Rabbi Yochanan ben Zakkai, Rabbi Meir, and Rabbi Akiva were buried there, their graves still to be seen.

However, when the Muslim conquerors came in the eighth century the town was already in decline. We hear little of the city, except at the time when it was conquered by the Crusader leader Tancred, who built a fortress which is still to be seen there. In 1835 a visitor reported that "there is not even one boat on the Sea." In 1873 one tourist spoke of crossing the lake in the "only boat on the entire Sea of Galilee." Things became better at the beginning of the present century as Arab fishermen and, somewhat later, Jewish fishermen, began to catch fish in commercial quantities.

Even today, with fishing at its highest level in many centuries (principally through the efforts of Kibbutz Ein Gev on the eastern shore) the lake is more famous for its new, luxurious hotels in Tiberias and the crowds of Israelis who line the shores in tents on Sabbaths and holidays than for its fishing. And because the Gospels are filled with stories about the activities of Jesus around the sea thousands of Christian tourists crowd Tiberias, Capernaum and the shores of the lake throughout the year.

That was one of the reasons for the interest in the finding of "Jesus' boat." In fact, the Israel Tourist Department in Jerusalem rejoiced that even if it could not be proven that the newly-discovered ship was used by Jesus it would be possible to establish another important tourist attraction for Christians by displaying the new boat.

Happily, the members of Kibbutz Ginosar, who were already building a large museum as a tourist attraction, were given the privilege of building an enclosed reservoir where the boat would be preserved in water and chemical liquids and it is today on view for a small fee near the kibbutz motel.

Guides at the museum will tell you that it is highly doubtful that Jesus used this boat but "altogether possible." And why not?

2 SO LARGE A BOAT

What really struck me when I first read the story in the newspapers about the kibbutzniks from Ginosar finding this ancient boat was the *size* of the ship.

I mean, for many years, as a pastor of a Baptist congregation in Jerusalem, I had read and reread the Gospels and thought of Jesus and his disciples going from place to place around the Sea of Galilee. Many of the Gospel stories I had used to illustrate my sermons or to show their relevance to our lives today.

But for some reason I had always thought of the fishing boats as about the size of most of the little boats fishermen use today.

In fact, when many years ago we were searching for a name to call the new gallery the Baptists were opening in Tel Aviv, we chose the name suggested by Israel Pincas, an Israeli poet. He said that "dugit" would be a nice name for our gallery.

Now in Hebrew *dugit* means a small, rather cute, short, fisherman's boat. At Israel's request a Tel Aviv artist drew up a logo which I print here:

Chandler Lanier, one of our Baptist pastors in Tel Aviv, has used it in publications for many years. Everyone likes it.

It just had not occurred to me that Jesus would have needed a much larger boat than the little *dugit* which one or two fishermen would have used. Even the boats I had seen being used at the Sea of Galilee were seldom more than fourteen to seventeen feet, but the ship that had been found was some 7 1/2 feet wide and more than 27 feet long.

That is a good-size fishing boat.

On second thought maybe it was not really a typical fishing boat at all. Maybe it was a ship employed to carry twelve to fifteen people commercially from place to place. When we read that

> ... one day Jesus got into a boat with his disciples and said to them, "Let us go across to the other side of the lake ..." (Luke 8:22)

it may mean that he had *hired* a large boat and that not only his twelve disciples but a crew of three or four, who operated the ship, were with him in the boat.

We read that

> ... as they were sailing, Jesus went to sleep. A strong wind blew down on the lake, and the boat began to fill with water, putting them all in great danger. The disciples came to Jesus and woke him up, saying, "Master, Master! we are about to die!"
> Jesus got up and gave a command to the wind and to the stormy water. They quieted down and there was a great calm. Then he said to his disciples, "Where is your faith?" (Luke 8:23-25).

We know from the ancient historian Josephus that boats of considerable size were built at the Sea of Galilee and that actual battles were fought between Romans and Jews in their ships not long before Jerusalem was destroyed.

So it should not have been such a surprise to me to think of Jesus traveling with twelve to fifteen men around the Lake of Kinnereth in a boat larger than a typical fisherman's craft.

In any case the finding of the "Jesus boat" has compelled me to correct my idea of the size of the ship he used from time to time in his ministry.

I like that. It is good to get some ideas straightened out.

3 I FISH IN GALILEE

Right here I need to tell you how I got interested in fishing in this famous lake called Kinnereth, or Kinneret.

It all started with two of my sons when they were very small.

During two years, in 1961 and 1962, I lived with my family in a great old house belonging to the Scottish Hospice, just a hundred steps up from the harbor at Tiberias. My wife Margaret and I had six children, three of which were older and were boarding school students at the Baptist Village near Petach Tikva. The oldest was David and with his younger, teenage sisters Lenore and Barbara he came home to Tiberias only on the weekend. Danny and Robert were eight and six years old at the time and their younger sister, Debbie, four.

One day Margaret and I took Danny, Robert and Debbie up to the Plain of Gennesaret (the Greek-derived name of Ginosar) for a swim. We passed down through the ruins of old Magdala (*Mejdel* had been the Arabic name and it was the village from which Mary Magdalene had come) and parked under the enormous eucalyptus trees near the shore. It was a balmy day with the western afternoon winds blowing gently towards the lake from the banana orchards and Margaret and I sat watching our children play on the sandy shore.

The surface of the lake was at the time higher than usual and little waves covered the roots of the eucalyptus trees, making a shallow area where small perch or bream lay sunning themselves at the edge of the shadows. Being boys, my sons could not resist climbing a couple of the trees and hanging lazily from the limbs. After a while we noticed that they had climbed down and gone up again with strings which they lowered with hooks to try to catch the perch.

And they did succeed somehow in catching a small fish or two and then shouting out at the top of their high voices, now and then, "I got one! Look, Mommy, Look Daddy."

As a lad growing up in Oklahoma, in the United States, I had spent many a Saturday with hook and line trying to catch the perch in our small ponds and creeks. Suddenly a memory long laid aside under piles of "more important things" asserted itself and I decided to try some fishing myself.

People in the Middle East often fish with just a line and hook, using for bait a tiny piece of bread. My ideas were Oklahoma ones. I bought some bamboo poles, a spool of nylon line and with Danny and Robert and sometimes their older brother David I dug for fishing worms or caught grasshoppers near the mouth of the Jordan.

Sure enough the little perch bit frantically at the worms or grasshoppers on my hook.

We learned to wade into the water and drop a baited hook near a half-covered shrub or oleander bush. I even made a little raft of big, factory, plastic bottles and we anchored it with a rope to a rock and fished from it.

Slowly we began to "get the hang of it" and to learn a little about the kind of fish the Sea of Galilee has in it.

The books I consulted rarely told much about the fish in the lake but one day at Yehuda Avni's ranch — Vered Hagalil — north of the Sea, I met a man who knew a lot about the fish in the lake. He called himself a "limnologist" (from the Greek for lake — *limny*) and he was an American expert in this field, lent to the State of Israel as a consultant on lakes.

From him I learned that the Kinneret was only on the average about one hundred and twenty meters deep (four hundred feet), that one of its problems was that its bottom was covered with so much silt that few springs were strong enough to throw their waters up through the silt to give oxygen to the fish population, but that in spite of this some sixteen or seventeen separate species of fish lived in the sea.

He told me that of the native fish there were at least eight species of "mouth-breeders." These are little bream or perch which largely live on the algae at the surface. Both the mother and the father come up and stick their noses out of the water, somehow signalling to the baby fish in their mouths to swim out to eat.

On a calm day you can often see these noses surfacing by the hundreds. If you try to approach them as you are swimming they disappear below with their alerted offspring safely in their mouths.

And there are lots of catfish which bear the scientific name *Clarias machro*.

They grow up to three feet in length. One time in the Plain of Ginosar my boys and I watched in fascination as some of these creatures noisily flipped and flopped over each other in shallow water while breeding. Fishermen in Tiberias sometimes catch catfish in their nets and, although they are not kosher, they report that some of the physicians in the area eat them because of the large amount of iodine found in their flesh.

One of the parables or illustrations used by Jesus comes close to mentioning the catfish:

> The Kingdom of Heaven is like a net thrown out in the lake, which catches all kind of fish. When it is full, the fishermen pull it to shore and sit down to divide the fish: the good ones go into their buckets, the worthless ones are thrown away. It will be like this at the end of the age: the angels will go out and gather up the evil people from the good, and throw them into the fiery furnace (Matthew 13:47-50).

Apparently the "worthless fish" are catfish while the "good ones" are those which have scales and fins. The "good ones" are, no doubt, the kosher ones, valid for eating by any Orthodox Jew, including Jesus.

4 TO PALESTINE IN 1939

I first came to the country we now call Israel when it was called Palestine.

The date was February 4, 1939 and I had just been graduated from the University of Oklahoma where my father had been treasurer for many years. I had until then lived with my father and mother just three blocks from the university campus. I was never to return to live with them again.

My reason for "going to Jerusalem," as my mother put it, was to fulfill a desire to learn Hebrew in the land where Jews again were speaking this ancient language.

My father attributed my desire to go to far places as a kind of wanderlust which, he said, is in the veins "of all the Lindseys." Nonetheless he was sympathetic, even though he had warned me at 16 when I felt my call to preach in the country districts around my home town, that I should remember the dream a young man like myself had had long before this. He saw in his dream, high in the heavens, three bold, golden letters: G P C ! He understood them to mean, "Go Preach Christ." Others who heard him preach decided the startling letters really meant, "Go Plow Corn!"

One of the reasons my father's parable did not affect my feeling of call was the pastor of my home church, Dr. E. F. Hallock, whom all of us called "Preacher" affectionately. His was a university church packed constantly with young students. My mother and father had been faithful members of this church, the First Baptist Church of Norman, Oklahoma for many years and their pastor, and mine, Preacher Hallock, had helped me through the waters of baptism when I was eleven years old.

He had also spent many hours teaching Bible to me and to a number of other students at the student center run by my church. During all my college years I had attended this center with other livewire youngsters whose motivation was deeply religious. The young woman who directed these out-of-curriculum classes, Susan Daniel, had encouraged us all to "hear as much as you can from Preacher Hallock who has so much to give."

It was he who gave me the deep, personal interest in the Bible I have never lost. Already at 18 I was holding two services a day in out-of-town schoolhouses where I would gather country teenagers and younger to preach to them the "things of the Lord." When I did not know what to preach, Preacher would go over a sermon he often preached, and teach me how to preach it.

Preacher believed in two big things needed by every believer: prayer and Bible reading. He read the Bible through twice yearly and constantly looked for a "promise" from the Word which he could lean on in his busy life.

He taught us that God was interested in the simplest prayers we could pray. "There is no prayer too small for Him," he said over and over, and he would quote that verse from the Old Testament: "before they call I will answer them" or Jesus' words, "Ask and you shall receive, seek and you shall find, knock and it shall be opened unto you" (Matthew 7:7).

Preacher Hallock was an intelligent, highly-educated man who, as a young man, had lost his childhood faith but regained it when his first son, Edgar, recovered from his cerebral meningitis within minutes after five thousand people prayed for him at an interdenominational tent campaign in Topeka, Kansas.

He told us stories like these:

> "When my son Edgar was five years old we had prayers around the breakfast table. His mother and I had always allowed him to pray his own prayer. Little Edgar prayed that morning for his parents, thanked God for his home and ended his prayer with these words: 'and, dear God, please send me a little white dog today.' Of course, we did not quite know what to do. But that afternoon two little boys appeared at our front door and when we opened it they showed us a little white dog and asked us if we wanted it!"

Preacher used to say, "When you read the Bible God is speaking to you. When you pray you are speaking to God. A bird has to fly on two wings. Your wings are Bible reading and prayer."

Under his influence I started reading the Bible. I read it by chapter, by verse, by book, by theme, by attention to the stories of the personalities in it, by the very words, many of which I did not fully understand.

As a young preacher, almost as young as the teenagers I so often preached to in the little tenant schoolhouses around my hometown, I remember some of my difficulties trying to tell of what God could and did want to do for them. As a Baptist and evangelical I felt it my duty to speak of truth and right ways of doing things and of the power of Jesus through his Holy Spirit to help us overcome unhappiness, wrong, unforgiveness and wrongdoing. All this was included, I knew, in the spiritual salvation available to people of all kinds and ages.

In the New Testament words like salvation, redemption and reconciliation were frequent and spoke to my evangelical heart. However, when I looked for these words in the Old Testament, which for me was fully as much the Word of God as the New Testament, I could not seem to find them.

It took me a long time to find equivalents for these great words in the Old Testament. Only gradually did I come to see that if I took a concordance and looked up the word "righteousness" in the Psalms or in Isaiah or even in Genesis I could discover that this word was the real expression equivalent to the word "salvation" in the New Testament. In the same way I learned eventually that to make a covenant with God was one way Israel's prophets talked when personal salvation or redemption was in mind. And there were other ways of talking, other words, which were fully as powerful and meaningful as those I knew from evangelical preaching and the New Testament.

But all this was largely in the future. I needed more study.

One day I asked Preacher Hallock how I could ever really know the Bible.

"Well," he said slowly, "you will need to go to a good theological seminary of course. There you will have expert teachers who can help you to be a good preacher and teacher. But the most important thing is that you will need to study the Hebrew and Greek languages, because the Old Testament was written in Hebrew and the New Testament in Greek."

These helpful words came before I had even started to university. At the University of Oklahoma at that time it was possible to major in the study of Greek but there were no classes in Hebrew. I decided that at least I should get a good foundation in Greek. With a small number of students I studied for four years the writings of Xenophon, Plato, Socrates, Aristophanes and Homer. It was all very hard work but I wanted to be able to read the Greek of the New Testament.

I did not yet know that it was equally as important to know Hebrew when reading large parts of the New Testament. I am now certain that at least many parts of the Gospels were translated from Hebrew!

But how was I ever to know Hebrew? From a few Jewish students I came to know at least the alphabet. Through them and through reading I then found out about the Jewish colonization of Palestine. I learned that although Hebrew had largely been a dead language for many hundreds of years it was now being revived as a spoken language in the "yishuv," the Jewish areas of Jerusalem, Tel Aviv and Palestine.

I then borrowed a page from my study of French as a modern and spoken language. I had learned that I had a certain aptitude for language. How would it be, I wondered, if I could somehow get to Palestine and study Hebrew in, say, a kibbutz or school where I would be practicing the language on the streets and in the shops and among other students of my own age?

This idea fascinated me. I began to pray and plan to get to Palestine somehow.

But where would I get the money?

Preacher's training again came into focus. "Find a promise in Scripture," he always said.

And one day it came.

I was reading the Book of Isaiah. The words the Lord God spoke to Cyrus the king of Babylon suddenly stood out on the page.

> I will go before you and make the
> crooked places straight.
> I will give you the treasures of darkness,
> and hidden riches of secret places (Isaiah 45:1-3).

A few months before I was graduated I got a job selling coupons for a photographer. It went well. Some good-hearted people heard of my plan to go to Palestine and at first thought it a strange idea but later handed me a few dollars here, a few dollars there. My parents saw my determination and helped.

A few days after completing my university studies I was aboard the large Italian liner, the *Conte de Savoia*, headed for Palestine!

Three weeks later I woke up one morning and looked for the first time from the deck at the city of Haifa and at that long, low sandy-looking range of mountains stretching behind her from Dan to Beer-sheba.

With fifty other tourists of my own group I was soon aboard a khaki-colored, Arab-driven bus rolling to Jerusalem.

It was February 4, 1939.

5 MY BEST FRIENDS

Polititians and all kinds of people have often been known to speak derogatively about Jewish people while in the same breath saying, "Some of my best friends are Jews." When this happens Jewish people smile, well knowing that the person speaking is probably a little anti-Jewish at heart.

I who had grown up on the plains of Oklahoma in a town which had perhaps four native Jewish families among 10,000 inhabitants was suddenly and unceremoniously immersed in a city of more than one hundred thousand people, most of whom were Jews. They were shopkeepers, government clerks, carpenters, plumbers, teachers, day laborers, stone masons. By religion many were Orthodox Jews, but most were purely secular in their habits and interests.

And they — at least most of them — were speaking Hebrew! The ancient language of the Bible. The language of Moses and Joshua, of Samuel and David. The language of the prophets!

I was excited, and through a Swiss Jewish lady I met who shared many of my evangelical beliefs, Miss Irene Goldschmidt, I was soon living in a little apartment in Geula in Jerusalem with a Hebrew-speaking family, with Zebulon and Ruth Weinstock.

The Weinstocks were sturdy, simple people who lived, like so many others in Jerusalem, on an extremely small income which he made teaching the occasional foreigner a bit of Hebrew or working as a maintenance man in one of the churches in West Jerusalem. The plan was that I should eat with them, sleep on a couch in the living-room-dining-room and get Zebulon to teach me the rudiments of Hebrew.

The Weinstocks were like mother and father to this twenty-one-year-old boy from America.

Zebulon took me around Jerusalem on walking tours. He took me to the Old City, to the Ultra-Orthodox area called Mea Shearim which was just down the street from our neighborhood, to the Western Wall (sometimes known as the Wailing Wall) near the central mosque on the Temple Mount, to the famous Great Synagogue in the Old City and to many other points of Jewish interest. He also introduced me to many young people and others who helped me in my first attempts at pronouncing and spelling Hebrew.

In a few weeks it seemed I could honestly say, not "some of my best friends are Jews," but "*all* my best friends are Jews!"

Of course I came to know and appreciate many young Arab Christians as well. Some of them visited the little Baptist chapel where I and my family were later to live and minister for many years. But the Weinstocks kept me struggling to learn the new language and to fit into Jewish Jerusalem.

They had a beautiful little daughter named Aviva. She was three years old and her long hair was kept in a braid by her mother. I learned a lot of my first Hebrew words from her.

Aviva would open the door for me when I would wander into the flat after riding my bicycle here and there across the hills of Jerusalem. When she did so she would shout, her blue eyes shining like silver, "Hineh Bob, hineh Bob!" and she pronounced my name as if it were Bobe, rhyming with "robe." *Hineh* is the word so often translated in our English Bible, "behold" or "lo." Thus she was saying, "Behold, Bob" but the Hebrew meant, quite simply, "Look, here is Bob!"

Learning Hebrew this way was just what I had wanted!

Later, with Zebulon helping me, I wrote out the forms and conjugations of dozens of verbs and expressions and began to read the easier portions of the Hebrew Bible. I was even encouraged to pray spontaneously in Hebrew at the breakfast table, a thing I did with many mistakes amid frequent moments of embarrassment.

Thus it happened that in November, 1945, when Margaret and our first two children, David and Lenore, came back to Palestine with me after studies in the United States I already had a speaking knowledge of Hebrew.

We settled into Baptist House at 4 Narkis Street in West Jerusalem and began our long stay in this land.

Year went by after year. There was much to do to help the struggling believers who came to the Baptist Chapel. We had, eventually, in all, six children and most of these went to Israeli kindergartens and schools and spoke Hebrew like all the other youngsters.

We still laugh and say, "All our best friends are Jews!"

In summarizing this chapter I find I must simply state that in my experience it is necessary to translate the Greek texts of Matthew, Mark and Luke to Hebrew word by word to recover the earliest form of the story of Jesus.

6 GALILEE AND HEBREW

Right from the beginning, as Margaret and I and our children lived on Narkis street in the heart of Jewish Jerusalem, we felt a close relationship with the people in our neighborhood and indeed the whole "yishuv." Learning Hebrew was an important key.

It helped when I found it my duty to purchase the property now known as Dugith Gallery in Tel Aviv. It helped when our family managed the new Baptist Village and its nineteen Arab orphan children for three years in 1956-60. It helped as I took on the task of editing a number of Hebrew translations of books like C. S. Lewis' *Miracles* and Ronald Bainton's *Church of Our Fathers.*

It helped later when I was given the job of editing a Hebrew hymnbook of songs mostly translated by various people from English hymns.

But where I really needed everything I could learn about the Hebrew language was when I found myself taking on the job of translating the New Testament.

Not that a translation of the New Testament had never been made before. Two outstanding such translations had been made by Franz Delitsch, a famous German Hebrew scholar, and by Isaac Salkinson, the first Hebrew translator of some of Shakespeare's works. But these had been completed at the end of the last century well before Hebrew had been revived as a spoken language. Their language was, of course, often archaic, though the more literal of the two, that of Professor Delitsch, was highly prized by some Israeli teachers. Professor Joseph Klausner used to say that he liked the exactitude of the translation of Delitsch but felt the New Testament should be rendered in a more Mishnaic Hebrew — the spoken language of many Jews in the time of Jesus.

I started trying to translate the New Testament at the Gospel of Mark. Mark is the shortest of our Gospels and is widely supposed to be one of the sources of Matthew and Luke, though in the order they appear in the first pages of the New Testament Matthew comes first, then Mark, then Luke, and finally John. All are written in Greek and when they were first gathered together around the turn of the first century it appears the favorite with Greek-speaking people was the Gospel of Matthew, causing it as a rule to be placed first in the ancient manuscript copies of the Gospels.

Now if you have not opened the New Testament to read it let me ask you to do so now, because that is the only way you will be able to understand how important it is to know Hebrew even to read the Greek original. And it is the only way you will easily understand what I am about to write.

The Book of Matthew begins with these words:

> Abraham begat Isaac.
> Isaac begat Jacob.
> Jacob begat Judah and his brothers.
> Judah begat Perez and Zerah.
> Perez begat Hezron.
> Hezron begat . . .

It is an ancient genealogy, just like those we find often in the Book of Genesis, the first book in the Bible. This old genealogy ends with:

> There are fourteen sets of fathers and sons from Abraham to David, and fourteen from David to the time when the people were carried away to Babylon and fourteen from then to the birth of the Messiah.

After giving the genealogy of Jesus, Matthew — as we call the writer of this Gospel — turns to tell in some detail about how Jesus was born in Bethlehem to Mary when she and her husband Joseph journeyed by foot, and presumably by donkey, to Bethlehem to be counted in the population registry. The story moves quickly on. King Herod, paranoid dictator that he was, tried to kill the baby he had heard would one day be king, but Mary and Joseph and baby Jesus fled to Egypt. After Herod died, we are told, they returned to Galilee to the village they lived in, Nazareth, just twenty miles from the Sea of Galilee.

This is a very Hebraic way of starting a book, as anyone who has read Old Testament or other ancient Hebrew books can verify.

But our only original for it is in Greek!

Ah, yes, but let us translate word by word the Greek text to Hebrew. Remarkable! It is just word for word like Hebrew!

When you first begin to feel that back of a Greek text is a Hebrew version, which you do not actually have but only *feel* was there, it is a bit spooky, even a bit frightening.

It is also exciting. You wonder whether by translating the Greek to Hebrew you may not just discover some big truth you would not have recognized from the Greek alone.

And that was the feeling I had when I started to translate the Gospel of Mark, a much shorter story than that of Matthew but nonetheless full of Greek sentences and paragraphs that sound when translated word by word like Hebrew sentences and paragraphs.

By this time it was the spring of 1960 and my family and I had moved from Jerusalem to the huge old house just above the shoreline of Tiberias. Coupled with my excitement about trying to understand more about Jesus by translating Greek texts back to Hebrew was the excitement of living just a hundred steps above the Kinneret, where so many of the stories about Jesus had taken place.

After getting the family settled I fixed up a rough, plaster and stone house adjoining the big house, collected all kinds of books which could help me in my research, particularly books which show the Greek texts of Matthew, Mark and Luke in parallel, and happily set to work.

During the day we looked across the sea as the sun poured mercilessly down on the blue expanse of water and danced on the beige and purple mountains beyond. At night we heard the constant slap, slap, slap of the waves just a hundred steps below us.

It would be another 25 years before the "Jesus boat" would be discovered, but looking north and south and around the sea which Jesus loved while trying to study the Gospels as they reveal him was inspiration enough.

The Gospel of Mark shows evidence of having descended from a Greek story of Jesus which had in turn been translated from a Hebrew original. Nevertheless the writer has inserted Greek phrases which do not go back to Hebrew. Actually, it is easier to translate the text of Luke back to Hebrew than that of Mark. When Matthew is giving Markan parallels he usually has the same non-Hebraic phrases but when his material does not parallel Mark his texts usually translate from Greek to Hebrew very easily.

7 DID JESUS SPEAK HEBREW?

I did not realize it but I had a lot to learn about the Gospel of Mark. It was true that for the most part the sentences in the story Mark told had word order like that we find in Hebrew and often the expressions were not like Greek at all but like Hebrew.

For instance, in the first chapter of Mark we find

> And it came to pass in those days that Jesus came from Nazareth of Galilee and was baptized by John in the Jordan (Mark 1:9).

Anyone who has read much in the King James version of the Bible (1611) will recognize that Hebraic idiom "and it came to pass." Moreover, the word order is often in Greek just like Hebrew word order.

Let me explain. In Greek it is not nearly so important where you put the verb or the subject or the object in a sentence. You can say,

To John James gave the book.

Or you can say,

James to John the book gave.

This is because the endings of the nouns in Greek are really case-endings and they tell you, as in Latin, whether the noun is an object, a subject or in a prepositional relationship.

But, as in English, Hebrew has a very fixed word order. In narrative, Hebrew first gives, usually, the word

And.

Then it puts the verb next, as in Mark 1:19,

And went he from there a little ways.

Then adds the next verb,

and saw James and John his brother.

Even more clearly is Hebrew word order found in Mark 2:19,

And said to them Jesus.

In English we would put the subject first and usually follow it by a verb.

Hebrew in narrative turns this around. Scholars call this Hebrew habit "the priority of the verb." As far as we know no native Greek ever wrote Greek with Hebrew word order, but the Jews about two hundred years before Jesus translated the entire Old Testament to Greek and they made the translation bear *the same word order found in Hebrew!*

Today we would call such a literal translation a bad translation. Happily for us when we want to get back of the Greek to what Jesus said in Hebrew we find that the ancient translators *preserved the Hebrew word order.*

There are many other indications that most of the stories and parables in the Gospels were simply translated from Hebrew to Greek. The bad news is that we have only the Greek text today but the good news is that we have a Greek text that often only makes sense if we retranslate it to Hebrew.

So, as I discovered, our first task is to try to see if any given sentence can be put back to Hebrew.

However, with great surprise, I found that Mark's Gospel often did not show Hebrew word order and idiom but actually presented texts which had a lot of Greek expressions as well as Hebrew-like idioms.

For example Mark often starts a story or sentence by writing "and immediately." In fact, the particular Greek phrase behind this expression is *kai euthus* and it has no ancient Hebrew equivalent!

Still, Mark uses it over *40* times!

For a long time this oddity escaped my understanding. Finally, I compared the places where Mark uses this expression opposite some parallel place in Luke and found that Luke never uses it except once and that not in a story he shares with Mark.

Now it is usually said that Luke copies much of the Gospel of Mark. If so — and since he does not totally reject this expression — why does he not copy *kai euthus* if he is copying Mark in so much of his material?

Two things emerged from this question for me. The first was that the evidence in this matter is that Luke did not copy *kai euthus* because he did not see it! The second was that Mark had introduced a Greek expression quite deliberately and that it could not have been a part of the Greek text as translated from the Hebrew story.

Testing other such expressions I came to the same conclusion: Mark may have copied often from Luke, but *Luke cannot have copied from texts of Mark like those we have.*

On the other hand, the fact that Matthew several times has *kai euthus* exactly opposite the parallel sentence in Mark suggested that Matthew was using Mark as one of his sources.

I made other tests. Similar conclusions surfaced. In the end I concluded that scholars had wrongly thought for many years that *both* Luke and Matthew copied part of their story from Mark. The truth — I decided — was that Luke wrote his Gospel before Mark wrote his and that Mark wrote his Gospel with the help of Luke's story. Matthew came later and used Mark for part of his material.

From Luke to Mark to Matthew was my conclusion.

Strengthening this was a test I now made on the parallel stories of Mark and Luke. I discovered gradually that very much material found in Luke had preserved the earliest Greek translation from the Hebrew. Mark had made many editorial changes and additions like that of *kai euthus*. As Matthew copied part of his material from Mark he sometimes rejected but often accepted a Greecism like *kai euthus* from Mark.

On the other hand, if Matthew presented some story or parable *not found in Mark* his Greek text translated to Hebrew beautifully, at least most of the time.

Now Matthew and Luke have many unique stories of their own but also many in common that are not found in Mark. It was clear they had a common source for the story of Jesus other than Mark. Moreover, in this common material Matthew and Luke gave texts that easily translated back to Hebrew.

In the end I came to the following rule: if you want to get back to the most literal Greek text of the original story of Jesus you must first test the text of Luke, translating it back to Hebrew. You can do the same with the stories in Matthew which do not appear in Mark — they are usually highly Hebraic.

In short we can get back to the earliest stories and words of Jesus through Luke and Matthew.

Following this rule it is very often thrilling and exciting to take a story, translate it to Hebrew carefully, and stand back and just marvel at what it says.

For example Luke preserves a saying of Jesus after he sent out his disciples to heal the sick and remove demonic spirits from the troubled. They came back excited at the fact that at their mention of his name the spirits would leave the sick on command. Jesus responded this way:

> "It is true that I have given you authority so that you can walk on snakes and scorpions. No power of the Enemy (meaning Satan) will be able to hurt you. But don't be glad because the evil spirits obey you; rather be glad because your names are written in heaven" (Luke 10:19, 20).

As so often, in these words of Jesus preserved in Luke you can take the Greek text and translate it word by word to excellent Hebrew.

This particular response of Jesus is not found in either Mark or Matthew but the following saying is recorded in both Luke and Matthew — Jesus is speaking about God whom he so often calls "Father."

> "My father has given me all things. No one knows the son like the father and no one knows the father like the son. And to whomever he wishes the son can disclose him " (v. 22).

Strangely enough Christian interpreters of this passage, failing to translate the Greek back to Hebrew, have supposed that Jesus is really calling himself "the" son and his father "the" father in some very special, theological way. For this reason they capitalize the word son (Son) and the word father (Father). Had they understood that this passage uses a Hebrew idiom "the father" and "the son" to mean "a father" and "a son" they would have understood what Jesus said much better.

For instance, in Ezekiel, chapter 18, God says

> "Behold, all souls are mine; the soul of *the* father as well as *the* soul of the son is mine: the soul that sins shall die" (v. 4).

What the Lord was saying through Ezekiel was that *any* father or *any* son belonged to him. The use of the definite article "the" is a use we call *generic*. It means "any" in such usage.

Actually we have the same usage in English. We say, for example,

"The barber cuts hair, the shopkeeper sells produce," or, "The teacher in every school must try to control the students and the students must be obedient and listen."

Thus the Hebrew retranslation shows us that Jesus is really saying,

> "My Father has given me all things. No one of course knows a son like a father. Nor does anyone know a father like a son, and the son can talk with authority to anyone about his father and tell this person all about him."

Naturally, Jesus is talking about God as his real, special Father but he is illustrating his authority to talk about him by the simple fact that a father and his son have a very special relationship which makes it possible for the son to describe and portray what his father is like to anyone he wishes to do so.

Jesus here makes a remarkable claim, but my point just now is that *it is through Hebrew idiom that we get back to the real meaning.*

Mark used Luke for most of the units he transmits. Taking his unit or story order from Luke, Mark nonetheless rewrote almost every sentence, borrowing for his editorial changes words and expressions we find in the book of Acts, in the epistle of James, in some of Paul's letters and in some other ancient sources. In Professor David Flusser of the Hebrew University I discover a friend and scholar who can test the meaning of what I am finding.

8 I MEET DAVID FLUSSER

When I came to what was for me a revelation as to which of our Gospels is the earliest and which best preserve the Greek words which literally rendered that first Hebrew story of Jesus I looked around to see if any other students of these books had come to similar conclusions.

What I looked for, first, was someone who had seen that our Gospel materials descend from some Hebrew biography of Jesus, and, secondly, someone who had concluded as I had that Luke and Matthew had carefully preserved much of an earlier Greek text which was itself the descendant of a very literal Greek story of Jesus.

All this was of supreme importance to me for it was now perfectly clear that I could not recover the words of Jesus — and indeed that early Hebrew story — without this basic analysis. I saw more and more that Mark had mainly followed whatever stories he found in Luke and re-edited them using a system the rabbis call *gezira shavah* and perhaps other rabbinic methods of interpreting.

In essence this system — so beloved among the rabbis — allows the interpreter to pick up any passage in the Bible which has a word or idea somewhat like the passage being interpreted and use it to make interesting or clear the particular verses or sentences he wants to interpret.

For example the rabbis often talked about "the Kingdom of Heaven," by which they meant "the Kingdom of God." They were afraid of transgressing the command not to "take the name of the Lord in vain" so, as was their habit, they said that if the actual name of the Lord is not said you cannot transgress this commandment at all: use some evasive synonym and you will not break this law. The expression in Hebrew is *malchut shammayim*, Kingdom of Heaven, Heaven being an evasive synonym for God.

Now Christians know the phrase Kingdom of Heaven or Kingdom of God only from the New Testament, for Jesus often spoke of God's Kingdom.

And, in truth, the words "Kingdom of God" are not found at all in the Old Testament. This phrase, of course as "Kingdom of Heaven," was apparently developed by the sect of Jews called the Pharisees — it is not used in the Dead Sea Scrolls. In essence they meant by it that any Jew who would seriously follow the Torah (the Law) had accepted the Lordship of God, that is, was prepared to do whatever the Law demanded of him. They did not — as so many Christians have supposed — mean by *malchut shammayim* some kind of future political supremacy by which the Messiah and Israel would rule the earth from Jerusalem. They, of course, believed that God rules the whole earth but when they used this special expression "Kingdom of Heaven" they did not mean God's general rule of the whole world. They meant that any Jew who began to keep the Torah and the rabbinic interpretations of the Torah had come under the rule of the Law and was now in God's Rule or Kingdom. He had taken upon himself "the yoke of the Kingdom of God," or simply, "the Kingdom of God."

Now, as I said, the actual phrase *malchut shammayim* is not found in the Old Testament but this did not bother the rabbis. Wherever they found God mentioned as *melech* (King) or the verb *malach* (to rule or reign) they said that this hinted or referred to *malchut shammayim*.

In the frequent Bible quizzes which are held for high school students all over Israel one of the questions sometimes asked is: when is the Kingdom of God first mentioned in the Bible? Almost every school child over fourteen years of age knows the answer. "It says," they will say, "in Exodus, chapter 15 that *Adonai yimloch leolam*" (the Lord will rule forever).

Here the actual phrase "Kingdom of Heaven" is not used. For the rabbis it is sufficient that the verb "to rule" (malach) appears, so they say that this is the first mention in the Bible of the Kingdom of God!

For an English-speaking person, of course, this method of interpretation is foreign. Our word for "rule" or "reign" says nothing specific to us about a king or a kingdom. All the more so for the non-Hebrew-speaking person who knows the New Testament and its specific use of the phrase "Kingdom of God."

In the minds of the rabbis — and young Israelis have imbibed this part of rabbinic teaching — *malchut* (kingdom), *melech* (king) and *malach* (to rule) are thought of as equivalents. You can find verses here and there in the Old Testament which use them, and by the system of *gezirah shavah* find the Kingdom of God in all kinds of places. More importantly, if you do not know much about the subject you are studying, you can find out much more by finding various related words or phrases in quite distant contexts and come up with wonderful interpretations!

Now this method of *gezirah shavah* is quite near to the method our Gospel writer Mark used. Mark would look at a story he was copying (usually from Luke), note some interesting word and recall that in such and such a verse in the Old Testament a similar word was used, or that such a word was used in the book we call the Acts of the Apostles, or in some of Paul's letters. Often he would then actually consult the passage he remembered and come back and rewrite the sentence he found in Luke, inserting instead of Luke's words the words he had picked up in what we would call a distant context.

So far as I know no one has ever noticed how extensive was this method Mark used but it helped me to understand why it was almost always easier to translate Luke to Hebrew than Mark. Happily, although Matthew had copied from Mark at many places in his Gospel he had also often copied from much the same Greek text Luke had used so that in at least those parts Matthew had not copied from Mark his text almost always translated to good Hebrew.

To get the earliest story and stories about Jesus we must go to Luke and Matthew.

But look as I would in the extensive literature about the Gospels, I could not find the conclusions I had reached.

It was at this time that I came to know Professor David Flusser, of the Department of Comparative Religions in the Hebrew University.

It turned out that Flusser had long had a deep and abiding interest in the Gospels and in the figure of Jesus which they portrayed.

When we met and discussed what I was finding his understanding was immediate.

He had been reading recently some German works which spoke frequently of the editorial "redaction" of Mark and had been impressed with many things in this Gospel which reminded him of rabbinic teachings but also had elements which indicated that Mark had added

Dr. Robert Lindsey and Dr. David Flusser

non-rabbinic words and ideas which were more Greek than Hebrew.

So it was that in 1962 I found myself spending many hours with Flusser in Jerusalem explaining what I was finding. We conversed in Hebrew and argued endlessly over this and that point so important to each of us. Like other scholars he had long supposed that Luke as well as Matthew had often copied from Mark. As we struggled with this and that difficulty he became convinced that I was on the right track.

We became fast friends, he the Orthodox Jew whose concern with the person of Jesus never left him, I the Oklahoma Baptist who by now was almost as much Israeli as American and just as deeply concerned to discover all I could about this Messiah of Jewish and Christian history.

To my delight Flusser was a man of deep religious piety, it was that which had attracted him to Jesus, I suppose. Though trained in a Roman Catholic college in Czechoslovakia, he had as a young man become acquainted with a keenly evangelical Christian group known as the Bohemian Brethren and it was among them that he felt he had discovered a close link with the early Jewish church of Jesus. The anti-Jewish attitudes of traditional Christian churches he simply did not find among the Bohemian Brethren and this made him wonder if the old conflict between Jews and Christians could ever be defended by "real" Christians.

Often, in those first days as we worked on Gospel questions Flusser would say to me, "Lindsey, you know what all our philological research is about, don't you?"

I would act as if I did not know.

"We want to know," and he would lean over the table, "who THE LORD was!" And, of course, he meant Jesus and was using the title Jesus' disciples gave him.

I was to see very, very much of Flusser during the next 25 years.

For the modern mind the figure of Jesus is more than shocking. By the age of twelve he is conscious of his role as the Messiah of Israel. At the age of thirty he is baptized by John as the Holy Spirit descends upon him and a voice from the heavens tells him he is God's Son as prophesied in Psalm 2. He meets a quite literal Satan afterwards who calls him the Son of God — a synonym among Jews for the title of Messiah. We may be ever so modern but, if so, what are these things we call poltergeists?

9 THE SHOCK OF JESUS

I am sure my friend Flusser would agree with me when I say that the closer one gets to the figure of Jesus in the Gospels the more startling this figure is. Jesus is most certainly not just a romantic shepherd blithly playing his reed flute while watching his sheep on the hills of Nazareth. Nor is he the youth of eight who, as the apocryphal Gospels tell it, made a clay pigeon one day and then brought it to life so that it spread its clay wings and flew away.

It is clear that he was gentle and patient, that he loved children as well as grownups, and that he knew the Hebrew Scriptures by heart (as did many of his fellow countrymen). There is no doubt that he had worked as some kind of craftsman or carpenter with his father for many years before he began the famous ministry and just as little doubt that he spent every Sabbath in the synagogue as he grew up, missing only when he was away from Nazareth in Jerusalem at one of the feasts.

We have one piquant story about him when he was twelve years old. It is told in the second chapter of Luke.

With his parents he had gone up to Jerusalem to celebrate the yearly passover. After several days, when the Galilean Jews normally left to return to their homes, Mary and Joseph — his legal parents — walked with the pilgrims a day's journey and discovered that night that Jesus was not with them. They seem to have assumed that Jesus was with playmates of his same age and should naturally have been with the entire group.

They hurried back to Jerusalem — still crowded with pilgrims since some returned later than others — and spent three days searching for him.

As the story goes they found him in one of the study rooms in the Temple compound. He was "sitting with the rabbis, listening to them and asking questions." It seems the rabbis were as much interested in him as he in them, for the story states that "all who heard him were amazed at his questions."

His mother was annoyed and said, "Son, why have you done this to us? Your father and I have been terribly worried trying to find you." Jesus' answer, like that of many an independent boy of twelve, was,

> Why should you have looked for me? Don't you know I have to be in my Father's house? (Luke 2:41-49).

The element of shock is there in the earliest story we have about Jesus. "My father" in Hebrew is *avi*. Although we have some evidence that on rare occasions some teachers spoke of God as *abba* (an Aramaic loanword to Hebrew in the period) it was normal for Jews to speak of God as "*our* father" or *avinu*, in the collective sense rather than in the purely personal *avi*.

Apparently the explanation of Jesus' use of *avi* "my father" lies in the fact that in several Old Testament passages known by Jews in that period as prophetic of the coming messianic King, the Messiah was thought of as a kind of son of Israel's God.

In the famous prophecy of Nathan to King David in II Samuel 7:14, God says of this future King not only that he will be David's son but, to quote,

> "I will be a father to him
> and he will be a son to me."

In Psalm 2 God is described as saying to this Messiah King-to-be,

> "You are my son.
> This day I have delivered you as a baby" (verse 7).

And, finally, in Psalm 89 this future, special leader is pictured as saying to God,

> "He will speak to me, saying 'Avi!'" (verse 26).

There seems no question but that Jesus at the age of twelve was completely convinced that his role was messianic. He does not say, of course, "I am the Son of God." His answer is far more biblical: "I have to be in my father's house." But the meaning is really the same. And the title "Son of God" is equivalent to "Messiah."

But if one is shocked by these words in the mouth of a twelve-year-old boy what do you do when you come to the first stories of Jesus when he is, as Luke says, "about thirty years old." Jesus goes from Nazareth to the Jordan River to a place where crowds are gathered around John the Baptizer who is calling Jews from Jerusalem and other areas to repent and immerse themselves in the Jordan under his authority.

When Jesus appears John tells him it would be more correct if Jesus baptized him than that John should direct him to be immersed in the muddy stream. Jesus says to him, "Allow me this privilege for I want to affirm this redemptive ministry of yours" (Matthew 3:13-15).

According to John, Jesus is someone very special (he seems to have believed that Jesus was the coming Messiah and King) and he is not quite prepared that he should come to be baptized by him. The story goes on that as Jesus was dipping in baptism in the stream

> the heavens opened up and the Holy Spirit as a dove came down and settled on Jesus' head. Then a voice came out of heaven, and said, "You are my son. This day I have delivered you as a baby" (Luke 3:21, 22).

(See the manuscript evidence showing the voice from heaven was actually quoting Psalm 2:7.)

Even stranger to us today is what happened immediately after this very Jewish baptism, for we read that,

> The Holy Spirit led Jesus out into the desert and after forty days in which he fasted, he, being hungry, was approached by Satan and tempted with the words, "Since you are the Son of God, take these stones and make them into bread!" (Matthew 4:2-4).

Jesus' answer to the age-old enemy of man was to quote a verse from the Torah,

> "Man shall not live by bread alone but by every word which proceeds out of the mouth of the Lord."

Then follow two Satanic temptations, one of which involves Satan's placing him on top of the pinnacle of the Temple and trying to get Jesus to dive down and show his colors as Messiah to the people of Israel, and the other, which tells of Satan's showing him all the kingdoms of the world and offering them to him "if you will only bow down to me" (Matthew 4:5-11).

Jesus, of course, rejects Satan's offer, quoting passages from the Torah. Prophecy of old, in Isaiah, speaks of the coming King and says,

> It is too light a thing that you should be my servant to raise up the tribes of Jacob and to restore the preserved of Israel. I will make you a light to the nations *(goyim)*, that my salvation may reach to the ends of the earth (Isaiah 49:6).

The role of the Messiah was clearly understood to be that of saving Israel but also of being a savior for the *goyim*.

Now all these stories are loaded with references to Old Testament Scriptures. They seem heavy to us today. Few Christians or Jews nowadays know the old prophecies like Jews of the first century knew them and they may seem far from us. Jews sometimes say to Christians in our time, "You Christians are always interested in Old Testament prophecy. To us it is more important to know the rabbinic commentaries and the Mishna. After all that is Judaism today." True, but it once was not so. The ancient books of the rabbis of the first three centuries of this era are chock full of references to Old Testament prophecy as well as more legal things. Christians — because the first ones were all Jews — have inherited the Jewish interest in Old Testament prophecy from the Jews of the first century.

But quite beyond the heaviness of these stories of Jesus as a lad, the baptism of Jesus, and the Satanic temptations does it not strike you that all these are extremely far from where you and I live today?

What modern man or woman can take these suggestions of supernatural voices and demonic apparitions seriously? The fact is that most Jews and Christians of today suppose such stories may have been meaningful to people two thousand years ago but hardly to us today. We do not believe in "ghouls and ghosts" and "things that go bump in the dark!"

Or do we?

As I write I have before me a copy of the *Reader's Digest* of January, 1985 (International Edition) which displays an article about a "poltergeist" which appears to have caused havoc in the home of a teenager in Columbus, Ohio, in March, 1984.

What happened in this suburban home is in many ways just as strange as these early first stories about Jesus. Tina, the teenager,

> had turned off the lights in the empty dining room, but now they were on again. So were the lights in the deserted and previously unlighted hallway. With no one upstairs, the shower began to run.

> Back in the kitchen, the washer and dryer sounded odd, and Joan (Tina's mother) could see by the dials that they were going through the cycles too fast. The hands on the electric clock raced wildly.

According to the story an electrician was called in. He taped the electric switches again and again but each time they would flick back on. "I used two rolls of tape and then tried adhesive bandages." The lights continued to turn on. "Everyone," he said, "everyone in the family was where I could see them, and no one could have touched a switch." The lights came back on. After three hours, Claggett, the electrician, gave up.

Later, according to the story, pictures fell from the wall, an expensive set of stoneware crashed piece by piece, chairs moved without help from anyone and couches were upended. Experts of all kinds were called in. A newspaper photographer actually photographed the telephone whizzing by Tina as she sat on a chair and the photograph was widely published, bringing all kinds of people to investigate the phenomenon.

The story is much longer but is worth reading. It is but one of the more widely publicized stories about a special kind of spirit called a poltergeist. Indeed, a whole literature about poltergeists has sprung up within the past fifty years, about their tricks of moving furniture around and generally causing confusion in homes where troubled teenagers live.

I asked Flusser whether he had trouble believing in the supernatural.

"Look," he answered, "I am a modern man even if I am an Orthodox Jew. Until I was 26 years old I thought my father was right when he took me out at age 6 to a graveyard and told me, 'That is the end, son, there is no more.' Later I began to think differently."

"Shall I tell you one of my own experiences?" he asked me. "I was getting ready to leave Czechoslovakia to come to Jerusalem years ago. I had my plane ticket. But a few hours before I was to leave, something said to me, 'Don't go. Don't go,' and I cancelled my flight. That plane was shot down and all the passengers perished!"

Jesus shocks us but that may just be *our* fault.

The picture painted of Jesus by our Gospels is that of a genuine superman who has appeared on earth to confront supernatural spirits of evil infecting the bodies of men and beasts. Jesus drives out these spirits without invoking the name of God or employing magical rites, but by his own authority. A world-view which makes room for God and angels, Satan and demons, is not unscientific, as Carl Jung and my friend Jack Taylor testify.

10 SUPERNATURAL THINGS

There is no escaping it. Jesus cannot be explained as the usual kind of messiah, the dictator of this or that banana republic, not even as a higher level warrior like Napolean who tried to conquer all of Europe. And of course he is much more than a reformer.

This is plain from the first scene we have in his ministry as recorded in Matthew and Mark (a bit later in Luke).

Jesus goes to Capernaum, on the north shore of Lake Kinneret, a busy, commercial town which must have had a large synagogue in it (the one shown presently was built in the third century of our era). It was probably built of large, black, roughly-hewn, basalt (volcanic) stones. It was a Sabbath and he doubtless went to pray. Both men and women sat or stood in the hall, for in contrast to later times men and women mixed fairly freely in the synagogue.

Suddenly a man started shouting, "What do you want of us, Jesus of Nazareth? You have come to destroy us! I know you, you are the Holy One of God!" (Luke 4:33-36). The man is demonized and the evil spirits are using his voice as they confront Jesus.

Jesus speaks directly to the demon, "Shut up and come out of him!" The spirit throws the man on the floor and leaves him. The man rises up. He is well and happy.

The exorcism of spirits was common among Jews at this period, as we read in the Talmud. It is still a part of the culture of most of the world. All kinds of things are done to relieve people tormented by demonic powers: parts of their fingernails are cut off and buried, hair is pulled out, fire is applied to hurting parts. The names of this and that deity are often invoked to cure the poor people.

Jesus later sent out his disciples to "heal and cast out demons," as we saw earlier. They exorcised evil spirits by speaking to them and "rebuking" them in the name of Jesus. And succeeded. Many evangelicals continue the practice with much success today.

But Jesus' exorcisms were not done in a "name." Jesus did not name any deity. He had the authority to confront these supernatural tormenters in his own power. As someone has said, we today must invoke the name of Jesus in dealing with evil spirits. Not Jesus. He commands and they flee.

This fact was immediately perceived by the people in the synagogue. "What is this?" they say, evidently using the expression in Hebrew *davar*. The Greek translator has misunderstood and rendered *davar logos*, literally "word" which it often is in Hebrew but here means "thing." "This man," they continue, "gives orders to the evil spirits and they come out!"

What surprises them is not that the spirits are driven out of the man — they had seen people delivered from demons often enough before — what surprises them is that Jesus deals with these lower denizens of the netherworld as if he is a commander punishing unruly soldiers. It is this ready and demonstrative authority which is such a surprise to them.

The same authority appears when Jesus leaves the synagogue and comes to the house of Simon, the fisherman, later called Peter. Simon's mother-in-law has a fever. Jesus goes over and "stands over her" and "rebukes the fever" as if the fever itself was as real as an evil spirit. The fever leaves immediately and the woman gets up and serves the guests and the people of the house (Luke 4:38-39).

No wonder is it that in the evening, after sunset, when the Sabbath is over, sick people from all over the village are brought and Jesus lays hands on them and each is healed. Jesus deals with demons causing bondage or sickness as well, and they come out screaming, "You are the Son of God!" The fact that Jesus came of the line of David and was thus entitled to be called "the Son of David" is not what worried the spirits: they were afraid of being "tortured" and dealt with roughly by a supernatural power of greater authority than they (Luke 4:40-41).

The Franciscan monks have excavated an ancient building at Capernaum which they believe must have been the house of Simon Peter. There are signs that the house was modified by the early Jewish followers of Jesus and sometimes used as a house of prayer. You can visit these ruins today and they are of great interest.

Once again — we moderns are shocked at the very mention of

something we would rather not talk about: demonic forces we cannot see and can only think of as "spooky."

More scientific and curious than we are was the famous Swiss psychologist, Karl Jung, who was student and collaborator with Sigmund Freud. Freud considered him a person of high integrity and ability but broke with him when Jung began serious study of what Freud called "the occult."

In his autobiography Jung tells of his interest in the mystical world, due, first, to a dream he had at the age of four in which he found himself descending through a large hole in a field and in the middle of a vast crowd of people worshipping a huge, pulsating phallic organ. He early asked himself how a child of four could have had knowledge of such things.

He tells also of a thick, hard-wood table-top which mysteriously broke with an explosive bang one day in his home when he was a teenager. There was no explanation for this strange occurrence, just as there was no way the family could comprehend what happened when suddenly all the silverware in his mother's home, knives, forks and spoons, bent completely out of shape in the drawer where they were kept.

Jung spent several years investigating such occult happenings. While he was doing so mysterious things occurred in his own home. On one occasion he and his family watched from their dining room the front doorbell being depressed again and again by invisible fingers, as the bell rang loudly in their ears.

Jung called these odd forces the "anima" which in Latin simply means the "spirits."

I am reminded of my friend Jack Taylor, a Baptist pastor who served a large congregation in Texas some years ago. He had been trying to understand the forces or powers of evil as they are described in the Bible when a young man, who sang in his church choir, approached him one day and asked to come for an interview. Some days later he came to Jack's office.

"Son," Jack said, "what can I do for you?"

"Pastor," said the boy, "I've got a demon."

Jack was taken aback. He had never had anyone visit him and say such a thing.

"What kind of demon?" Jack countered, not really knowing how he would be able to deal with this situation.

"It's a demon of homosexuality," said the boy, matter-of-factly.

Jack had never had anyone admit homosexuality either. However, he took out his New Testament and the two read several stories about the way Jesus healed persons in bondage to evil spirits. They then knelt and asked God to help the boy. Jack decided to speak directly to this demon of homosexuality, of course in the name of his Lord.

A tussle immediately followed, the spirit apparently throwing the boy to the floor while the boy himself wriggled and writhed as if in torture. Jack got down on his knees and kept saying, "Leave this boy, you spirit of homosexuality, in Jesus' name."

A voice came from the throat of the boy, "He is mine. I live here. I am not leaving!"

Exactly like the Gospel stories.

At last the spirit said, "Well, if I have to leave, he's going with me!"

With that the boy lunged for an open window of the second-story office they occupied. Jack grabbed the feet of the boy to prevent his jumping and called for some of his church staff to help him. They came running and several of them held the boy down until Jack's command in his Lord's name had succeeded.

Remarkably enough, the boy recovered fully, was relieved of his strong drive to homosexuality, married, and, Jack says, has a normal family life today.

Once again, the world in which these Jewish fishermen lived is unlike that we know in this age of science and pseudo-science, and their culture is not ours, but it may be that with a bit more curiosity and research we will find that the ancient consciousness of God and angels, Satan and demons, is much closer to reality than we have supposed.

Once we get over our unfamiliarity with the ancient world and its daily experience with the supernatural, good and bad, we can, perhaps, understand better other stories so common in the life of Jesus.

Sometimes, at the beginning of one of these stories of healing for instance, we find it said about Jesus that as he looked at some crippled or fevered person he "had compassion on him." In one particular story a woman comes to him all bent over and unable to stand erect and Jesus heals her, saying as he does so, "Woman, you have been set loose from your infirmity!" The head of the synagogue objects that Jesus is healing on the Sabbath and says, "Are there not six days in which one can do what he wants without healing on the Sabbath?" Jesus unhesitatingly blames the crippled condition on an outer, supernatural force. Jesus answers . . . "This woman has suffered this crippling from the Devil for eighteen years. Should not this daughter of Abraham be healed, even on the Sabbath?" (Luke 13:10-17).

People need healing. So often have they been battered around by systems, governments, bosses, spouses and even children, not to speak of the Enemy of us all.

The eyes of Jesus must often have shone with great compassion, a compassion fully matched by his understanding of the causes of human misery.

Jesus does not walk around arrogantly saying he is the Messiah, in so many words, nor does he have to. His miracles and approach to exorcism speak for themselves. But in Nazareth he declares he is the Messiah by quoting Isaiah 61:1, 2 and applying these words as explanation of himself and his unusual ministry. Of much importance is his interpretation that with him God has inaugurated an age of healing and grace.

11 STARTLING CLAIMS

I cannot write of the visit of Jesus to Nazareth and the opposition he ran into in his own hometown without telling how we studied this story as found in Luke 4:16-30 in Flusser's New Testament seminar several years ago at the Hebrew University in Jerusalem.

You see, Flusser taught on the life of Jesus from the Gospels in an advanced seminar in the University for many years and I was present during a great many of these sessions. He and I had collaborated since 1962, the year I moved with my family back to Jerusalem after spending two years in Tiberias attempting to translate the Gospel of Mark anew.

We talked constantly both privately and in the seminar about problems we met in trying to understand Jesus, as the texts of Matthew, Mark and Luke described him. Often Flusser would choose a story, lecture on the Greek text and indicate rabbinic and Hebrew suggestions connected to it. Students would comment and ask questions. Frequently Flusser would turn to me at the end of the discussion and ask me to comment. Sometimes we disagreed, or argued this or that point vociferously, but as a rule we came to important conclusions affecting our mutual understanding of the story.

Little by little we built upon our accumulated experience and little by little many of the difficult problems encountered found their solution.

Now one of the short narratives, which is actually longer than many, is that which tells of Jesus going to Nazareth after having become more and more famous as a healer around Capernaum.

As both Flusser and I agreed there is not a more Hebrew-like Greek text in all our Gospels. The story has descended in Greek but can be easily turned back word by word to Hebrew. Nevertheless there are little points of interpretation which are of great importance to understanding Jesus as we bring this story back to Hebrew. And not a few problems.

The story begins simply enough.

Jesus, who apparently is visiting his mother, Mary, and his brothers James (Yaakov), Joseph (Yossi), Judah (Yehuda), and Simon (Shimon), comes early on the Sabbath to worship at the village synagogue. After the Torah is read, it is the scroll of the Prophets which is handed to Jesus and he is asked to read from it.

Each ancient synagogue, no matter how small, tried hard to come by at least a good copy of the Torah and one of the Prophets (which included the books of Joshua, Judges, I and II Samuel and I and II Kings as well as the books of Isaiah, Jeremiah, Ezekiel and the so-called minor prophets). It was a precious scroll which Jesus opened.

He found the place in the Prophets from which he would read, Isaiah chapter 61, the first two verses. Like Christians later, Jews popularly believed that the coming Son of David would one day say these words:

> The Spirit of the Lord is upon me,
> Because the Lord has anointed me
> To preach good tidings to the poor.

At this point Jesus made a change in the ancient reading. Where the original said,

> He has sent me to heal the brokenhearted

Jesus dropped the expression "to heal the brokenhearted" and went on to read,

> To proclaim liberty to the captives,
> And the opening of the prison

But even here he seems to have read in such a way that the people understood this last phrase as,

> And the opening of the eyes of the blind,

which is a possible reading of the Hebrew.

So instead of reading

> And the opening of the prison to those who are bound

he reads, apparently,

> And the opening of the eyes of the blind

and adds

To set the oppressed free,

which is a phrase he lifts out of an earlier portion of Isaiah (58:6) and inserts here.

Finally, Jesus returns to Isaiah 61:2 and ends the quotation,

To proclaim the acceptable year of the Lord,

dropping, as he does so, a further sentence from Isaiah 61:2:

And the day of vengeance of our God.

Although it may seem strange to us today, this special way of reading a passage from the Prophets — dropping one phrase to insert another biblical phrase — was a common practice among Jewish rabbis and teachers. In the sectarian documents of the Dead Sea Scrolls, which comment on many biblical texts and constantly refer them to people and events happening at Qumran or Jerusalem, the writers make small changes in the biblical material as interpretations flow from their pens. The reason is that in making a deliberate change or insertion the writer is bringing out some special point he desires to make and some interpretation which may not have been exactly that of the prophet himself but suggests some contemporary matter or event.

The passage in the original context of Isaiah obviously had to do with the Judeans who were being promised deliverance from captivity but Jesus is talking about a quite different kind of deliverance.

The Enemy, Satan, has brought sickness and disease on the people and Jesus has come to heal them physically and deliver them from the power of the devil. By making changes suitable to what he wants to put across he is able to quote a famous Scripture yet apply it not as meant originally but to explain himself and his mission.

Christian ministers and sermon-makers often misunderstand both this Jewish method of interpreting a Bible passage and what Jesus meant by saying the Lord had sent him to "preach good tidings to the poor," or, as good tidings is often translated, "the Gospel." Very often the calling of the minister is said to be largely that of "preaching the Gospel" and the supposition is that this means that the Christian minister's main task is to stand behind a pulpit and preach two or three sermons weekly.

But, of course, this is not what Jesus means by saying he had come to preach the Gospel (good tidings) to the poor. He is really saying that he has good news for the oppressed. Through him they can find healing and deliverance from the Enemy. It may very well be that the Christian evangelist who calls men to make a decision for Christ and his kingdom is engaged in helping a person to the source of blessing and power by calling on him to follow Jesus but Jesus certainly meant much more. He had come to touch the bodies of people and make them physically and spiritually whole.

We read that after Jesus had finished his interpretive reading of Isaiah 61:1, 2 he closed the book and gave it to the attendant *(chazan)*, sat down and — after a pause in which every eye was upon him — said,

> "Today your ears have heard the fulfillment of this Scripture."

It is sometimes said that in view of the fact that Jesus did not go around saying loudly, "I am the Messiah," he may not have thought of himself as the Messiah. In fact this idea has been advanced by so many people that it has become a kind of cliché in the mouths of many who should read these stories in the Gospels more carefully.

The people who came to the synagogue in Nazareth that day so long ago clearly had no doubt that in this very Jewish way of referring to Isaiah 61 Jesus was claiming messiahship.

Without saying it in so many words Jesus is declaring that he is the expected Messiah. "This Scripture is talking about me. The Lord has anointed *(mashach)* me. I am the Messiah *(mashiach)*."

Before a Jewish audience all kinds of messianic pretenders had come and gone and would do so for years after the time of Jesus. The sophisticated pretender would avoid saying directly, "I am the Messiah." Bar Cochba a hundred years later would call himself "Nasi" (Prince) rather than Messiah and inscribe this messianic name on the coins he issued. It would remain for Rabbi Akiva to call him the Messiah. To have said blatantly "I am the Messiah" to a Jewish audience in the first century would perhaps not technically have been considered blasphemy (since the claimant would not actually have called himself God) but it would have been thought of as extremely bold and *near blasphemy*.

Jesus is thus doing two things in reading and making Isaiah 61:1, 2 a central text that can explain what he wants to say to those in the synagogue. He is saying that he is the expected Son of David, Messiah, and that his ministry or method as Messiah is to heal the sick, dispel demonic forces, give eyes to the blind, make the lame walk, and in this way bring "good news to the poor."

He will emphasize this special method of ministry again when in Matt. 11:2, 3 John the Baptist sends messengers to ask him, "Are you the one we wait for or do we have to wait for someone else?" Jesus will reply by asking the messengers to inform John that

"The blind receive their sight
And the lame are walking.
The lepers are cleansed
And the deaf are hearing,
And blessed is he not offended in me." (Matthew 11:5, 6).

We will see later that John's mistake was that he thought the coming Messiah would *on appearance* fulfill ancient Scriptures promising the pouring out of the Holy Spirit on all people and the setting up of thrones of judgment. Jesus made it clear that *his first task as Messiah was to heal* and that meant that *before* there would be an outpouring of the Holy Spirit and the Messianic judgment there would be a period of Messianic healing.

It was, of course, promised in Isaiah that the Messianic period yet to come would be a time of great physical blessing for the people.

Then the eyes of the blind shall be opened,
And the ears of the deaf shall be unstopped.
Then the lame shall leap like a deer,
And the tongue of the dumb sing (Isaiah 35:5, 6).

Jesus was saying, "The time has come. The Messianic period is here. Healing and deliverance is the program for the hour."

He is saying even more. As we noticed, he quoted the first phrase in Isaiah 61:2: He was

To proclaim the acceptable year of the Lord,

but deliberately dropped the next sentence. He was *not* to proclaim

The day of vengeance of the Lord!

The day of judgment, in which the Messiah would sit as the great and final judge, would not come for — who knows? — a long time. Meantime Jesus would walk from village to village visiting the synagogues and healing all he would find who wanted healing. It is the acceptable year of the Lord.

As the Gospel of John sums it up in Jesus' words:

I have not come to judge the world but to save the world (John 12:47).

To emphasize once again how Jesus used Isaiah 61, let me put down side by side the passage in Isaiah and the words of Jesus as he quoted and interpreted it.

ISAIAH 61:1, 2	LUKE 4:18, 19
The Spirit of the Lord is upon me, because the Lord has anointed me to bring good tidings to the poor;	The Spirit of the Lord is upon me, because he has anointed me to bring good tidings to the poor;
he has sent me to bind up the brokenhearted,	he has sent me
to proclaim liberty to the captives, and the opening of the prison (or the eyes);	to proclaim liberty to the captives, and the opening of the eyes of the blind;
	to set free those who are oppressed (Isaiah 58:6)
to proclaim the acceptable year of the Lord and the day of vengeance of our God.	to proclaim the acceptable year of the Lord.

So far as I can see Jesus never varied from this understanding of his mission and clearly left it as a heritage for the mission of his followers. Jesus would send out his disciples later to heal and deliver people from the powers of evil. The book of the *Acts of the Apostles* describes the first post-resurrection followers as praying for the sick and possessed as well. Have we modern followers largely missed the way Jesus interpreted bringing the good tidings to the poor for our emphasis on "preaching the Gospel" with many good words but no cleansing of the leper or raising of the dead?

In the story of the rejection in Nazareth the phrase "The words of grace which proceeded out of his mouth" more probably mean "the words of disgrace that proceeded out of his mouth." Leaders of the synagogue in Nazareth find Jesus' claims seditious and heretical and they apparently think he should be stoned as a false prophet. He challenges his opposition and moves on.

12 TOO MUCH FOR US!

It would be easier to understand this story if we were to expect that the people of the town, and especially the leaders of the synagogue, were to take offences at Jesus' words the very moment he declared that these words have found their fulfillment this very day as you are listening to me" (Luke 4:21).

In this case their words, "After all (the meaning of the Hebrew when we retranslate the Greek negative) this is *Joseph's son*!" would be an expression not of their seeming surprise but of their horror. "We all know Joseph and he is a good man. How can his son get so big-headed as to think he is the Messiah himself? Maybe he has performed some miracles not far from us but does that make him the Messiah?"

Let me remind you that we were studying this story in Flusser's seminar and that meant we were looking into every possible problem connected with the text. There was always the possibility that the Greek translator had misunderstood some Hebrew word or phrase and mistranslated it.

The value of a seminar is that you always have students who may know something the professor does not know and the value of studying a passage from the New Testament with the help of Israelis who have studied rabbinic sources can often bring light to so Jewish a book.

As the seminar proceeded week after week, one young woman who was studying early rabbinic literature at the university grew more interested with each hour of seminar. For one thing, she pondered the fact that this episode ends with the people trying to throw Jesus down from the cliff Nazareth was built on. This reminded her of some of the suggestions of the Mishnah: when punishment was to be that of stoning (for whatever reason) it was thought kinder to push the condemned off of some high place — often a house — with the hope that he would die from the fall and the stoning be without agony when it followed.

Perhaps, she reasoned, the people of Nazareth planned to throw Jesus down from the cliff as a preliminary act before actually stoning him.

She then looked at the expression "they were astonished at the gracious words which issued from his mouth." Translating back to Hebrew she noted that the Greek "words of grace" are literally in Hebrew *"divrei chesed."* This expression could easily be understood by a Greek writer translating to Greek as "words of grace." But the word "chesed" in Hebrew can also mean "a wicked thing" or a "disgrace." In Leviticus 20:17 we read, for instance,

> If a man takes his sister ... and they remove their clothes and see each other naked, it is a wicked thing *(chesed hu).*

In Proverbs 14:34 we read,

> Righteousness exalts a nation
> But sin is a reproach *(chesed)* to any people.

Perhaps, said she, the people were not astonished at the "words of grace" coming from the mouth of Jesus but at what they interpreted as "words of disgrace," or "words of apostasy."

This suggestion led me to look at the word in Greek translated into English as "spoke well." Here the word is *martureo* and while in Greek it normally has the meaning of "testifying in favor" of someone the moment you translate it back to Hebrew you find it means "testify against" (*heidu b.,* compare I Kings 21:10).

Thus the passage may easily mean:

> And all of them *spoke critically* of him and were astonished at the *words of apostasy* coming out of his mouth.
>
> Then they said, "After all, this is Joseph's son!"

To put it more popularly the people in the synagogue said something like, "Good heavens, this is Joseph's son!"

When I suggested this kind of translation the young woman — let us call her Gerda — mentioned the fact that in the Mishnah the reasons for stoning varied but that it seemed the people in Nazareth were thinking of various strictures against false prophets or would-be-prophets in the Torah. In Deuteronomy 13 the people of Israel are warned against anyone who does signs and wonders or indeed anyone who tries to lead the people to worship another God than that of

Israel. They are to stone him with stones "until he dies" (v. 10).

"I would have expected," said Gerda, "that the people would have demanded some proof of Jesus' claims, a thing the rabbinic considerations would suggest."

That idea rang a bell with me. I immediately thought of a passage in which Jesus was asked to give some sign or miracle (Matthew 12:38, *cf.* Luke 11:16; 12:54). He answered,

> "When you see a cloud coming up in the west, at once you say, 'It is going to rain,' and it does. And when you feel the south wind blowing, you say, 'It is going to get hot,' and it does. You can look at the earth and the sky and tell what it means. Why, then, don't you know the meaning of the present time?" (Luke 12:54-56)

In another place we read,

> "It is an evil generation that seeks a sign and no sign but that of Jonah will be given to it, for just as Jonah became a sign to the people of Nineveh so the Son of Man will become a sign to this generation."
>
> "The men of Nineveh will rise up at the judgment with this generation and condemn them, for they repented at the preaching of Jonah, and behold, more than Jonah is here."
>
> "The queen of Sheba will arise at the judgment with the men of this generation and condemn them, for she came from the ends of the earth to hear the wisdom of Solomon, and behold, more than Solomon is here" (Matthew 12:39, 40, 42).

Since many of the sayings of Jesus have been preserved without their original context it seems highly probable that these passages should be inserted here. In them Jesus calls himself the Son of Man, a messianic title taken from Daniel 7:13 which we will again notice later. We hear him saying, not, "I am the Messiah" but words that mean the same. Jesus says he is "more than a Jonah" and more than a Solomon."

It is a stupendous claim among a nation that honored its kings and prophets. On the other hand Jesus shows no petty dogmatism or capriciousness. He reasons with the people even while noting their serious and strong opposition.

> "You will no doubt quote this proverb to me: 'Doctor, heal yourself,' (like our English proverb, 'Barber, why don't you cut your own hair!') 'what we have heard you have been doing in Capernaum do here.' But I will tell you this proverb, No prophet is accepted as such in his own home town" (Luke 4:23, 24).

In the end Jesus drives home the seriousness of their rejection of him and his claims by illustrating how God's miracles and signs are reserved for those who are willing to accept the ministry of his chosen prophets.

> "There were many widows in Israel during the time of Elijah, when there was no rain for three and a half years and there was a great famine throughout the whole land. Yet Elijah was not sent to a single one of them, except a widow in Zarephath, in the territory of Sidon" (Luke 4:25, 26).

> "And there were many lepers in Israel during the time of the prophet Elisha, yet not one of them was made clean except Naaman the Syrian" (v. 27).

Especially strong in Jesus' rebuke is his illustration of miracles the God of Israel did through his prophets Elijah and Elisha to people not of Israel. Non-Jews got the blessing, not Israel (which at the time was strongly idolatrous).

It is no wonder that the leaders of the synagogue rose up and pushed Jesus with them towards the edge of the city's cliff.

Perhaps as they walked they realized that their action was not according to the Torah. Jesus had not blasphemed or profaned the name of God nor had he called upon the people to follow another God than that of Israel. The people of Nazareth were just being overly sensitive. Had we been in their place would we have been any better?

When they came to the edge of the cliff, he turned and, without a word, walked through them and went on his way.

Incidentally, the story of the rejection at Nazareth (Luke 4:16-30) — highly Hebraic and much longer than its parallels in Mark and Matthew — apparently preserves the "longer story" form which we shall find is evidenced by the remarkable fact that our present shorter units can often be recombined to get an earlier, more original and longer story.

In the earlier part of his career Jesus moved from village to village healing in the synagogues, no doubt in both Judea and Galilee. On at least one occasion he was hailed as the messianic Prophet "like Moses" (Deuteronomy 18:18) and in the healing of a paralysed man he used words of forgiveness reserved strictly in the Law to God. He speaks of himself as "the Son of Man" and thus claims the highest and most deity-laden messianic title of the Scriptures.

13 HEALING EVERYWHERE

It is often supposed that Jesus began his career largely through public teaching, lecturing and preaching. This is surely a mistake. Jesus did go about teaching, but clearly *after* he had become famous as an exorcist of demonic powers and healer of broken, diseased bodies.

He followed the same pattern when he later sent out his chosen band of twelve apostles. They were given power to heal and cast out evil spirits and their only "teaching" lay in interpreting what was happening when the healing occurred: "The Kingdom of God has come here."

God had penetrated into man's misery and was healing wherever the apostles had been sent.

This is the reason so many of the first stories in Matthew, Mark and Luke have to do with two points: the identification of Jesus as the Messiah with supernatural character and power, as proved by his healing and confrontation of evil, and the happiness of those who are healed, or watch others as they are healed.

The fame and credibility of Jesus grew precisely as his love and power to heal showed itself in village after village.

For it was in going from village to village, at which time he often performed miracles in the little synagogue of each town, that characterized the early activity of Jesus. This period of ministry was apparently largely a personal one. The "crowd" we so often hear about in the early stories seems to be a synonym for the "local inhabitants" of this or that town in which the event or miracle occurs. Indeed the Greek *ochloi* (crowds) is exactly equivalent to the Hebrew *ochlosin* which the Hebrew of the period borrowed from Greek and meant what we call "the local folk" of a given place.

Later there were so many people crowding around Jesus and his disciples, especially along the shores of the Kinneret that you could speak of real crowds following him from place to place. But not at the beginning.

We also easily suppose that the earliest stories about Jesus occurred almost solely around the Sea of Galilee. However, Luke appears to have known about an early Judean ministry, for he writes (in 4:44) that Jesus went actively preaching in Judea, but says nothing in detail about this ministry.

What seems highly probable is that a number of our early stories actually took place as Jesus went from village to village in and around Judea as well as in Galilee.

For instance, at the end of the story about Jesus' raising the widow's son as he passed a funeral procession when entering a village called Nain we read that Jesus "came and touched the bier" and spoke to the corpse of the young man, "Young man, I say to you, rise up!" The dead man got up and Jesus gave him to his mother while "fear seized them all and they glorified God and said, 'A great prophet has arisen among us. God has visited his people!'" — The short account ends with:

> And this report concerning him spread through *the whole of Judea* and all the surrounding country (Luke 7:11-17).

Not far from Affuleh, near Kibbutz En Dor, is a little village which is shown by the tourist guides as the Nain of this story. However, the possibility that the young man was raised in Judea is strengthened by the fact that there was a Nain in Judea (mentioned by Josephus).

Moreover, we read that Jesus healed a leper ("cleansed a leper" is the biblical phrase) on one occasion and told the man to go to the priest and bring an offering to celebrate his cleansing. Presumably the leper was somewhere in the neighborhood of Jerusalem for that was the only place an offering of an animal could have been made in this period.

There are other stories given in the early part of Luke which cause one to ask whether they may not have occurred in Judea in this early period.

We read of how Jesus healed a man who suffered from a "withered hand" (our Hebrew-Greek calls this ailment a "dry hand") and of a crippled woman he "loosed from Satan" who had been all bent over for eighteen years, both of these on a Sabbath and over the objection of the ruler of the synagogue who religiously quoted the Torah, "Six days shall you labor and on the seventh day you shall rest." These healings may have occurred in Judea, though we have no proof of it (*cf.* Luke 6:6-11; 14:1-6; 13:10-17).

Of very special interest is another story which may come from the early Judean ministry Luke mentions. A paralyzed man is brought by his friends to the house where Jesus is laying hands on the sick. So many have crowded around Jesus inside the house to get his healing that a hole is made in the roof and the man let down by his friends in front of Jesus. Strangely, Jesus does not simply lay hands on the man and heal his paralysis but says to him,

> "Man, your sins are forgiven you" (Luke 5:20).

Until I began putting these stories back into Hebrew I was never able to understand the way some in the crowd looked at Jesus in shock for having said these words. Had I not all my life been told to forgive anyone who did something wrong against me, especially if such a person asked me to forgive him?

No, these critics said, "He is blaspheming. Only God can forgive sins!" In other words they were saying Jesus was using words only God could use.

Then one day I realized that if you put this text back into Hebrew you are reminded of certain passages in the Torah (mainly in the 4th and 5th chapters of Leviticus) in which a person who has committed an "unwitting" sin, for example, has done something against God's will by transgressing a thing forbidden in the Torah and only afterward recognizes his sin. Such a person was told to bring an offering to the priest who would in turn sacrifice two turtle doves or an animal on the altar, at which time it was said God would forgive the person. The phrase used, over and over again, is,

> And forgiven is he.

It is this phrase which Jesus uses here. He says to the man, quite literally,

> "Forgiven are your sins" (Luke 5:20).

Moreover — and this is important — the word used in Hebrew for "forgiven" is the Hebrew *salach*, literally, *nislechu lecha chatoteicha* (forgiven are your sins). Today, in Hebrew, a person may say to another, "*Ani soleach lecha*" (I forgive you), but in the time of Jesus this expression for forgiveness was *only used of God's forgiving someone* (*cf.* Leviticus 4:26, 31, 35).

This is a good illustration of the way the knowledge of modern Hebrew may cause one to go astray when looking at the language of Jesus. You must always use the Hebrew of that period, because modern Hebrew, like modern English compared to that of Shakespeare, is not always the Hebrew of the first century.

Once again, Jesus is not using the hackneyed phrase, "I am the Messiah," or "I am God's special apostle," or "I am like the Angel of the Lord in the Tenach, and speak in my own name as that of God." He is picking up a phrase only God could use and deliberately talking as no man would normally dare to do.

The story ends by Jesus' response to his critics, a touching and beautiful illustration of his, shall I say, teasing sense of humor,

> "What is easier — to say to this paralyzed man, 'Take up your bed and walk' or to say, 'Your sins are forgiven!'"

As you think of it, Jesus' confidence in his role as a divine Messiah — not a warrior about to lead Israel's armies against the Romans — is simply astounding. As some have said from time to time, Jesus can only have been one of three things: a madman whose intelligence belies his madness, an impostor or con-man who not only fooled hundreds of honest Jews in his time but also a billion followers of today, or the Messiah he claimed to be, an honest, loving "Lord" who was better than anyone ever expected him to be.

The last words of Jesus in this story drive home his claims.

> "So you will know that the Son of Man has the authority on earth to forgive sins . . ." (he said to the paralytic) "Take up your bed and walk" (Luke 5:23, 24).

This the man did as he half-stumbled, half-walked through the crowd while people tried to make way for him to get out of the press of bodies waiting for the touch of Jesus.

We have already met the expression Jesus uses in speaking about himself — the Son of Man. It was clearly taken from Daniel 7:13, 14 where Daniel tells of a vision:

> And behold, with the clouds of heaven
> there came one like a son of man
> and he came to the Ancient of Days
> and was presented before him.
> And to him was given dominion

and glory and kingdom,
that all peoples, nations and languages
should serve him.
His dominion is an everlasting dominion
which shall not pass away,
and his kingdom one that shall not
be destroyed.

In the Hebrew Jesus spoke he seems to have inserted the Aramaic expression *bar enash*, the Son of Man, from reference to this passage, and used it as his favorite self-title. Rabbis of the period counted this passage a messianic one, often speaking of the "cloud-man," *anani*, because of Daniel's words. As we shall see, in statement after statement in which Jesus called himself the Son of Man, his emphasis is on his special apostolic divinity and this claim to forgive sins just as his Father forgives sins is underlined by his use of the deity-laden expression Son of Man. Of such a man it can be said:

His dominion is an everlasting dominion
which shall not pass away.

By inviting followers to call him Lord and to itinerate with him in Galilee and Judea Jesus organized a Movement which he saw as made up of those he called disciples and which he called "the Kingdom of God." This was a special phrase originally used by the Pharisees and included only those who accepted and kept the Torah. Scholars have erred in thinking Jesus meant political rule over Israel or the world.

14 A NEW MOVEMENT

A great many foolish things have been said and written about Jesus. For example one scholar has written:

> Suppose we try to picture a typical day in Jesus' life. It was not lived by schedule probably; his social contacts like those of Socrates were of the most accidental sort. He was neither a systematic teacher of his disciples, nor careful in his evangelistic planning. He wandered hither and thither in Galilee. He sowed his seed largely at random and left results to God. More depended, he believed, on the soil, than on the sowing. Probably much that is commonly said about the general purpose of Jesus' life and the specific place in that purpose of detailed incidents is modern superimposition upon a nearly patternless life and upon nearly patternless records of it.

Strangely enough this same writer cannot help but notice that little item about how Jesus left Capernaum and, when found walking away early in the morning by many from the town, said,

> "I must also bring good news to other towns, for for this reason I was sent" (Luke 4:43).

He admits there may have been more planning for the future by Jesus but says he is not sure.

The evidence is that Jesus did a number of things which can only be explained by his feeling of planning and purpose.

One of these was what we label the "calling" of disciples. In rabbinic sources we hear often of famous rabbis who gathered *talmidim*, learners, around them and taught them Torah and rabbinic traditions about the Torah. The difference seems to be that Jesus not only called *talmidim* to learn Torah from him but also eventually to be granted powers of healing and exorcism in his name so that they could perform the same kinds of miracles he performed.

A number of stories in our Gospels tell about Jesus inviting this or that one "to be his disciple" and it is from this band of itinerating followers who go with him from place to place that he afterwards chooses twelve to be his *shelichim* or apostles. It was, of course, this latter group of specially chosen leaders who eventually headed and guided the movement Jesus founded.

One moving story records how Jesus came to the edge of the Kinneret one morning followed by a large number of people, got into a fishing boat owned by Simon, and requested to be rowed out a ways from the shore. He then taught the people in what may have been a kind of natural amphitheatre (voices carry well across calm water). Afterwards he asked the fishermen if they would lower their nets to bring in a catch of fish. Simon agreed, with the comment, "Lord, we have worked all night and caught nothing — nevertheless, at your word I will do so" (Luke 5:5). When they did let down the nets they caught so many fish the two boats involved almost sank from the enormous number of fish.

"Lord," said Simon who was also called Peter (a Greek name meaning Rock), "depart from me for I am a man of iniquity." He was prostrate at the feet of Jesus when Jesus gently said, "Don't be afraid! From now on you will be catching men!" (Luke 5:8,10).

Simon, the story goes, "left all and followed him." So did his brother Andrew, along with two other fishermen, James (Yaakov) and John (Yochanan). These early *talmidim* were apparently soon joined by many others. We hear of three men, one after another, who approached Jesus wanting to become disciples (Luke 9:57-62):

> One man said to him, "I will follow you wherever you go!" Jesus said to him, "The foxes have holes and the birds have nests but the Son of Man has nowhere even to lay his head."
>
> To one man he said, "Follow me." But he said, "Lord, let me first go and bury my father" (he meant, presumably, to wait to join Jesus till his old father had died). Jesus told him, "Let the dead bury their dead but you go and proclaim the Kingdom of God."

The third man had a similar excuse and Jesus said to him, "No one who puts his hand to the plow and looks back is fit for the Kingdom of God." He was talking about the small Near Eastern plow a farmer guided with one hand as he directed his animals with the other.

It is clear that in inviting and accepting many *talmidim* to go with him from place to place as he continued to work miracles of healing and exorcism Jesus was forming a band of followers who were prepared not only to learn from him but to carry out any requirement of life or duty he laid upon them. These are the people in our Gospels who call Jesus "Lord." When they join his learners he says they have "come into" or "received" the Kingdom of Heaven, that is, the Kingdom of God.

The Kingdom of God is the place where God is reigning, or, if you wish, the person or community he is ruling. Jesus explains that when he casts out a demon "the Kingdom of God" has come upon all those present, that is, God has taken charge of a situation in which formerly the devil ruled. God has penetrated the very spot in which men find themselves under Satan's control.

Modern Christians have had great difficulty in understanding what Jesus meant by the Kingdom of Heaven. They have often supposed that since the rabbis used the same expression, *malchut shammayim*, the Jews in general had some kind of idea that the Messiah would some day, defeat all of Israel's enemies and "set up" the Kingdom of God. Such thinkers talk about Jesus as having expected the "inauguration of the Kingdom of God" at some future time, before or after he had himself died. One of those who wrote with such a misconception was the famous Albert Schweizer.

There were Jews and rabbis who did hope for a messianic figure that would one day defeat Israel's enemies and bring peace on Israel. *Melech hamashiah* or King Messiah they sometimes called him. But the rabbinic writings — apparently guided by the early Pharisees — have a much more distinct and non-military meaning to the expression *malchut shammayim*.

For them, this Kingdom was, in essence, the *rule of God*, most often described as equal to the personal acceptance of God's reigning over a given person. The rabbis speak of repeating the *Shema* (Deuteronomy 6:4) as taking upon oneself the "yoke of the Kingdom" or, even very often, of "taking upon oneself the Kingdom of Heaven." What they mean is that once a man says the *Shema* he will go on to keep the commandments (Deuteronomy 11:13ff).

Now this is a distinctly *spiritual* understanding of the expression Kingdom of Heaven or Kingdom of God. A man *decides* to "do the will of God" and at that moment God comes to take charge of him and all that he is.

This basic meaning of *personal acceptance of God's rule* over the believer or follower is carried over by Jesus in his use of the expression.

It has a distinctly spiritual meaning. The Gospel of John, which often epitomizes the very thought of Jesus, puts it this way when Jesus is asked by Pilate the Roman governor if he is not, after all, a King,

> "My Kingdom is not of this world. If my Kingdom were of this world, then would my servants fight" (John 18:36).

I shall never forget a talk I once had with a young rabbi on this subject. With my family, which then numbered only Margaret and our two first children, David and Lenore, I was aboard a ship coming across the Mediterranean en route to Jerusalem and the rabbi and I struck up a friendship. Somehow I asked him how Jews understand the expression Kingdom of Heaven. Standing on the deck as the boat rocked from the gentle swells of that inland sea he welcomed my question, for he had often discussed it with Christians.

"Look," he said, "Christians have got a basically wrong idea about what Jews mean when they talk about the Kingdom of God."

I must have looked puzzled, for he went on to explain his criticism.

"What the rabbis meant — and we Jews believe today — is that to get into the Kingdom of God a person has to decide to do what God wants him to do, and that is all laid down in the Torah and the Mishnah. Anybody who keeps the commandments as laid down in these books has let God start ruling him — *he is in the Kingdom of Heaven!*"

"Somehow," he went on, "Christians have gotten the idea that when all the Jews get back to Israel or Israel's army takes more and more of the Middle East to incorporate it into Israel that is what Jews hope for and think of as 'setting up' the Kingdom of God. This is simply not true."

"Why, we can have the Kingdom of Heaven wherever we are, just so we keep the commandments God gave us!"

Through the years I have often thought of this conversation when some evangelical Christians have come from time to time to Jerusalem to announce that they are expecting Jesus to return within a few weeks and rebuild the ancient Temple in order to live there and rule the world. Such Christians have been taught that Jesus will take up the sword of worldly power and literally fulfill all the messianic pictures of an earthly, military leader. They suppose that the Kingdom of God Jesus talked about has not come because the visible, earthly trappings of a military empire led by him have not come into being.

This interpretation of the second coming of Jesus appears to have come late into Christian history. A Roman Catholic priest in Chile nearly two hundred years ago outlined the principal points of this scheme and although his book in Spanish (printed in 1812 after his death) was both in the last century and this condemned by the Holy See it was taken up earnestly and popularized by some Protestant evangelicals in the early part of the nineteenth century and has many thousands of devotees until today.

The name of the Chilean priest was Emmanuel Lacunza. He wrote that according to many Old Testament prophecies "which have not been fulfilled" Jesus the Messiah will set up his throne in a rebuilt Temple, will daily supervise the sacrificing of animals as in ancient times and will then distribute to all present *the elements of the mass.* Certain evangelicals, first in Great Britain and then in the United States, picked up the scheme of Lacunza, modified some of his specifically Roman Catholic ideas, and over the years have published hundreds of books following Lacunza's basic interpretations.

Christians need badly to listen to Jews when it comes to learning what expressions like the Kingdom of Heaven mean. The expression Kingdom of Heaven — or Kingdom of God (Heaven, as we have seen, is an evasive synonym for God used by Jews in the first century in order not to "take the name of the Lord in vain") — is not found in the Old Testament but was used by the rabbis. Almost certainly Jesus borrowed this term from Pharisaic use and gave it his own, special meaning.

And what was this meaning?

Apparently two basic ideas converge in Jesus' use.

First of all, he meant, quite simply, that in his own performance of healings and miracles God was manifesting his presence and power. When a person was healed as Jesus laid his hands on him the Kingdom of Heaven, the Rule of God, was shown to have come into effect in the person healed.

We read that on one occasion Jesus was causing a demonic spirit to leave an afflicted person and some people present criticized him, saying that he was operating under the power of Beelzebul, the chief of the demons. Jesus' answer to this criticism included these words:

> "If I am using the power of Satan to get rid of Satan's own servants that must mean there is rebellion in his camp (his kingdom). On the other hand if I cast out demons by the finger of God this means that the Kingdom of God has come down onto you!" (Luke 11:17, 20).

It is clear that for Jesus the direct confrontation he made against the enemy of man meant that the love and power of God *had supernaturally impinged* at the place where many miserable people on this earth were living. This was the real battle he came to fight. Men — in this case his own flesh and blood — were in bondage to a bigger enemy than the Romans and they needed salvation. When a satanic spirit was driven out by Jesus the Kingdom of God took over — *God took charge at that point.*

Moreover, this struggle, this fight, was being fought under Jesus' own leadership. It was being fought on a limited battlefield, the place where the demon had been vanquished.

For Jesus the Kingdom of God was not some sort of generalized, indefinite rule of God over the whole world, real as that might be. The Kingdom of God was located where Jesus was, where he was leading the battle. He was himself the "King" of the Kingdom of God.

The second meaning Jesus had for the Kingdom of God follows from this definition. Wherever a person would join him at his call he became a part of the Kingdom. By following the leadership of Jesus he is *both ruled by God and is ruling* with the Messiah in the sense that he is battling disease and death, Satan and sin. Jesus can even speak of those people following him as "the Kingdom of God" or as being "in the Kingdom of God."

On one occasion, contrasting John the Baptist with his own followers, Jesus says,

> "The smallest in the Kingdom of Heaven is greater than John" (Luke 7:28).

Jesus was drawing together large numbers of people into his "Kingdom of God," into his movement. John did not join Jesus' band and learn at his feet as a *talmid.* He continued his own work of calling for repentance, but in this special meaning of the Kingdom of Heaven as God's flock led by Jesus, John tragically did not participate.

When Jesus stated that he had come not to "destroy the Law and the Prophets but to strengthen them" (Matthew 5:17) he said that not "one jot or tittle would pass away from the Law until heaven and earth pass away," using as he did so a rabbinic hyperbole which referred to the smallest letter of the Hebrew alphabet and its little hook on the end of the letter. He added to which,

> "Whoever relaxes one of the least of these commandments and teaches men so shall be called 'least' *(katon)* in the Kingdom of Heaven, but he who does them and teaches them shall be called 'great' *(chamur)* in the Kingdom of Heaven" (Matthew 5:18, 19).

Clearly, he is talking about his followers. They are in his movement, in God's "Kingdom."

Let me say it again: for Jesus the Kingdom of God is not some specious, grandiose way of talking about how God is ruling the entire world, controlling kings and empires and allowing or preventing national and international disasters but is strictly — in this second sense — a term used to designate those *who are in the Jesus movement.*

That is why Jesus can contrast Satan's Kingdom with God's Kingdom, or as I translated it a few lines ago, Satan's "camp," which has as its opposite, God's "camp." Satan rules his camp, God rules his camp. Satan has his followers, God has his.

That is why Jesus can later use the *Edah* (Church) as synonymous with the Kingdom of Heaven (Matthew 16:18, 19). That is why Jesus will later tell the authorities of the Temple,

> "...The Kingdom of God will be taken from you and given to a nation bearing the fruits of it" (Matthew 21:43).

He does not mean that the Sadducaic priests in the Temple have some kind of authority to rule in the name of God or his Kingdom and are about to lose it; he means that his own followers as "the Kingdom of God" will be moved out of the milieu which was Israel before 70 A.D. and sent to be his "witnesses in all the world" (*cf.* Acts 1:8).

It is probable that the Hebrew word for kingdom, when translated to our western languages, is what makes it so hard for Christians to grasp what the Hebrew-speaking Jew of the first century understood so easily. *Malchut* is a kind of verbal noun in Hebrew. *Malchut Shammayim* is often "God's ruling" and, secondarily, "the area God is ruling." This latter meaning is why we are able to speak of the *malchut* as a movement or "camp." We western people, however, think of a kingdom as a territorial and political entity ruled by an army or a police force fully equipped to defend one's "national" rights. For this reason all kinds of liberal as well as fundamentalist Christian interpreters of the Bible have easily supposed that Jesus looked forward to becoming a king ruling over all the Jews of ancient Israel in a quite literal, physical way and why many evangelicals today expect the Temple to be literally rebuilt when Jesus returns so that he can rule the world from Jerusalem.

This misconception — which began with Lacunza so long ago — can only be described as a colossal distortion of what Jesus meant when he spoke of *malchut shammayim*. It led, for instance, to the idea that Jesus presented himself to Jews generally as their physical and supernatural king and offered them the right to become the political and religious "Kingdom of God" ruling the entire world. According to this idea the Jews rejected Jesus' offer of "the Kingdom" and this led to the crucifixion of Jesus by the Romans, the result of which spiritually was that the Kingdom of God was relegated to a shelf while the great period of "grace" was begun in which the world will in part be evangelized in the name of Jesus the Messiah before Jesus returns.

Further concomitants of this view dictate that when Jesus comes back he will temporarily catch his believers up "in the air" while the Jews in their revived state of Israel fight most of the nations of the world in the "battle of Armageddon." At that time he will descend from heaven and personally rescue the Jewish people, and set up his messianic kingdom in Jerusalem for a thousand years. God will succeed in the future in "setting up the Kingdom of God" on earth in accordance with the Old Testament prophecies and the people of Israel will completely evangelize the world in the name of Jesus the Messiah, a thing the *goyim* could never do in the period of "grace."

If Christians could once grasp that Jesus meant by the Kingdom of God a "people bringing forth the fruits thereof," a voluntary movement which he later called the *Edah* (witnessing congregation or Church where God was in charge empowering and working his miracles) they would be able to overcome a great deal of misunderstanding and be able to give up many false expectations.

But here I must tell about how my friend Flusser made a big breakthrough in understanding a famous text about the Kingdom of God.

It is incorrect to translate Matthew 11:12 as "The Kingdom of Heaven suffers violence." Jesus is hinting at a famous messianic verse in the prophecy of Micah (2:13) and is saying that his Movement — the Kingdom of God — is "breaking forth" or expanding like a mustard seed or like leaven in bread. Actually he is not only talking of his Kingdom Movement but about himself as King.

15 THE BREAKER

From the beginning of this book I have been claiming that when we return many of the Greek passages in the Gospels back to Hebrew and when we compare those passages to rabbinic usage we do sometimes get an exciting light on what they really mean.

We have already noticed that on one occasion when Jesus was talking about John the Baptizer he stated that "the smallest in the Kingdom of Heaven" was "greater than John." On the same occasion the following words are recorded:

> "From the days of John until now the Kingdom of Heaven suffers violence, and the violent take it by force" (Matthew 11:12).

Almost anyone who reads these words wonders what they mean, commentators included. I remember many years ago trying for hours at a time guessing about one solution or another. A well-known volume entitled *THE JERUSALEM BIBLE* has these notes at the bottom of the page where this passage occurs:

> Various interpretations have been offered. The violence may be:
>
> 1. . . . the bitter self-sacrifice of those who would take possession of the kingdom;
> 2. the misguided violence of those who would establish the kingdom by force (the Zealots);
> 3. the tyrannical violence of the powers of evil . . .

It is clear that none of these solutions makes much sense. I remember thinking once that perhaps what Jesus meant was that only the very aggressive could manage to get into the Kingdom of God. That was so unlike the man from Galilee, who said,

> "Come unto me all you who labor and are heavy laden and I will give you rest" (Matthew 11:28).

that I decided my solution was as bad as the others I had seen.

One thing that intrigued me several years ago was the possibility that the Greek word which is usually rendered "suffers violence" *(biazetai)* might not have a passive sense but an active sense. Perhaps, I guessed, it represents the Hebrew word *poretz*, but I concluded it was just a random thought of mine and doubtless a bad guess.

Imagine my surprise when one day as I came to see Flusser for a couple of hours of study he looked up to me from his desk, cluttered with books, and said, "Lindsey, I think I know what *biazetai* means! In fact, I know what it means!"

"Fine, what is it?" I could only ask.

"Look," he said seriously, "I was looking up something Radak mentioned." Radak is the name by which a famous medieval rabbi and commentator is known.

"I am all ears," I said.

"*Biazetai* is a translation of *poretz*!" he almost shouted, waving a Hebrew Bible at me. Radak mentions an old interpretation of Micah 2:13. Look at Micah 2:12 and 13."

I read it:

> I will surely gather all of you, O Jacob . . .
> like sheep in a fold,
> like a flock in its pasture,
> a noisy multitude of men.
>
> The breaker *(poretz)* will go up before them;
> they will break through and pass the gate,
> going out by it.
> Their king will pass on before them,
> The Lord at their head.

It was clear what the prophet was saying. God was comparing Israel to a flock kept up at night behind a temporary rock wall. In the morning the shepherd "breaks open" a gap in the wall and the sheep run pell-mell through the opening. But since he is really talking about people, the shepherd or "breaker" is both "their king before them" and "the Lord at their head."

"Radak retains this old midrash on the Messiah," said Flusser. "He says that 'the Breaker' is Elijah who precedes the coming of the Messiah, the 'king' is *melech hamashiach* and 'the Lord' is of course the God of Israel."

Typical rabbinic exposition of a messianic passage.

"All the people of course know this text of Micah 2:13 refers to the Messiah," continued Flusser. Jesus hints at it as he so often does in other passages. We have to read it as follows:

> "From the days of John until now the Kingdom of Heaven is breaking out" *(poretzet*—feminine form of poretz)

My earlier guess was right after all! Jesus is not talking about the Kingdom of Heaven "suffering violence" (although our Greek author Matthew probably supposes this meaning since he adds "and the violent seize it") but *breaking forth or breaking out, expanding, and growing as many more come into the movement.*

There are a number of lessons to be gathered from this "breakthrough" of Flusser.

One is that the use of the tool of retranslating to Hebrew can often be combined with rabbinic usage and interpretation and a difficult passage exposed and expounded correctly.

Another is the suggestion that, as so often, Jesus avoids speaking directly of himself and therefore speaks of "the Kingdom" breaking forth but not of himself as the King. In actuality anyone who knows the Micah passage will understand that *Jesus is really saying that he is the Shepherd, Breaker, King and Lord.*

Still another lesson is that Jesus is contrasting the movement John had led with his own Kingdom of God: Jesus' movement began in the wake of John's charismatic preaching and at the beginning was no doubt small, yet when John died the movement continued to grow and expand by leaps and bounds. It is highly probable that two of Jesus' parables about the growth of the Kingdom of God were uttered shortly after this part of Jesus' discourse about John:

> "What is the Kingdom of Heaven like and to what shall I compare it?
>
> "It is like a grain of mustard seed which a man took and sowed in his field, and it grew and became a tree, and the birds of the heavens came and made nests in its branches.
>
> "The Kingdom of Heaven is also like leaven a woman took and hid in three measures of meal until it was all leavened" (Matthew 13:31-33).

The final lesson is more of a question. Was Jesus thinking only of the expansion of his movement "since the days of John" or was he prophesying of the enormous growth his movement would continue to have throughout history?

In any case it seems impossible to agree with the judgment that Jesus "was neither a systematic teacher ... nor careful in his evangelistic planning, "wandering hither and thither in Galilee" in a "nearly patternless life."

He appears more to be the Master Planner.

The rabbis argued endlessly and often productively about the implications of each command in the Law. Jesus also hallowed the Torah and pointed out its rich meaning for ethical behavior. By combining two passages in Luke and one from Matthew we can restore his teaching about the meaning of "neighbor" (the Hebrew equivalent means both friend and fellow human being) and thus sample his method of underlining the importance of the Torah.

16 TEACHER OF TORAH

One of the few "teaching" episodes which may have occurred in Jerusalem in what we have surmised was Jesus' early Judean ministry is a remarkable account of a one-on-one encounter between a lawyer or *sofer* and the rabbi from Galilee. It is unrelated to any miracle or exorcism. There is, moreover, no suggestion that the story comes from the later time when disciples *(talmidim)* were involved.

There is also a certain, delightful absence of the feeling of crisis and debate which one so often senses in the various stories of confrontation which characterize the last week or so of the life of Jesus. Almost certainly the story took place in the unhurried atmosphere of the early ministry of Jesus, whether in Judea or in Galilee.

Luke (10:25-28) tells the story in the following words:

> "Rabbi, what must I do to get (literally, 'inherit') eternal life?"

Jesus is addressed by this scholar of Torah and tradition as "rabbi," which literally means "my teacher." By the time the rabbinic literature was written down (200 A.D.) this turning to a teacher and addressing him as "my teacher" *(rab-bi)* lost its simple Hebrew meaning of "my" teacher and became simply rabbi so-and-so, rabbi Meir, or rabbi Yochanan, or rabbi Ben Tov. It is one of the characteristics of the Gospels that they at times preserve Hebraic terminology current a hundred or more years before much of the rabbinic material was published.

Jesus answers the man,

> "What is written in the Torah? How do you read what you find there?"

The man responds by saying,

> "You shall love the Lord your God with all your heart, with all your soul, and with all your strength, and your neighbor as yourself."

The *sofer*, or scribe, has neatly combined two famous "You shall love" Torah passages (Deuteronomy 6:5 and Leviticus 19:18), a combination that was already known before the time of Jesus.

Jesus replies,

> "You have answered right. Do this and you will live."

As Luke records this story the scribe then asked Jesus, "Who is my neighbor" and in Jesus' answer he told the story well-known to all as "the Good Samaritan" — the story of a Samaritan who helped a Jew who had fallen among thieves on the road to Jericho.

I must happily credit my friend Flusser with what I believe is an important reconstruction at this point. He noticed that in what we call the Sermon on the Mount there is a long discussion by Jesus of his interpretation of the Torah and it ends up by discussing the "who is my neighbor" question (*cf.* Matthew 5:43-48). He suggests that we lay out the following sequence of passages:

1. Luke 10:25-28
2. Matthew 5:17-48
3. Luke 10:29-37

"This sequence," says Flusser, "makes excellent sense and accords with what some of us have found when we have taken scattered units and recombined them to demonstrate their earlier, more original, form."

And so it does. See how Jesus continues to answer the scribe by turning to those standing around who have heard the conversation of the scribe and the one he calls rabbi ("my teacher").

> "Do not think that I have come to do away with the Torah and the Prophets. I have not come to do away with them, but to strengthen what they teach (Matthew 5:17).

Then he talks about "whoever relaxes one of these least commandments and teaches others to do so," and then speaks of "whoever does them and teaches them." The first kind of person will be called least *(katon)* in the Kingdom of Heaven while the second type of person will be called great *(chamur)* in the Kingdom of Heaven. We have already noticed this passage but let us remind ourselves again that Jesus simply means that in this continuing body of disciples which he calls the Kingdom of God those who have a reverence for all that the Torah is meant to teach are the ones who will be respected. The words *katon* and *chamur* are rabbinic expressions related to the way some people can suppose a small commandment is of less value than a great one — the rabbis said no commandment was small — Jesus says that the person who makes "small" anything in the Torah will be called "small" and *vice versa*.

Now come discussions of five typical commandments of the Torah (Matthew 5:21-48). However, most are from the Ten Commandments and all are what you can call central, ethical commandments which have far-reaching importance to human beings. Jesus is here criticizing the way people abuse the commands even while glibly quoting them.

Thou shalt not murder

He begins by talking about the law against murder (in English it is translated "kill" but the Hebrew says "murder," and there is a difference!). He does not say that it is "written" one should not kill but only that "it is said, you shall not murder." He is mimicking the way this commandment comes out of the mouth of most every Jew of the period: "Yes", they would say, "no one should murder!"

"Ah yes," says Jesus, "and what if you just get angry at your friend and call him a bad name?" That too, he is saying, is back of the command not to murder, for if you get so angry you can murder someone (or want to) you are already starting to transgress and sin.

Thou shalt not commit adultery

"You have heard people say this, too," says Jesus. "I tell you if you look at a woman to want to have sex with her (and she is married) you have already committed adultery with her!" Cut off the reason for doing wrong before you transgress in the central sin.

Do not swear falsely

People quoted this commandment too. It is a prohibition against injuring another through lying. In ancient times a person who was willing to swear by this or that was thought to be reliable. If he swore by his god or a religious symbol like the Temple, or Jerusalem, he was inviting trouble if he did not carry out his oath. Long before the time of the Second Temple, however, swearing had lost its meaning as a preventive to lying.

Jesus therefore says one should not "swear at all, neither by the earth nor heaven nor Jerusalem" nor by whatever else occurs to the swearer. "You should say No or Yes. Anything more comes from the evil one."

Eye for eye, tooth for tooth

He is still quoting these strong commandments but in the way people say them. It is easy to say, "This one or that one killed someone: let us kill him!" or, "He shot my father, I will kill him!"

Jesus then quotes apparently from Psalm 37:9, 11. "Cease from wrath and give up anger, do not be so angry that you do more wrong." Nay, go even farther when someone does you wrong: If he strikes you on your right cheek turn the left one so he can strike it. If he makes you go a mile with him (a common thing the Roman soldier often did to force someone to help him carry his luggage) go with him still another mile! When you follow this way of dealing with wrong you can often succeed in curbing the meanness of the person who would mistreat you.

Thou shalt love thy neighbor

Now we see how people think on the popular level when they repeat the command to "love one's neighbor." "Love your *friend* (the Hebrew has *rea* which can also mean friend) *but hate your enemy*!" By a clever play on the double meaning of *rea* people would quote the commandment but cancel its ethical meaning.

Jesus picks up those words "and hate your enemy" and turns them back on the person who would misuse the commandment of the Torah. "You must not hate your enemy. You must do something much bigger to fulfill this commandment of loving your neighbor. You must actually *love* your *enemy* and pray for him if you want to fulfill this commandment."

It is clear what Jesus is saying. The Law, he says, tells you more than at first it seems to be telling you. You have to ask what God means by these commandments, for the outward prohibition reveals only the end danger of a process of ethical deterioration. That is why Jesus calls *chamur* (great) the man in his Kingdom who upholds them and *katon* (little, least) the man who makes "little" of them.

The rabbis added many prohibitions which were intended to protect a person from transgressing this or that commandment of the Torah. Their additional prohibitions were labeled a "fence around the Law" *(siyag latorah)*. Jesus seems not to be putting a fence around the Torah but insisting that behind each given commandment there lies an ethical and psychological danger or need which must first be faced before the outward and final prohibition even comes within the range of possibility.

To sum up the way Jesus probes the conscience as he teaches the Torah:

Murder is terrible but beware! Anger is almost worse and must be dealt with before it bears the deadly fruit of murder.

Adultery is terrible but long before it takes place outwardly it takes place in the heart.

Swearing falsely to a neighbor's hurt shows how dangerous is lying but in any case swearing itself has become meaningless as a protection against lying so let a man's word be simply Yes or No.

People callously say "eye for eye, tooth for tooth" but, like murder, a man must learn to bite his tongue and not increase evil by taking revenge. Two wrongs do not a right make.

The Torah says that you are to love your neighbor as yourself. Popularly people like to add, "Ah yes, and that means you should hate the one who hates you!" Turn this around, says Jesus, and consider even your enemy your neighbor! Pray for him and do good to him.

Finally, we return to Flusser's reconstruction.

The scribe hears all that Jesus has said and asks the needling question, "And who is my *rea*, my neighbor?" Jesus answers with this parable:

> "There was a man who was going down from Jerusalem to Jericho, when robbers attacked, stripped him, and beat him up, leaving him half-dead. Now a priest was going down that road and when he saw the man he walked on by, on the other side. In the same way a Levite also came along, went over and looked at the man, and then walked on by, on the other side. But a man who was a Samaritan came along that way and when he saw the man he was filled with pity. He went over to him, poured oil and wine on his wounds and bandaged them. Then he put the man on his own animal and took him to an inn, where he took care of him. The next day he took out two silver coins and gave them to the innkeeper. 'Take care of him,' he told the innkeeper, 'and when I come back this way I will pay you back whatever you spend on him'" (Luke 10:30-35).

At the end of this story, Jesus concludes,

> "In your opinion which one of these three acted as neighbor *(rea)* to the man attacked by robbers?"
>
> The scribe says, "the one who was kind to him." Jesus replied, "You go, then, and do the same " (vss. 36, 37).

In the story the priest and the Levite are really prisoners of their own liturgical regulations: they are not allowed to touch a dead body and this half-dead body of a man thrown by the wayside may defile them. Jesus contrasts them with the good Samaritan, who simply as a human being takes pity on a fellow human being.

There is a lesson in this for all of us who participate in religious and liturgical acts (even a Quaker meeting has a certain liturgy) but how easily these acts can imprison us and make us no longer sensitive to a hurting world!

Of course the contemporaries of Jesus believed that God was good but they found it harder to believe he was immediate. Through humorous similes and parables Jesus taught that God was near and would hear the persistent prayers of his faithful servants.

17 WAS JESUS A REFORMER?

In the story of the good Samaritan, which Jesus deliberately tells to a strict, very religious interpreter of the Torah there is certainly implied criticism of religious systems which try to regulate societies according to what they think is the will of God.

We noticed before that in criticizing the people of Nazareth for their failure to believe in his role as Messiah and Deliverer Jesus referred to miracles performed by Elijah and Elisha on non-Jews when plenty of ethnically-pure candidates existed right among the people of Israel themselves. Do these and other examples of Jesus' prophetic stance among his own people mean that he was primarily a reformer?

If we mean by a reformer someone who wants to pull people in the direction of a right understanding of the goodness and immediacy of God, a goodness and immediacy which had been covered over by a mass of religious regulations and tradition in which this is "permitted" but this is "forbidden," one has to say Yes. If we mean by a reformer one who hopes to bring an entire nation into some kind of modification of the existing religious practices one has to say No. There is no indication that Jesus was that kind of reformer.

While preaching everywhere and demonstrating God's concern to break through into the life of his people as he tirelessly moved from town to town Jesus took a quite different path. He seems to have seen no possibility of changing the encrusted ways of an official religion and tradition, and to have done so would no doubt have meant a semi-political revolution ending in the kind of reform Turkey went through under Ataturk. Under Ataturk the blaring megaphones of the mosque have been silenced and the mullahs displaced but the inclinations and habits of the multitude have largely remained as entrenched in tradition as ever.

Jesus' way appears to have been to find the men, simple or

profound, who would be willing to "leave all and follow him." He was to make out of them a Kingdom — a movement — which would build on the good of Israel's past and revelation but eventually burst the bonds of locality and nationality.

If we even for a moment consider our own religious traditions, both Jewish and Christian, we can easily come up with illustrations of the near hopelessness of our best religious institutions and practices.

Some of my Israeli friends, both Orthodox and non-Orthodox, express a certain sadness when they read the *Tenach* (Old Testament) and note that Abraham our father, *Rabbenu* Moses, David the King and all the prophets get direct words from Israel's God and pray or speak to him without using a prayer book. They say that in today's synagogue service there is almost no possibility for the worshippers to say a personal prayer, though such a possibility once existed.

"We have lost something," they say, "but no one knows how to revamp tradition and return to the spontaneity of old."

The same thing has happened over and over again in the history of the Christian Church.

How different is the story of the early Jewish-Christian Church. Almost every page of the New Testament glows with the sense of God's immediacy and love. Prayer is personal as well as corporate and God answers the prayers of his people. When Peter is thrown into prison by one of the Herods and condemned to die the next day the Church in Jerusalem gathers to pray, and the very same night an angel visits Peter in the prison and says, "Get up!" Prison chains fall off and the angel leads Peter through open doors to the street where he proceeds alone to the house of a "brother." He knocks and so casual is the story that it tells of a young girl named Rhoda who comes to the gate to open it but on seeing Peter is so excited she runs back to the believers without even opening the gate!

Who says the Bible does not record some comic things that happened to ordinary people in the course of quite supernatural events?

But modern Christians, no matter how orthodox their religious convictions, tend to relegate the possibility that God might do something as miraculous as what he did to Peter to "that ancient beginning of our faith two thousand years ago." Quite marvelous theories are seriously presented which suggest, for example, that when the canon of Scripture (including Old Testament and New Testaments) was completed in the first century, miracles "ceased" because the was no longer any need for them — since we have the Scriptures and that is enough!

We are like the people at Sinai when out of fear of the "smoke and thunder" coming from the holy mountain they kept their distance and said to Moses, "You listen to the words of God. We are too afraid!"

Several years ago one of my Baptist colleagues who lives in the Tel Aviv area was visiting in the United States with his wife and family. A lady in the church they were attending fell sick with cancer and was given only three months to live. David and his wife, Jean, were fresh from Israel and a fellowship where they had experienced real answers to many prayers and they wondered if they should take some initiative in going to see the sick lady to pray for her.

The three months she had been given to live were almost over when David and Jean got up the courage to go to visit the lady. Because there is a passage in the *Epistle of James* in the New Testament which advises the early believers to ask the elders of the local congregation to anoint the sick with oil since "like Elijah" the fervent, effectual prayer of a good man will be answered, David took along a little vial of olive oil, "just in case."

To their surprise the lady asked them whether they thought that passage in *James' Letter* was still applicable for today. That was their signal to use the oil and pray over her, which, of course, they did.

The next day the lady called David. "You know," she said, "something seems to be happening to me. My feet are not black today!" David said, "Mine are not black either!"

To make a long story short, this lady immediately recovered from cancer and her disease was said to be "in remission" by her doctor. The people of the church were happy, but a little in shock. They believed in God but they were not used to having answers that were so miraculous!

More difficult was the whole experience for the lady's husband, however. He was happy that his wife was well but he was not used to seeing the Almighty step into his life so dramatically. He felt, as he confessed, a kind of confusion, though why he felt this way he could not really tell.

His wife, who was perhaps a stronger believer than he, decided she would ask her Lord to do something to make her husband more certain that God is willing to penetrate supernaturally into our lives.

It never occurred to her that a table they had had in their front room for some years and which had been put in their basement because the top had warped so badly that it could not be repaired might have something to do with helping her husband.

But one day soon after her healing her husband came up from the basement and said to her, "Honey, you know the table we put down in the basement?" She replied, "Yes," having almost forgotten it.

"Did you have it repaired?" he asked.

"No," she said.

"Well," he said slowly, "we've got some kind of miracle. That top is no longer warped. It is perfect."

To the amusement of the wife and everyone who later heard the story the husband brought the table up from the basement and placed it in the very center of the living room. As friends came by to see them he related the story of the table.

To relate to his wife's healing seemed too difficult. The healing of the table was quite a different story!

Settled practices, habits and tradition can often be very good indeed but they can also prevent us from finding reality and the joy of truth, no matter how emancipating it may be. Jesus still shocks most of us when he talks of prayer and says so casually,

> "Ask and you will receive.
> Seek and you will find.
> Knock and it shall be opened to you.
>
> For everyone who asks receives
> And he who seeks finds,
> And to him who knocks it will be opened" (Matthew 7:7, 8).

Jesus welcomed into his prophetic Kingdom of God any who would commit themselves to his leadership and this included many who were considered outcasts in the society of his day. Two stories about two tax collectors can be restored to show how effectively Jesus shared his concern for those ridiculed by an uncaring — though religious — society. In expressing this concern he uses words only attributed to God in Ezekiel.

18 HIPPIES ARE WELCOME!

For a moment let me skip ahead a bit.

So far as we can tell from the records, Jesus continued to welcome *talmidim* into the Kingdom even up to the last few days before his epochal entry into Jerusalem.

In Jericho a man awaited the arrival of the Galilean pilgrims with Jesus among them and because he was "short of stature" climbed a sycamore tree to see him (the sycamore trees in Israel grow fruit on their bark and their branches have few leaves). Jesus spotted him and told him to come down out of the tree, for, as he said, "I am going to your house today." The man was so excited he ran home, had a meal prepared for Jesus and his people, and made an about face as a wealthy tax-collector, promising to restore fourfold any moneys he had taken wrongly. Like all those joining the Movement, he called Jesus Lord (Luke 19: 1-10).

Like tax-collectors everywhere at all times, tax-collectors in the period of the Second Temple were much hated and some of the more religious types criticized Jesus for allowing such despicable characters to share his teaching and table. Jesus defended his inclusion of such people by saying that these outcast Jews were the very ones who needed to be welcomed and healed. One is reminded of a letter Billy Graham once wrote to a lady who said she would like to be a believer in the Savior Billy preached but she was not "good enough." Billy wrote her that she was in the main class of people God is interested in saving.

In Jericho, the tax-collector, whose name was Zacchaeus (Zaccai), was labelled by some present "a sinner." When Zaccai declared his repentance and his willingness to make restitution for any unfair tax he had collected, Jesus said,

"Today salvation has come to this house, since he too is a son of Abraham, for the Son of Man has come to seek and save the lost" (Luke 19:9, 10).

He means by "the lost" people who have like sheep strayed away from their master. In actuality he is quoting words spoken by God to Ezekiel, in that prophet's book, chapter 34. As usual, when Jesus calls himself the Son of Man, he is emphasizing his role as what Flusser calls "that of the eschatological prophet." In simpler words, Jesus as the Son of Man does not hesitate to speak as if he were God himself, because he is "David," God's special son, just as he does not hesitate to accept the title "Lord." In the first verses of Ezekiel 34 God says he will himself "seek the lost sheep of Israel"; in the last verses of the same chapter he says "David" will seek the lost (literally, "be their shepherd").

In his reply to his critics Jesus seems to have used two illustrations which have become famous.

The first is a parable about a certain Pharisee and one of those outcast tax collectors the "better people" called "sinners." The two went up to the Temple to pray.

"The Pharisee stood and prayed in this way with himself, 'God, I thank you that I am not like other men, extortioners, unjust, adulterers, or even like this tax collector. I fast twice a week, I give tithes of all that I get.' But the tax collector, standing far off, would not even lift up his eyes to heaven, but beat his breast, and said, 'God, be merciful to me a sinner'" (Luke 18:9-14).

And Jesus added,

"I tell you, this man, and not the other, went home right with God."

The second illustration suggests that when the "better people" will not accept the invitation to God's blessings he will find someone who will.

"A man once gave a great banquet and invited many. And at the time for the banquet he sent his servant to say to those invited, 'Come, for all is now ready.' But each and every one began to make excuses. The first said he had bought a field and had to go to see it. Another said he had bought five yoke of oxen and had to check them over. Still another said he had just gotten married and therefore could not come. This the servant reported to his master.

"Then the owner of the house said to his servant, 'Be quick. Go out in the streets and lanes of the city and bring in the poor and maimed and blind and lame.' The servant did so and said, 'My lord, I have done this

> and there is still room.' Then the master said, 'Go into the paths and hedges and compel people to come in so my house will be filled. I tell you, none of those people who were invited shall have a taste of my feast!'" (Luke 14:15-24).

We also have a shorter story about another tax collector named Levi whom Jesus called and who made a feast for him and his disciples (Luke 5:27-32). On this occasion, too, the disciples were criticized by some apparently strong traditional, religious people, because they were "eating and drinking with sinners."

Jesus answered them by saying,

> "Those who are well do not need a physician, but those who are sick. I have not come to call saints to repentance, but sinners" (Luke 5:27-32).

He apparently then told two parables which are not found in the context of this story about Levi but appropriately match these words of Jesus.

> "Which man of you will have a hundred sheep and if he has lost one will not leave the ninety-nine and go after the one which is lost, and when he finds it, lay it on his shoulders with joy. Then when he comes home will he not call all his friends and neighbors and say to them, 'Rejoice with me, for I have found my sheep which was lost'?
>
> "I tell you that in the same way there will be more joy in heaven over one sinner who repents than over ninety-nine saints who need no repentance" (Luke 15:4-7).

That is the first parable, and, as usual, to give further punch to the subject, Jesus adds a second illustration.

> "Or what woman who loses one of her ten silver coins will not light a lamp and sweep the house, looking carefully till she finds it? Then will she not call her friends and neighbors and say, 'Rejoice with me for I have found the coin I lost?'
>
> "I tell you that in the same way there is joy among the angels of God over just one sinner who repents" (Luke 15:8-10).

Like all societies Jews who lived in the land of Israel in the days of Jesus made distinctions between those considered "respectable" and those not considered such. The "sinner" was either the immoral person or the person engaged in a dishonorable occupation such as tax-collectors, excise-men, *etc.* By loving and accepting the outcasts Jesus could gladly say that “the tax-collectors and harlots go into the Kingdom of God before” the “saints,” that is, the respectable (Matthew 21:31).

Jesus would have reached out to the hippies of a generation ago.

What is meant by "hidden stories" is the remarkable fact that our Gospels of Luke and Matthew have preserved parts of units or stories so well that we can often recombine these units to restore the earlier form of this or that narrative. I tell here how this surprising discovery was made.

19 HIDDEN STORIES

You may have noticed that in the two stories I have just repeated I have attached two "twin" parables in each case to two short stories but in each case the short stories now stand very far in the Gospel of Luke from the appropriate "twin" parables. In the story of Zaccai (Luke 19:1-10) the attached parables appear in Luke 18:9-14 and in Luke 14:15-24, while in the story of Levi (Luke 5:27-32) the two parables occur in Luke 15:4-10 — ten chapters apart!

Therein hangs a story.

If I am not wrong it was the end of January, 1979. In Flusser's seminar at Hebrew University on Mount Scopus we had spent four weekly seminars discussing various matters regarding the rather strange fact that Jesus seemed to have spoken the same words in telling the gentle joke about how he had come to call sinners, not saints, to repentance in two very different and distant contexts, Luke 5 and 15 — very far apart! As Flusser kept saying, it does not seem probable that Jesus would have made such a remark on two separate occasions.

Then I had, as we say, a bright idea (in view of the consequences of this idea I sometimes think it was a kind of revelation).

"What," I said to Flusser as the other members of the seminar looked on with a "what now" kind of look in their eyes, "what if we would take this statement of Jesus about his not having come to call saints (righteous) to repentance but sinners, pull it out from where it is, and put it in front of the parables of the lost sheep and lost coin?"

Flusser looked askance at me but we did what I suggested.

Taking the story of Levi we placed it just before the parable of the lost sheep. At the end of the story Jesus says,

> "The well do not need a physician, but the sick. I have not come to call saints to repentance, but sinners" (Luke 5:31, 32).

Then we placed the parable of the lost sheep immediately afterwards:

> "Which one of you will have a hundred sheep and if one is lost will not leave the ninety-nine and go to find his sheep, and when he has found it he will ... come and say to his neighbors and friends, 'Come rejoice with me ...'? So there is more joy in heaven over one sinner who repents than over ninety-nine saints who have no need for repentance " (Luke 15:4-7).

Not only the idea is here but the very words "need," "saints," "repentance," and "sinners" are in both passages, although in Luke's Gospel they stand ten chapters apart.

"Lindsey," said Flusser, "you are right. These two passages once stood together as a single story!"

It was the beginning of a series of what both Flusser and I now think of as extremely exciting discoveries. The very next day I found that the famous story of the rich man who came to Jesus to join the Kingdom (Luke 18:18-30), must originally have preceded a parable passage in Luke 14:26-33 (I later noticed that Matthew 13:44-46, the parables of the Mustard Seed and the Leaven, evidently once stood also in this reconstruction between the Luke 18 and Luke 14 passages). Today we can count nearly 20 reconstructions of this kind.

I have already mentioned a number of times in this book that by putting together a story with a teaching of Jesus and a couple of parables we have, apparently, hints of a longer and earlier story. For the sake of improving the continuation of themes I was getting ahead of myself. But I must now, as it were, help you to know "where I am coming from," as we say.

Incidentally, I have to call this finding a Jerusalem discovery, for although many a Christian minister combines the sayings and stories about Jesus in his sermons almost automatically at times there seems to have been no suggestion before our discovery that our Gospels have preserved sections of longer stories so well and so completely that nearly two thousand years later we are able to pick up these scattered parts and rebuild longer and earlier units which must once have stood in both the Hebrew original and the subsequent Greek copy of it.

It took a while — and the discovery of several other hidden stories — to begin to understand what made it possible for us to bring together many scattered units in Matthew and Luke and so recreate earlier and longer stories.

Gradually I began to realize that there must have been a scroll written prior to the scroll known to our writers and that it must have displayed many stories in the life of Jesus which had three kinds of materials in each:

1. An opening incident
2. A teaching discourse of Jesus
3. Two parables.

I would find, for instance, a discourse of Jesus on some theme, often given by both Matthew and Luke. I would then look for a short story suggesting a similar theme. Finally, I would try to find two parables or illustrations spoken by Jesus. I would then put these together as

1. opening incident
2. discourse
3. two parables.

Presto, another hidden story came to light!

Sometimes one of the units would be from Matthew, while two were from Luke, Luke usually preserving the opening incident. Both of them often displayed the same discourse though less frequently the same parables.

Students have often suggested that the discourses and parables must originally have been given in definite contexts, but that these have not been preserved in our Gospels.

By this method we were finding such contexts.

Matthew and Luke had so well preserved the parts of the earlier stories that we were finding it possible to recover the hidden original, especially after retranslating the Greek to Hebrew.

What this meant in terms of the history of transmission of our materials slowly became clear. According to the Greek fathers of the second-century Church the first story of Jesus and his words was written in Hebrew. We must therefore imagine a first handwritten scroll composed presumably by Matthew, the tax collector (also called Levi).

Let us call it the

HEBREW STORY OF JESUS

From this original comes a literal Greek translation, the

GREEK STORY OF JESUS

At this point someone seems to have noticed many simple, straightforward, short stories of Jesus' healings and exorcisms, apparently in the period when he was beginning his ministry. In these stories there was little one could call instruction or teaching or parable illustration.

But of the time when Jesus began gathering disciples the *GREEK STORY* provided longer narratives about Jesus, narrative units which included an opening incident which was then followed by a teaching discourse to those present and ended, usually, with two parables.

Evidently what then happened was that a Greek copyist decided to transfer the narrative-incident sections of the longer stories to the series of miracle-and-healing narratives, gathering at the beginning of the new scroll he was making all the short story units.

After this he seems to have separated the teaching units from the longer stories and grouped them together (often listing them partially under common words found in the different sayings). This is apparently why we have such a collection of sayings and discourses as that we call the Sermon on the Mount (Matthew 5, 6 and 7).

Finally, this new editor seems to have collected all or most of the twin parables which normally ended the longer stories and placed them in what might be called the third section of his scroll.

We thus get what we may call the

REORGANIZED SCROLL

of materials which no longer gives a chronologically topographical, typical, Hebrew story of Jesus and his teaching in the way the Hebrew original and the first Greek copy did but becomes a kind of anthology of units of material from which each reader learned about Jesus.

Apparently the popularity of this new scroll — perhaps because it had Jesus' teachings and parables so neatly grouped together for purposes of memorizing them — seems to have brought about the displacement of the earlier *GREEK STORY*. It is quite clear that our writers Matthew and Luke (and probably Mark as well) knew and used the *REORGANIZED SCROLL* and did not know the earlier *GREEK STORY*.

The next step appears to have been made by what I have called the First Redactor. From the Gospel of Luke, which clearly has two distinct sources (seen most easily by what are called the Lukan "doublets," that is, passages which are found twice in Luke) we see that someone before Luke, using the *REORGANIZED SCROLL*, attempted to produce an account that continuously told the story of Jesus. This Redactor sometimes selected pithy sayings of Jesus from the longer discourses and presented them as "Lists" of sayings. He also introduced small editorial notes here and there to keep the story moving.

This document, probably a scroll, we can call the first

RECREATED STORY OF JESUS

because it attempts to recover the earlier, continuous *GREEK STORY*. However, it is clear the author, our Redactor, knows only the *REORGANIZED SCROLL*, for he records some stories without recognizing that they were once attached to sayings and parables.

Luke is the first of our writers and he uses as his two sources the *REORGANIZED SCROLL* and the *RECREATED STORY OF JESUS*.

Mark follows Luke and mainly uses his text but usually cuts out Luke's doublet passages and occasionally takes material from the *REORGANIZED SCROLL*, revising it by making many verbal changes just as he does with Luke.

Finally, our Greek writer Matthew follows Mark but uses the *REORGANIZED SCROLL* plus Mark's Gospel as his sources.

For the sake of those accustomed to philological diagrams I give the following chart of the relationships on the following page as I see them:

SOURCES OF OUR GOSPELS

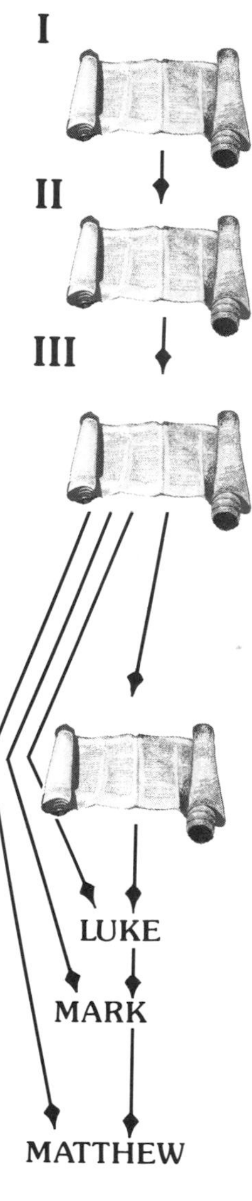

HEBREW LIFE OF JESUS

Written by Matthew of tradition, continuous story by eyewitness.

LITERAL GREEK TRANSLATION OF THE HEBREW LIFE OF JESUS

REORGANIZED SCROLL (RS)

A revision of the Greek continuous story—narratives gathered and placed first, then discourses, then parables. This involved separating narrative, discourse, and parable elements in longer stories from the original form of the stories.

Our Gospels descend from the reorganized scroll, but our writers know there was an earlier continuous life story of Jesus.

FIRST RECONSTRUCTION (FR)

Someone took a number of units from RS and reconstructed a short continuous story of Jesus without knowing stages I or II.

LUKE used two sources: FR and RS.

MARK knowing RS sees FR in Luke and largely lifts FR out of Luke to make his Gospel.

MATTHEW uses two sources. From Mark he gets his unit order, from RS he gets additional material including small word corrections to Mark.

For early Hebrew-Greek stories in triple tradition (Matthew, Mark, Luke) we go to Luke mainly. For early material in double traditional (Luke, Matthew) or unique Luke and Matthew we find both non-Marcan Matthew and Luke, as a whole, excellent.

The claim of many scholars today is that our Gospels are collections of story-units which were largely invented by Greek-speaking Christians late in the first century. The possibility of restoring earlier, longer narrative units by recombining parts of these units preserved in Luke and Matthew shows that our Gospels are largely the product of simple literary transmission, not oral development. They still retain what is an essentially accurate picture of the original story of Jesus. A case in point: the restored narrative connected with Mary and Martha.

20 WHY HIDDEN STORIES?

What I have just written is a kind of secret. Not a secret to be hidden, such as those kinds little girls love to hint at when they say, "I've got a secret and you don't know what it is!" but the kind of secret that explains something important and is available for the asking.

It is really important and let me tell you why.

Nearly two hundred years ago, in Germany, scholars began to question whether the stories in the Gospels were to be taken literally or not. Several things bothered them. One was the many accounts of miracles Jesus did. In essence they said that modern people do not believe that God interferes with the natural force of nature, though the Bible contends that he does, if he so wishes.

The Bible says that the prophet Samuel heard the voice of the Lord as a lad and that on one occasion he called for rain in the season of harvest (when there usually is no rain) to show the people of Israel that the God of Abraham was very much around.

The Bible says that the prophet Elijah supernaturally provided as much cooking oil and grain as a widow and her son needed in Zarephath and called down fire from heaven on Mount Carmel. It also tells us the prophet Elisha raised a woman's son from the dead and performed a number of other miracles in the name of the God of Israel.

In the Gospels we read that on one occasion Jesus was asleep in the boat in which he and some of his disciples were going from one side of the Kinneret to the other. A great storm came up and threatened to capsize the boat. The disciples came to Jesus and complained that he was sleeping and "we are about to be drowned!" Jesus awoke, stood up and commanded the wind to cease, which it promptly did. Then, as if this were a daily event they should have been prepared for, he said, "Where is your faith?"

Now that kind of story, said the critics, must have been one of the many legends that grew up around the memory of the Lord the early Greek Christians believed in and followed. Maybe some remarkable things happened in connection with Jesus but the telling of the story over and over caused all kinds of extra details which were not original to creep into the accounts.

One modern scholar who made a long and careful analysis of the Gospel materials came to similar conclusions.

Rudolf Bultmann, the scholar I am talking about, said, quite frankly, "We live in an age when people no longer believe in demons and evil spirits. We can hardly relate to such stories if we think highly of Jesus. Very probably the best explanation of such stories is that they accumulated around the memories of Jesus because the people themselves believed in such things."

This basic disbelief in miracles and the rejected thought that God can penetrate the normal cause and effect of what we call nature and do whatever he wishes actually became a serious reason for skepticism about the Gospel story.

Combined with this was the observation that the various units and narratives preserved for us by the Gospels are displayed in quite different locations in Matthew, Mark and Luke. "There must be some reason for this," said Bultmann, and along with two or three other German scholars of note he concluded that the units themselves were probably first just little stories which were taught by Greek Christian teachers to young adherents of the early Greek-speaking Church.

Bultmann supposed that each unit had, therefore, a "history of its own." Very little of such material went back to Jesus. We no longer can hear his voice. Worse, we cannot know much with certainty about Jesus at all. So he said.

And many have followed his skepticism.

Before I met Flusser in 1962 he had already come to the conclusion that scholars like Bultmann had misread and misinterpreted the materials we have in the Gospels. One thing in particular had impressed him about the Gospel stories: they could not have originated in a Greek-speaking community, that is, at least all those found in Matthew, Mark and Luke. The accounts were simply too Jewish, too much in thought and outlook like the rabbinic materials in and around the period of the Second Temple, as Jews called the temple built by Herod. In a thousand years no non-Jewish Greek community could have produced these materials.

In 1968 Flusser wrote in German a book simply named *JESUS* which was published a year later by Herder and Herder in English, sadly with many typographical mistakes. At the beginning of the English version (p. 7) Flusser writes,

> The main purpose of this book is to show that it is possible to write the story of Jesus' life. True, we have fuller records about the lives of contemporary emperors, and some of the Roman poets, but, with the exception of the historian Flavius Josephus, and possibly St. Paul, among the Jews of post-Old Testament times Jesus is the one about whom we know most.

The additional discovery that it is possible to reconstruct older stories by studying the Greek texts of Matthew and Luke and finding grammatical, linguistic and common theme links has for both Flusser and me eliminated any doubt that the oral hypothesis espoused so strongly and commonly by modern New Testament scholars is in error.

The fact is that we now know enough to insist that the problem of unit placement and unit authenticity can be settled much more easily and certainly than through appeal to any kind of oral hypothesis. Our materials have been transmitted to us from the first as literary documents. There was a Hebrew writer — doubtless the Matthew of tradition — who first wrote down the story of Jesus. He was certainly an eyewitness of many of the accounts he gives and his scroll was a Hebrew biography of Jesus, much like the stories in the Tenach of the lives of Elijah, Elisha, King David and others. His work was translated quite literally to Greek in a translation so literal that to understand much of it we have to retranslate the Greek texts we possess *back* to Hebrew.

Because someone took it upon himself to break up some of the biographical narratives found in the Greek translation of the Hebrew life of Jesus and to create a scroll or book which separated all narratives from the discourses and parables of Jesus our writers (and probably some writers before them) were obliged to put back the materials of the original Greek biography as best they could. They succeeded rather well in this aim but have left some materials still scattered even in their own works and this fact has made it possible for us many hundreds of years later to bring together a number of the earlier stories on our own.

As I say, this is exciting. We are able to see much better the way in which Jesus lived and taught, especially after he began to gather disciples.

A case in point is the story of Mary and Martha who, according to the Gospel of John, made their home in Bethany *(Beit-anya)*. We have as the "incident" which began this story a few sentences from Luke 10:38-41. Jesus entered a "certain village," says Luke, and Martha welcomed him into her house. Luke says she had a sister, named Mary, and Martha complained that Mary was not helping her in the "serving" (which must mean Martha was preparing food for more people than Jesus). Jesus said to Martha,

> "You are worried and troubled about many things, but only one thing is needed, and Mary has chosen the best, which will not be taken away from her."

According to the story "the best" that Mary had was the fact that she was "sitting at Jesus' feet and listening to his word."

Now the very word that Jesus uses in explaining to Martha what is making her nervous — worry — is the same word around which Jesus composes an entire discourse recorded by both Matthew and Luke (Matthew 6:25-34 and Luke 12:22-34).

Luke begins his version (which is almost word for word like that in Matthew) by writing that Jesus said to his disciples,

> "Therefore (probably the original expression connecting Jesus' word to Martha as both Matthew and Luke give it) I say to you, don't worry about your life, what you are going to eat and what you are going to drink, nor about your body, what you are going to put on it. Isn't life more than food and the body more than clothing?
>
> "Look at the birds of the air. They do not sow nor reap nor gather into barns, yet your Father in heaven feeds them. Are you not of much greater value than they?
>
> "Which of you by worrying can add one cubit to his height?
>
> "So why do you worry about clothing? Look at the flowers of the field, how they grow. They neither card nor spin and yet, I tell you, that even Solomon in all his glory was not arrayed like one of these.
>
> "If God so clothes the grass of the field which today is and tomorrow is thrown into the oven, will he not clothe you, O you of little faith?
>
> "Therefore don't worry, saying, 'What shall we eat?' or 'What shall we drink,' or 'What shall we wear?' for after all these things the Gentiles run, and your Father, after all, knows that you need all these things.
>
> "But put first the good of the Kingdom of God and his redemption and all these things will be added to you.

> "Therefore don't worry about tomorrow, for tomorrow will worry about itself. Sufficient for the day is its own trouble."

Now there are many fascinating things about this passage which appear as we translate word by word from the Greek text but I want to emphasize here that the reference to worry occurs six times in Jesus' short, little lecture. Martha's worry had been the feeding of a good many extra people. No doubt she was the strong, extroverted housewife who really did not mind Jesus' gentle rebuke and his use of her worry to expand about the danger of worry to his disciples in many things beyond that of "serving" a lot of extra guests.

By putting these two passages together on the basis of the word worry and a common theme we happily find out the "best" that Jesus was talking about concerning Mary's sitting at his feet. What he is insisting is that the disciples must all put "first things first" and in this case this is the Kingdom of God and God's redemptive concern for all people everywhere. They are in this Kingdom, this movement, as they follow Jesus. Now they must put God's desire that all men get into this Kingdom above their highest goal or need in life.

But where and what are the two parables we expect to finish his sermon?

No problem. They are there, though not together and only one of them standing in Luke near the second passage we used above.

The first is what we call the Parable of the Rich Fool (Luke 12:13-21). Notice the word "barn" which nicely connects with the same word in the place above where Jesus says that the birds of the air "neither sow nor reap nor gather into barns."

> "The ground of a certain rich man yielded plentifully. So he thought to himself, 'What shall I do, since I have no room to store my crops?' Then he said, 'I will do this: I will pull down my barns and build greater ones and there I will store all my crops and my goods. And I will say to my soul (this is a Hebrew way of speaking of oneself), 'Soul, you have many goods laid up for many years. Take your ease, eat, drink, and be merry.'
>
> "But God said to him, 'You fool! This night your soul will be required of you — then who will get all those things you have laid up?'
>
> "So is he who lays up treasure for himself but is not rich towards God."

This is a story about a man who has too much to eat. Jesus had warned that one should not worry about what he was to eat or drink.

But there is also a parable about a man who had too much to wear!

We call it the Parable of the Rich Man and Lazarus (Luke 16:19-31). Jesus tells of a certain rich man "who was clothed in purple and fine linen and had plenty to eat day by day" while at his gate a beggar named Lazarus was laid daily to beg even for the crumbs that fell from the table of the wealthy man.

So miserable was the poor man at the gate that his body was full of sores and the dogs came and licked them.

The beggar died "and was carried by the angels to Abraham's bosom." The rich man also died and in Hades "lifted up his eyes and saw Abraham afar off, and Lazarus in his bosom." This led him to cry out,

> "Father Abraham, have mercy on me, and send Lazarus to dip his finger in water and cool my tongue, for I am tormented in this flame."

But Abraham said,

> "Son, remember that in your lifetime you received your good things while Lazarus got only bad things, and now he is comforted and you are tormented.
>
> "And besides all this, between us and you there is a great gulf fixed, so that those who want to pass from here to you cannot do so while those from there cannot pass to us."

Then the rich man asked,

> "I beg you therefore, father, that you send him to my father's house, for I have five brothers. Let him testify to them lest they come to this place of torment."

Abraham said,

> "They have Moses and the prophets. Let them listen to them."

But the rich man argued,

> "No, father Abraham, but if one goes to them from the dead they will repent!"

And Abraham answered;

> "If they do not hear Moses and the prophets, they will certainly not be persuaded even if someone rises from the dead."

Now in the story of the man who had too much to eat the Greek has the same expression for "many goods" that is used in Abraham's statement here about the rich man having received in his lifetime "good things" (*ta agatha mou* back of which is obviously *tuvi* of Hebrew). The first passage of our reconstruction ties together with the second through the word "barns." The third ties together with the fourth passage through the word *ta agatha mou (tuvi)*.

And, of course, the four passages make good sense when put together.

In the story of the rich man and Lazarus it is clear that Jesus was using models about failure to repent and subsequent torment or blessing in the life after death so common in the writings of the rabbis. They spoke of Hades (or Sheol in Hebrew) as the place of the departed dead, one part of which was for the righteous and the other for the wicked. Sheol is a temporary place, according to the rabbis, and it will only be terminated at the general resurrection and the final judgment in *haolam haba* (the world to come). The righteous dead will, in their spirits, be carried away to the "bosom of Abraham" *(cheik Avraham)*.

In much the same way people in Christian countries tell about someone dying and coming at last to the gate of heaven where Saint Peter is imagined to be standing to allow (or not to allow) this person to enter. Often the model thus used stands to introduce some witty or laughable conversation between Saint Peter and the new candidate for heaven.

As we have seen, there are many indications that Jesus could say some witty thing intended to be laughable and funny. On one occasion he talked about the way people often criticize one another. "Why do you see the *splinter* in your brother's eye," he said, "when you cannot see the *log* in your own eye!" On another occasion when he was describing how difficult it was for a wealthy man to "leave all and follow" him he said, "It is easier for a camel to go through the eye of a needle than for a rich man to come into the Kingdom of Heaven!" (Luke 6:41, 42; 18:25).

In fact, whole books have been written to show Jesus' sense of humor.

The way in which Jesus moved from the actual conversation he had with Martha concerning her worry about getting a meal ready to the way people worry about food and clothing in general is itself interesting. Add to this his moving from the need to replace worry with faith and kingdom-dedication to a story about the over-confidence men get when they are no longer worried about food. There appears to be not only great fertility of imagination but also humor in suggesting such contrasts.

In some ways the description of the miserable Lazarus and the elegantly dressed rich man living in such close quarters on this earth has also a touch of exaggeration which is made stronger when they are described now far from one another. The essence of humor is exaggeration and incongruity and Jesus seems to be using these to dramatize the point he is making about the finality of death as the cut-off point for real repentance. Now is the day of salvation. Perhaps someone will listen if he hears the most dramatic and exaggerated story possible.

Jesus is the master physician and planner. He is also the master story-teller and teacher.

And what a sense of humor!

When rightly understood the "Lord's Prayer" is really the "Disciples' Prayer" and is full of Hebrew phrases found till today in the Jewish prayer book, read in the synagogue. More than anything else this prayer involves the worshipper in taking God's side in the struggle of good against evil, of God against Satan. I had personally to see that Jesus' teaching on prayer requires much boldness.

21 KINGDOM LEISURE

As I sit typing this book I feel a strong sense of privilege in being able to do so in one of the rooms of our little cottage in Poria Elite, high on the southwestern hills above the placid waters of the Kinneret. Margaret and I bought this house in 1962 at the time we were having to leave Tiberias after two happy years of research into the life of Jesus. We were obliged to go to Jerusalem and the Baptist chapel for work there.

We had saved very little money at the time but the forty houses in the sleepy little town, where even a grocery store did not exist, were inexpensive, and we wanted badly to keep touch with the Galilee and to bring at least our younger children, Danny, Robert and Debbie, to visit now and then. Besides, our oldest girls, Lenore and Barbara, like our oldest son David, had made friends in Tiberias and there was some possibility they would come back from college in the United States and want to see their friends.

I made a raft from a plywood platform and some factory-size plastic bottles and we used to put the raft on the top of the 1964 Chevrolet, and go fishing on the lake. We would catch an occasional catfish on worms Benjamin, the gardener at the Scots' Hospice, would help us dig, and often enough a string of perch. Our neighbors in Poria, Lilly Wreshner and Elsie Churchill, enjoyed any fish we could bring them, just in case we were too lazy to clean out catch.

The years have ambled by and all our children are now married and live in the United States. We have thirteen grand, grand grandchildren and love all of the spouses very much. They come to Israel as often as they can. Danny married a beautiful young lady who was born in Bethlehem and grew up in the Old City of Jerusalem. She, Samira, and Danny, had premature triplets several years ago, of which one,

Benjamin Luke, lived only eighteen days, but his two brothers, Mark and Matthew, have survived and long since wrapped themselves around our hearts like all the grandchildren.

I have just stopped my peck-peck-pecking and gone for a walk across the rise at the top of Poria near the old black, basalt ruins and stood looking from the south end of the lake to the north. It is a beautiful sight at four o'clock in the winter, the eastern bluffs picking up the dying embers of the sun, and the northern shore so hazily blue in the distance.

I thought of some of the stories I have not had time to tell in this little volume and of some I must yet mention.

It is clear that Jesus spent many days and hours moving from place to place, and village to village, and often in the very areas I am able to see from Poria. Usually the recovered stories we are able to put together show Jesus in company with his disciples. The mood of the opening incident and conversation often sets the tone for a leisurely talk by Jesus on some theme dear to him and needed by those he is training.

There is that time when one of his disciples turned to Jesus and said, "Lord, teach us to pray as John taught his disciples to pray." Jesus answered with words so completely Jewish (some found in the Jewish morning service till today) but now so common among all kinds of Christians that few Christians think for a minute that they are shared by the synagogue. Although we call these words "the Lord's Prayer" they more truly should be called "the Disciples' Prayer," for Jesus himself prayed to his Father by addressing him as "my Father" or "Abba" ("Daddy," in English) but taught his followers to address God as "our Father who art in heaven."

The so-called Lord's Prayer is the shortest kind of poetic utterance addressed to God to be imagined (Matthew 6:9-13).

"Our Father who art in heaven," it begins. Then follows,

> "Your name (let it) be hallowed.
> Your Kingdom come,
> Your will be done in heaven and earth."

That is almost half of the prayer. It obviously relates the worshipper to the purposes of his God.

The second part is petition:

"Give us this day our daily bread.
And forgive our sins as we forgive
those who sin against us,
And lead us not into trial
but deliver us from the evil one."

That is the entire prayer. Early in Christian history a further "thine is the Kingdom and the power and the glory" was added for liturgical purposes but it is not a part of the words Jesus seems to have taught his disciples.

In one of the tractates of the Mishnah there is an illuminating discussion about what kind of prayer a man should pray when he is in imminent danger. This rabbi said this or that, another rabbi something somewhat different. The question was what kind of quick prayer could be prayed in a time of danger and still get the essentials in it.

Very probably this search for the shortest prayer containing the most important things a man should say under duress developed into a tradition by the time Jesus suggested a prayer for his disciples. He therefore emphasizes only those matters of the greatest importance. And they are revealing.

In the first part of the prayer the disciples take sides, as it were, with God in what he wants done in this world. The history of the people of Israel in the Old Testament beautifully illustrates the fact that it is only the God of Israel who is to receive glory. We think of Gideon who dismissed at God's command thousands of his army and conquered the Midianites with only 300 men "so that the credit would belong to the Lord," and not to men. "Let your name be hallowed."

"Let your Kingdom come and your will be done in heaven and earth" shares the same form. The praying person knows that God intends to rule all men everywhere and he says to the Almighty that he wants exactly what God wants.

"Your Kingdom come" means not that the supplicant is expecting God to set up some kind of universal throne in Jerusalem or any other place on earth, as we know when we put this prayer into Hebrew. "May you rule more and more people just as you intend to" is what is meant.

And "your will be done in heaven and earth" is simply parallel to "your Kingdom come." The oldest and best reading does not say "your will be done in earth *as* it is in heaven." The biblical and Jewish understanding was, no doubt, that of Jesus. God's will and rule in heaven (here meaning what we call the supernatural) is not complete, for Satan and his hordes of evil are still out to battle God's purposes in the heart of man. Jesus is telling these members of his Kingdom that they have *the right and responsibility to encourage God* in his intention to rule all people everywhere *and even the evil, supernatural powers as well.*

"Our wrestling," writes the Apostle Paul later in one of his letters found in the New Testament, "is not with flesh and blood, but with powers and principalities in the heavenly (supernatural) places."

We stand again in amazement at the shock that Jesus' words, rightly understood, give us.

In contrast to everything said by statesmen, philosophers, politicians, psychologists and the mass of pundits our modern world listens to, Jesus calls to us from two thousand years ago and insists that our world simply cannot be explained by the conflicting interests only of men, machines, and ideas. There is something deeper, more penetrating, more relevant. It includes an almighty God and his angels, as well as a weaker, but significant Force of evil and his operators from below.

We who pray these words can never say them lightly once we see what Jesus really meant by them.

The rest of the prayer is highly practical. We pray for a livelihood — bread. We pray to be forgiven just as we give forgiveness. We pray to be delivered from the evil Satan (the evil one) would try to bring on us. Once again, we are face to face with the supernatural world even as we pray.

I have been wondering how I can say what I feel I must now write, for just as Jesus shocks us in so many ways I am sure my words will be shocking to many (on the other hand I am sure they should not be shocking and would not have been shocking to Jesus' Jewish audience two thousand years ago).

Several years ago I watched a minister pray for people who had pains in their backs. Some of them had a "scoliosis" which caused their backbone to take on a slight "S" configuration. This minister would seat the person to be prayed for on a chair, ask him to sit as squarely as possible with his back to the rear of the chair, and then kneel and take the feet of the candidate in his hands, measuring them to see if the heels (shoe heels) matched one another in length.

Often one heel extended farther than the other. He then prayed a simple prayer praising the name of Jesus while the person watched with astonishment as the heel lines came together. Sometimes the person would say, "Oh, I felt my leg moving!"

At first I thought this kind of praying for a person with back problems a gimmick, or a joke. Later, I watched as a man who had lost two inches of bone below his left knee was prayed for — the leg lengthened as if after an orthopedic operation, right before my eyes.

What shall I say? I had long taken seriously the Bible's contention that God is still working miracles (where he finds faith) today, and had not my own Baptist pastor in Oklahoma said the same thing over and over again? But to tell the truth I had never laid hands on anyone expecting God to work *right then*, much less straighten out a backbone.

My feeling was one of great shame. Here I am, I said to myself, a minister telling people about how God is still guiding, directing, healing, changing people for the good, but with all my words I had never really put them to the proof.

But there came a day when I prayed such a prayer for the first time — for a young woman who had a terrible limp from the time she had suffered a bout with polio as a child. Her left leg was nearly two inches shorter than her right. Feeling utterly foolish, I held that poor, emaciated leg up against the good one and simply said words of praise in the name of the Lord Jesus, my Lord and hers.

At first it seemed that left heel was determined to stay right where it was. I felt myself growing sweaty and wondering how I had ever gotten into such an embarrassing situation.

And then that weak, short leg began to move. In less than a minute the heel lined up with the other one. You can imagine how relieved I felt and how thankful to the One who can still do miracles.

Since that day I have prayed in this way for several hundred people and I can recall only two or three people whose heels failed to line up, no doubt for some reason I could not know.

I have learned many things in praying this simple prayer of praise over people suffering from major or minor scoliosis, but perhaps the most interesting one is that sometimes when I pray for such people the short leg will move out only — but exactly — half way. At such times I have learned to ask the person if someone may have hurt him and caused him to have unforgiveness in his heart.

Very often he or she will say, "Yes," and frequently begin to cry. I then say, "All right, you do not have to tell *me* who has hurt you but I ask you to tell the Lord that you forgive that person." Such people usually lower their heads and do just that. And the leg, as if on cue, will then slowly or quickly move right out and line up in length with the other.

This certainty that I have experienced just in praying for people who suffer from scoliosis has made it easier and less shocking to hear Jesus talk of prayer:

> "Ask and it will be given to you,
> seek and you shall find,
> knock and it shall be opened to you.
>
> "For everyone who asks receives,
> and everyone who seeks finds,
> and to him who knocks it shall be opened.
>
> "What man of you — if his son asks bread from him — will give him a stone? or if he asks a fish will he give him a snake? If you then, being evil, know how to give good things to your children how much more will your Father in heaven give good things to those who ask him!" (Matthew 7:7-11).

Once again we are putting together passages which seem once to have stood together. Happily we have two remarkable parables on prayer which, as usual, are not preserved in the context of these words on prayer, but are nevertheless obvious illustrations which fit them. In the first Jesus compares God's willingness to answer prayer to that of a reluctant neighbor who is bothered by another neighbor asking for some bread for guests that have come in late at night.

> "Who among you will have a friend who comes to him at night and say, 'Friend lend me three loaves of bread, for my friend has come to me from his travels and I do not have anything to put before him' and that fellow within will answer and say, 'Don't bother me, the door is shut and my children are with me in bed. I cannot get up and give some bread to you.'
>
> "I tell you, if he will not arise and give to him because he is his friend he will, because of feeling obliged, get up and give him everything he needs" (Luke 11:5-8).

Two things are especially funny in this story. The first is that in the Near Eastern and Jewish culture of the first century it is quite impossible to turn away a request of this kind from a friend or neighbor who asks bread at any time, at noon, at dusk, or at midnight. Jesus' disciples must have smiled broadly at the idea that a friend would say to another in such circumstances, "Don't bother me, the door is shut, *etc.*" This is something someone might say to himself but he would never, never say to a friend.

The second funny — and bold — idea is the ease with which Jesus compares his Father in heaven to someone who really does not want to get out of bed and help a friend at midnight. The entire Bible is, after all, a kind of letter which tells of God's love for his people and his desire to bring the world to himself. God takes the initiative again and again to save Israel at the Red Sea, or after forty years of incursions from the Midianites, or meets Moses at the burning bush and Gideon at the winepress. He approaches Abraham and tells him that not only will he himself receive great blessings but his descendants will be as the sand of the sea and in him "all the nations of the world will be blessed."

And Jesus himself had just said that God was not some rascal of a father who would give a stone when his son asked bread or a snake when his son asked for a fish. So why this comparison of our good Father in heaven with a hard-hearted neighbor?

The answer is simply that once again Jesus uses his perceptive sense of humor to get a laugh out of his students, who can more readily see how completely unlike a rascally father or reluctant giver God really is. Exaggeration and incongruity are the life of humor, and blessed is the teacher whose heart is full of it!

And now for that second, telling parable.

We call it rather witlessly the Parable of the Unjust Judge but it might more properly be called the Parable of the Grouchy Judge. Jesus says there was this "judge in a certain city who had no fear of God or man," and a woman came to him begging him to take her side against an adversary with whom she was in dispute.

At first the judge did not want to pay any attention to the woman but after a long while of her bothering him and begging help he said to himself,

> "Although I have no fear of God or man I may as well take the side of this woman just so she will not keep coming and wearing me out!" (Luke 18:2-8).

Of course this judge was not equipped with all the legal decisions and trappings of a modern court, with its advocates and pleaders, but had the right to make decisions of the kind Jesus is describing. Jesus applies his parable:

> "Listen to the words of this crooked judge! And don't you think God will take the side of his chosen who cry to him day and night, and have mercy upon them?
>
> "I tell you, he will speedily bring them justice!"

Once again, Jesus has his audience imagine the worst possible situation a person who is asking for help can think of, needing the help of a judge who *can* help but does not really want to do so. Of course God is not like that but if even a grouchy, old magistrate can yield to the pressure of a woman who is like a dog yapping at his heels how much more will the merciful and loving God of Abraham, Isaac and Jacob hear those whom he loves when they persist in prayer!

There is humor here, lots of it, and, with a smile (or was it a big laugh?) Jesus drives home his sermon on the efficacy of prayer.

We return to that central passage in Matthew where Jesus describes the Kingdom of Heaven as his growing Movement, which is the center of God's new dispensation of healing and redemption. John correctly saw Jesus as Messiah but in foretelling the role of the Messiah as the giver of the Holy Spirit and the future judge he skipped over the intervening era of deliverance and salvation. We are still in this great period.

22 ARE YOU THE ONE?

In our earlier discussion about the Kingdom of God and what Jesus meant by it I mentioned how it was that Flusser discovered that a right translation of Matthew 11:12 credits Jesus as saying that the Kingdom of Heaven is "breaking forth from the days of John" but at that juncture I did not write about how this fits into the picture of John the Baptist's wondering why Jesus was not doing the things he should do as Messiah. I may be repeating a bit at this point but it is important to consider the whole incident a little more.

Both Matthew and Luke record the story of John's sending two of his disciples to the place where Jesus was busy healing many people. The messengers from John ask Jesus in his name,

> "Are you the One coming or must we wait for another?" (Matthew 11:2-14; Luke 7:18-28).

John the Baptist, of course, had been present at Jesus' baptism in the Jordan, had seen the Holy Spirit coming down to light on Jesus' head in the form of a dove, and had heard the voice from heaven saying, "You are my son. I have brought you forth as a baby today!" He had also preached dramatically to bring the crowds from Jerusalem and Judea to repentance and prophesied of "One coming" whose shoes he was not even worthy enough to untie.

> "I baptize you in water,"

said John,

> "but he will baptize you in the Holy Spirit and fire. His winnowing fan is in his hand and he ... will gather his grain into his barn but burn up the chaff with unquenchable fire!" (Luke 3:16).

There is every reason to believe that John was certain that Jesus was the Messiah to come, yet for some reason not known to us he did not leave all and follow Jesus as leader and Lord of the new Kingdom. Instead, he continued his charismatic ministry and even gathered *talmidim* of his own. "Don't tell me," he cried to the crowds who gathered to hear him, "that you are all right because you have the security of good birth, being sons of Abraham."

John looked down at the tan, dusty stones of the river bank where he was preaching and they reminded him of loaves of bread. "I tell you," he continued, "God can take these stones (in Hebrew *avanim*) and make them into sons *(banim)* of Abraham!" Like the earlier prophets John could not stand cant and clichés and the claim of blood kinship to Abraham could never take the place of a change of heart, of repentance and determination to live honestly and morally and to prepare oneself for the Coming One.

> "I baptize you in water but he will baptize you in the Holy Spirit and fire."

It is clear that John knew the writings of the great Prophets and that he saw in them the promise of God that he would someday rain the Holy Spirit on "servant and maidservant" alike (Joel 2:29) and that when that happened God would then bring fire on the world, that is, bring it to its day of judgment. All this, John evidently believed, would happen with the coming of the Messiah.

But people reported neither the rain of the Holy Spirit nor the setting up of thrones for judgment in connection with Jesus' ministry. What was wrong? Why didn't Jesus get on with baptizing people in the Holy Spirit and start the judgment? Was he, or was he not, the Messiah? John's disciples ask Jesus,

> "Are you the Coming One, or do we have to wait for another?"

The answer of Jesus is to hint at other prophecies in the Scriptures which John has not taken into account. He says to John's disciples,

> "Go, tell John what you hear and see."

Obviously the two disciples John has sent have been around Jesus and his disciples long enough to have seen many of the miracles Jesus was doing. Because of this Jesus says,

> "Blind men are seeing, cripples are walking, lepers are being cleansed, and deaf people are hearing, dead are being raised up, and poor people are hearing the good news."

"And blessed is the man who doesn't find what I am doing wrong" (Matthew 11:3-6).

Jews in the period of the Second Temple were always interested in words and passages in the Torah and the Prophets which suggested the coming of the Messiah. I quoted one of these before but let me quote a bit more of two verses in the thirty-fifth chapter of Isaiah:

Behold your God will come with vengeance,
With the recompense of God,
He will come and save you.

Then the eyes of the blind shall be opened,
And the ears of the deaf shall be unstopped.
Then the lame shall leap like a deer,
And the tongue of the dumb sing (vss. 4-6).

We do not know how John responded when he got these words of Jesus but his knowledge of Old Testament prophecies undoubtedly gave him cause for thought. He probably said to himself, "Oh yes, God did promise healings in the days of the Messiah." Very probably John's question to Jesus did not represent a lack of belief that Jesus was the expected Messiah but was a way of putting Jesus on the spot: "Why don't you get on with the important things like the giving of the Holy Spirit? You are indeed the One we were expecting. What are you waiting for?" In any case it is interesting that Jesus and John found themselves communicating through a common knowledge of the divine Scriptures.

After John's messengers had departed Jesus turned to the crowd and said,

"When you went out to John in the desert, what did you expect to see? A reed shaking and bending in the wind? What did you go out to see? A man dressed in fancy clothes? People who dress like that live in palaces! Tell me, what *did* you go out to see? A prophet? Yes, I tell you, and much more than a prophet!

"John is the one the Scriptures talk about when they say, 'Behold I send my angel before your face, who shall prepare your way before you'" (Matthew 11:7-10).

Jesus is paraphrasing the passage in Malachi 3:1 in which the Lord says he will send his angel (or, messenger) and he will "prepare the way before me." The passage goes on to say,

> And the Lord, whom you seek,
> will suddenly come to his temple....

Without saying it directly Jesus appears to be saying that he, "the Lord," is also talked about in the passage in Malachi. *Haadon*, "the Lord," was the title given to Jesus by all who followed him, perhaps partly because of this passage.

His next words are just as striking:

> "I tell you, there has not arisen among the offspring of women a greater than John, yet the smallest in the Kingdom of Heaven is greater than he."

It is then that Matthew adds Jesus' words stating that "all the Prophets and the Torah prophesied until John, but from the days of John until now the Kingdom of Heaven is breaking forth ..." As we saw earlier, this is a hint at the words of Micah the Prophet when he wrote that

> The Breaker will go up before them.
> They will break through and pass the gate,
> going out by it,
> Their King will pass on before them,
> the Lord at their head.

Jesus is comparing his followers to the flock of sheep. Instead of calling himself the King he speaks of the Kingdom of Heaven but he means no less than that he is the leader and that his *talmidim* are growing in numbers and, as we say, "moving out!" He spoke of himself as "meek and lowly" and this characteristic apparently explains his reticence to use words like King in referring to himself.

Without question we can complete this reconstruction by adding the Parables of the Mustard Seed and the Leaven,

> "What is the Kingdom of Heaven like and to what shall I compare it? It is like a grain of mustard seed which a man took and sowed in his field, and it grew and became a tree, and the birds of heaven made nests in its branches.
>
> "The Kingdom of Heaven is also like leaven which a woman took and hid in three measures of meal until it was all leavened" (Luke 13:18-21).

From something small like a seed or a lump of leaven an enormous growth occurs. This movement of the Kingdom of God begins in a small way but it starts growing and nothing can stop it! In essence Jesus is prophesying, the first instance of several prophecies he will yet make.

There is something of tragedy in Jesus' description of the greatness of John the Baptizer. He is the last of the great prophets, yet more than a prophet because he paves the way for Jesus the Messiah. He is "Elijah who was to come" and he went out in the Spirit of Elijah to call all Israel to repentance. He knew Israel's Messiah and pointed to him. He is the end of one age of God's dealings with Israel and man, but also the harbinger of the new dispensation of the Messiah.

Yet he himself did not enter in. He did not come weeping and repentant and join the Kingdom of God. When B.C. time became A.D. time he hung behind and did not cross the line. Of those born to women none was ever greater than John, but the person considered of least importance *in the Kingdom of Heaven* was "greater than John."

Jesus obviously loved John very much but the Kingdom of God is a voluntary society. A person has to respond when the Spirit of God is calling. God does not compel the will of man. It would be very much unlike Jesus to "set up" a kingdom in which he rules both willing *and unwilling* subjects, as some of my Christian friends think. What would such a kingdom be? Would it not be a political madhouse or at best a police state, and do we not have enough of such states already? Have not Christians often enough tried to set up such a state only to fail miserably? Jesus would have none of it.

And what about that Kingdom of Heaven today?

> Is it not a herd of cattle stampeding for the feed lot?
> A cloud pouring torrents of rain on a thirsty land?
> A lake whose dam has burst and whose waters
> are cascading into the valley below?

In Africa for every two people being born eleven are becoming Christians. In South Korea, where fifteen years ago only eight percent of the populace was Christian, twenty-five percent are now followers of the lowly Nazarene and it is authoritatively suggested that by the year 2,000 *A.D.* half of South Korea will call Jesus Lord.

Margaret and I watched in 1973 as 2,500 South Korean soldiers were baptized by about fifty Korean ministers and their color-clad wives. A few weeks before this, 3,400 candidates for baptism were enrolled in one ceremony. Dr. Paul Cho, the pastor of a church in

Seoul, and the largest in the world, has 500,000 members and several hundred assistant ministers!

My first response to such facts is to sit and just marvel.

My next thought — after living all these years in Israel — is "Where are all these people going to get a proper understanding of the Bible, and especially of Jesus?"

It surely ought to be in Israel.

Planning to extend his kingdom of God ministry Jesus selected twelve helpers and sent them out to heal as he had done and to declare that God's Kingdom "has come near", which means in Hebrew, "God's Kingdom is here." The source of wrong ideas about God's Kingdom as political and military largely stem from failure to translate our Greek texts back to Hebrew.

23 JESUS SELECTS TWELVE

What do you do when you have hundreds of *talmidim*, not to speak of people crowding around you every time you come back to Capernaum, which has been your main center of operations?

Jesus seems to have had no question. Luke tells us that Jesus went up "into the hills" (*haharah* in Hebrew) to pray, and after a night of prayer called his disciples together and chose twelve men to send out "to heal and cast out demons." These men were to go from village to village in two's, stay for a while at the home of anyone who was hospitable to them, and heal the sick and demonized. As the people were made whole in each town the disciples had only one basic word of explanation: "The Kingdom of Heaven has come near!"

Now one of the commonest mistakes made by readers of the Gospels is to suppose that the disciples were really saying, "The Kingdom of God has not quite come, but it is coming, and we are working miracles to prepare for its coming."

This is when you need to know Hebrew!

The Greek text literally says, "The Kingdom of Heaven has come near." When we put this into English the first idea we have is that the Kingdom is delayed *in time*. But when we translate the Greek literally to Hebrew we find it means "The Kingdom of Heaven has come up to here *(karvah malchut shammayim)*!" In other words the normal meaning of the Hebrew phrase is *spacial*. Instead of meaning that the Kingdom is still to come it means "the Kingdom of Heaven *has come*!" (*cf.* 2 Samuel 20:16, 17; Genesis 20:4.)

Now that is exactly what Jesus said about his casting out of a demon: "If I by the finger of God cast out a demon then has the Kingdom (Rule) of God come down on top of you." However in this case, he used a different verb (Greek *ephthasen*, Hebrew *higia*) so that the scholars have never been able to deny that somehow Jesus did have an idea that "the Kingdom was here already in some 'realized' way." Nonetheless most of the literature about the Kingdom of God has erred by its failure to think Hebrew and to retranslate our Greek texts — when necessary — back to Hebrew.

It is really not difficult when you know the Hebrew *karav* (come up to here) to understand what the apostles were saying. They would pray over someone and he would be healed on the spot. Or they would rebuke an evil spirit and the demon would throw the person into physical contortions as it came out. *Then* the apostles would say, "The Kingdom of God has come at this place." In other words, they would say, "My friends, God has taken charge of this situation. He has broken through from the infinite to the here and now." As I wrote earlier, *malchut* is a kind of verbal noun in Hebrew. It is more "ruling" than "rule" in the static sense.

But this very strong sense of *malchut* as an active, ruling penetration of God's power into the physical situation where men live (demons enter the physical body of a person and control one or more functions if they can) does not prevent the expression "Kingdom of God" from being the name of Jesus' movement. The Kingdom led by Jesus is also "those ruled" by God.

It is this sense of a growing body of people "ruled" by God that has so often not been understood, yet even if we talk about the Kingdom of Scotland or the Kingdom of Wales we mean not just the territory that makes up such a kingdom but the *citizens* of the kingdom. So it really should not have been all that difficult to get clear.

Sometimes Hebrew idiomatic usage explains difficult texts where the Greek translator of the Hebrew original simply rendered the Hebrew so literally into Greek that it makes sense in Hebrew, but not really in Greek or English. For example, we have this saying of Jesus (it is not clear where it stood originally):

> "Not everyone who says 'Lord, Lord' to me will come into the Kingdom of Heaven, but only he who does the will of my Father in heaven."

This saying stands right next to one where Jesus says,

> "Many will say to me in that day, 'Lord, Lord did we not prophesy in your name, and cast out demons in your name, and do mighty works in your name?' And then I will declare to them, 'I never knew you. Depart from me you workers of iniquity'" (Matthew 7:21-23).

In this latter saying it is clear Jesus is talking about the day of judgment. These two sayings have apparently been put together by a late editor because he found each saying using the double "Lord, Lord."

But the first saying obviously originally had quite a different context. When we first read it we think that the expression "will come into the Kingdom of Heaven" means an entrance *at some future time*. However, when we put this back into Hebrew we recognize that we have here a proverbial kind of expression. Such sayings in Hebrew can use the imperfect, perfect or participial form of the verb. We cannot translate proverbial expressions in Hebrew as if the imperfect represented a true future or the perfect a true past. Both in Greek and English a proverbial expression must be put *in the present*. "A stitch in time saves nine." "A watched pot never boils."

Yet the Greek translator of Hebrew normally used Greek's future tense for the Hebrew imperfect and one of Greek's past tenses for the Hebrew perfect. In this way the proverbial form of the Hebrew is lost in translation. We should translate:

> "Not everyone who says to me 'Lord, Lord' *comes* into the Kingdom of Heaven, but only he who does the will of my Father in heaven" (Matthew 7:21-23).

There is no idea of the future. The point is that there were people in Jesus' experience who right then were trying to join the Kingdom by just saying "Lord, Lord." Jesus did not accept them.

Without doubt one of the reasons so many scholars have supposed that Jesus was in the habit of talking about "inaugurating the Kingdom of God" or "setting it up" some time in the future was due to their failure to take our Greek texts back to Hebrew where necessary.

We find interpreters making the same mistake about proverbial sayings in such remarkable sayings as those we call the Beatitudes (the *ashrei*) in Hebrew. As usually translated to English here are two of the eight in Matthew 5:3-5.

> "Blest are the poor in spirit
> for theirs is the Kingdom of Heaven.
> Blest are those who mourn,
> for they shall be comforted."

The first of these appears in the present tense in Greek so we have no trouble when we get a literal rendering into English, but the second has the present tense in "those who mourn" and the future tense in "they shall be comforted."

We should translate the second beatitude as

"Blest are those who mourn
for they *get comforted*!"

and the third as

"Blest are the humble
for they *inherit* the earth."

Again, the fourth as

"Blest are those who hunger...after righteousness
for they *find* satisfaction."

And so forth. *The beatitudes are typical Hebrew proverbs but the tenses must be rendered into English as present in form* so that we can see that they are proverbial.

Would you believe it? One well-known German semitic scholar who surely should have known better developed a famous theory which held that in giving these beatitudes Jesus was talking about a pie-in-the-sky "future" Kingdom and these were the blessings he was promising one and all for that yet-to-be Kingdom of the future! Almost certainly much of the idea that the Kingdom of Heaven was strictly a future matter for Jesus came from such mistakes in translation equivalents.

While we are still talking about the famous *ashrei* sayings of Jesus I should mention the fact that what we call the first and eighth beatitudes have apparently been almost universally misunderstood by translators. Most of the problem centers around the Greek word *auton* which could either go back to the Hebrew *lahem* (or *lahema*), "theirs" or to *meihem* (or *meihema*), "of these." Is it correct to render the first beatitude

"Blest are the poor in spirit
for *theirs* is the Kingdom of Heaven"

or would it be more correct to render it

"Blest are the poor in spirit
for *of these* is the Kingdom of Heaven?

Is Jesus saying that his followers *possess* the Kingdom or that they *make up* the Kingdom?

Exactly this question arose long ago in the story of how the disciples of Jesus shooed away the little children and their parents when the parents came to ask Jesus for his hands to be laid on the children in blessing. It is one of the most delightful episodes recorded about Jesus. The translators of the King James version (1611) wrote that Jesus said to the disciples,

> "Suffer the little children to come to me,
> for *of such* is the Kingdom of Heaven" (Luke 18:16).

Here "suffer" of course means "allow."

Later translators have rendered this verse as,

> "Allow the little children to come to me,
> for *to such belongs* the Kingdom of Heaven."

The reasoning seems to be that if we are going to translate the first and eighth beatitudes as if the Kingdom *belongs* to the followers we should let the children into owning the Kingdom of God as well!

But why would Jesus say that God's Kingdom belongs to anyone else but God? The very phrase "the Kingdom of God" means that it is God's operation or is the community over which he has charge, as we have been seeing.

Here again, because interpreters have supposed that Jesus thought the Kingdom had not arrived (based on false understanding of Hebrew phrases), the translators have erred and we get the unconfirmed conception that God's Kingdom can be owned by human beings.

No, the Kingdom of God is the place where the supernatural is penetrating the natural, or, secondly, it is the community of Jesus' followers where the Messiah and Lord is in charge.

Flusser, who has long studied and written in depth on the writings of the people of Qumran — the Essenes — has pointed out again and again how highly Hebraic in idiom and expression is the list of what we call the Beatitudes. The eighth beatitude should read, says he,

> "Blest are the righteousness-driven,
> for of these is the Kingdom of Heaven" (Matthew 5:10)

This is because the phrase *nirdefei tsedaka* seems to stand behind the Greek. These Kingdom people are inwardly pushed, driven, to get the saving power of God (God's righteousness in biblical terms) to a world that needs deliverance from evil powers and forces. How completely different is our usual understanding of this Beatitude!

So — just for the record — let us put down for our own benediction and that of the many dedicated Bible translators what the Hebrew-speaking Jesus really said: Here are the Beatitudes (Matthew 5:3-10), as I would translate them:

"Blest are those not dependent on self,
for of these God makes up his Kingdom.

Blest are those who mourn,
for they get comforted.

Blest are the humble,
for they inherit the earth.

Blest are those hungry for deliverance,
for they get satisfied.

Blest are those who extend mercy,
for they get mercy extended to them.

Blest are the pure in heart,
for they see God.

Blest are those who make peace,
for they get labelled "Children of God."

Blest are those who cry for the redemption of the world,
for of these God makes up his Kingdom.

It seems certain that Jesus' poetic and dramatic words here must have come as a response. We read that on one occasion a certain man "who sat at table with him" (Luke 14:15) let out a hearty "Blessed is he who eats bread (proverbial form: not "shall eat bread") in the Kingdom of God!" Obviously this man was expressing his thrill at sitting with others in the Kingdom of Heaven — the gathered followers eating with Jesus. Perhaps it was this man's excited shout that led Jesus to give these famous words of *ashrei* which are in reality an inspired description of those who *do not own his Kingdom but make up that Kingdom.*

This Kingdom — his Movement — is a NOW experience. Those in it are blessed and are being a blessing NOW. They get comfort NOW and mercy NOW. They see God NOW and get called God's children NOW. They get deliverance and inherit the earth — NOW.

And, by the way, these Beatitudes are chock full of Hebrew phrases Jesus borrows from some of the Psalms and the Prophets. If you can read Hebrew even a little compare Isaiah 66:2; 61:2; 66:13; Psalm 37:9, 11; 24:4; 84:8; *etc.*

Although it is clear that our Gospel writers had as their principal source a revised life of Jesus in which the earlier, continuous story had been transformed into sections as to whether they were narrative, teaching or parable in character, Matthew and Luke still retain between them most of the materials needed to outline faithfully the life and career of Jesus.

24 OUTLINING JESUS' LIFE

The fact that our Gospel writers clearly did not find it easy to reconstitute the older order of stories in the written life of Jesus means that we are obliged to depend on various strategies and hints to draw the main outline of Jesus' life. Happily, there are quite a number of clues to help us determine the principal turns and directions the ancient story took.

Let us put some of these down here:

1. The first stories or units spoke of John the Baptizer and his message.
2. The first units about Jesus concerned events such as his visit to the Temple as a child of twelve, his baptism by John in the Jordan, his bout with Satan after forty days of prayer, his first exorcisms and healings and various miracles which provided him the opportunity to proclaim his Messiahship.
3. The famous visit to Nazareth which appears to be the first account of events in which he carries on long, semi-teaching conversations with opponents.
4. The stories about calling disciples to the Movement or Kingdom of God show us Jesus encountering a person or situation which he uses as an occasion to teach his followers by words or example. Many of these stories were broken up by the author of the *REORGANIZED SCROLL* on the basis of incident, discourse and two parables.
5. The final stories which occur still in Galilee and on the road to Jerusalem emphasize the choosing by Jesus of twelve special people (the apostles) and his training of them for future leadership in his Movement.

6. The stories of Jesus during his last days in Jerusalem at Passover time are for the most part straightforward accounts of conversations with opponents in the courts of the Temple, though parts of some of these stories are found no longer located in their original contexts as Temple stories and must be regathered on the basis of incident, discourse and parables.

7. The stories which tell of the arrest of Jesus by the Temple authorities, the various interrogations before rabbinical and Roman persons, crucifixion, and resurrection retain a sequence which appear on the whole original and reliable.

If we add the accounts given in the first two chapters of the book we call the Acts of the Apostles we can state with Flusser that it *is* possible to write the story of the life of Jesus with the conviction that we are in possession of an outline of that life which is authentic.

There is one group of materials — now scattered across the Gospels of Matthew and Luke like parts of an exploded airplane lying across a field — which are sayings of Jesus that have almost no suggestion of context. These appear to have once stood together as the prophecies and instructions of Jesus to his disciples after his resurrection. Since in our Gospels there is little hint that these sayings were given *after the Resurrection* the fact that they exist and have not been recognized as such presents us with great surprises. But I have not included them in the list above and will deal with them later.

For now I would emphasize that I have talked mainly in this book of the stories about Jesus which were

1. Early miracle and healing stories
2. Stories of the calling of disciples
3. Stories of the training of the disciples.

There is a clear progression here, both in the sequence of the stories and in the way Jesus was moving with purpose to expand his Movement to include many others. It is difficult to see why anyone would suppose that Jesus had no plan or detailed purpose for his life or for the future of those he had gathered behind him.

Jesus' twelve shelichim come back excited about the power in invoking the Name of Jesus. It is in this connection that we need to understand Luke 8:10 where its position makes Jesus seem to be using parables to hide rather than clarify his message. The privilege of the apostles is to experience not the secrets of the Kingdom of God (see manuscript evidence on Luke's text) but the "secrets of God" — Razei El — and as such to be in on the secret and not need the words of an attractive and explanatory parable.

25 PRACTICING

Clearly part of Jesus' training of the disciples was his separating to himself twelve men whom he calls his *shelichim* (apostles). He is training now a select group of future leaders. They go out with the authority to confront Satan's spirits and heal in Jesus' name. In contrast to Jesus they must heal *in his name*: Jesus healed and cast out spirits "by the finger of God" but without appeal to a supplementary divine name.

Why twelve men? No one knows for sure of course but in the last week of Jesus' career he tells his apostles that their future task will be to "judge the twelve tribes of Israel" (Luke 22:30) and these words seem to suggest that Jesus thought of his growing Movement as representing a New Israel of which he was the leader. The failure of some Christian interpreters to recognize Jesus' symbolic use of such numbers as "the twelve" has often led to the conclusion that Jesus saw his apostles as eventually leading an Israel escaped from Armageddon with Jesus enthroned in the rebuilt Temple of Jerusalem. Such a conclusion does violence to the sophisticated use Jesus made of biblical words and symbols.

In Luke we read that Jesus sent out his twelve disciples (Luke 9:1-6) and a chapter later we read he sent out seventy disciples (Luke 10:1-12). Very probably this double sending is due to the fact that Luke had two sources, as we have said before, and the same sending out is duplicated because of Luke's use of more than one source. If so — and there seem to be excellent reasons for thinking so — instructions given by Jesus as the *shelichim* go out may be taken from either account.

The apostles are to carry "no purse, no bag, no sandals" and will go two by two. In whatever village they are to enter they must find a "son of peace" (Hebrew for a good-hearted person) and stay with him, letting their "peace rest upon him." They are to "heal the sick" and say to them, "The Kingdom of Heaven has come near," or, as we have said when we return this saying to Hebrew, "The Kingdom of Heaven is here."

If the people of a given village do not receive the emissaries they are to go out into the streets and say, "The dust of your town which clings to our feet we shake off against you." Jesus added, "I tell you, it shall be more tolerable on that day for Sodom than for that town."

It was a kind of field practice that Jesus sent these *shelichim* out to perform. You learn by doing and so they learned. They came back elated.

> "Lord, even the demons were subject to us in your name!" they said.
>
> He replied, "I have just been watching Satan fall like lightning from heaven! It is true that I have given you authority to tread on serpents and scorpions, and over all the power of the enemy, and nothing is going to hurt you. Still, don't rejoice in the fact that the demons are subject to you but that your names are written in heaven" (Luke 10:17-20).

The excitement in the report of the apostles as they watched the bodies of the sick and depressed relax and the mouths of the delivered smile again is easy to understand. But even more exciting was the fact that when the demons objected to the word of rebuke in the name of Jesus they nonetheless complied and gave up the battle. I know how the disciples felt for I have often been called upon to rebuke demonic powers in the depressed and at least at the first of such successes one is inclined to feel overconfident and not a little proud. Jesus puts the emphasis where it should be — the privilege of knowing "him whom to know aright is life everlasting."

But he does not hesitate to express his own joy at the success of his ambassadors. He has seen their enthusiasm and seen Satan being beaten in the ongoing battle of good and evil. He must have seen what would later become the greatest army earth has ever seen, not an army out to fight human armies of any kind but a heavenly army doing battle with Satan and his hosts. How regrettable it is that people calling themselves by the name of Jesus have often supposed their battle with wrong was a human one, accompanied with bombs and bullets and every other kind of military hardware! He has never led such a campaign and we can be sure he never will.

Jesus also tells these emissaries what a rare and unexpected privilege has been theirs:

> "Blest are the eyes which see what you see and the ears which hear what you hear.
>
> "I tell you, many prophets and saints have wanted to see what you are seeing, but did not get to see it, and to hear what you are hearing, but did not get to hear it (Luke 10:23, 24).

He must be referring to the prophetic descriptions the prophets saw of the Golden Age to come when "the lion will lie down with the lamb" and "the child play unhurt over the hole of the asp." How easily Christians have relegated these bursts of prediction granted by the Holy Spirit to some future, earthly age never yet begun (Isaiah 11:6, 8).

Jesus' view of the Age which he has inaugurated is one his followers have so often ignored. True, death and sickness and evil of all kinds fill the pages of our morning newspapers but do they really represent the vast majority of good things that go on every day for most of us? In some lands starvation and deprivation seem the only order but are not most of the lands where the words of Jesus have been taken seriously vastly different than they would have been if these words had never seen much application?

We take so much for granted.

For Jesus this was obviously the age promised by the Prophets. There was something new in the air. He was calling men to holy tasks. In his name redemption could not be delayed.

This was the period when the Kingdom of Heaven would grow and influence the world.

Some Christian interpreters of the Bible have divided up the history of the world into seven ages: or, as they say, dispensations:

Innocence is the first dispensation — before the Fall.
Conscience is the second — after the Fall.
The third is Human Government — Genesis 8:20, 21, a promise of no more divine cursing of the world.
The fourth: Promise through Abraham, Genesis 12:1-3.
The fifth: Law — the world governed by the Torah.
The sixth: Grace — our period, the acceptable time.
The seventh: Kingdom — when Jesus rules the earth for 1,000 years.

The first of these so-called dispensations seem more than arbitrary and a little contrived. But Jesus himself seems to have divided divine history into *three* dispensations or ages:

1. The Age of the Law and the Prophets — until John the Baptizer, whom Jesus recognized as the last of the prophets — although "more than a prophet" (Matthew 11:12, 13).
2. The Age of the Kingdom — "Whoever leaves home for the sake of the Kingdom of Heaven will have much more *in this age* . . ." (Luke 18:29, 30).
3. The Age of the World to Come — "Whoever leaves home for the sake of the Kingdom of Heaven . . . will have much more in this Age and in the Age to Come life everlasting" (Luke 18:29, 30).

For Jesus the Age of the Kingdom of God *is* the period of Grace, the acceptable time or year of God's favor. For him this is earth's Great Age. Through the Kingdom Movement God is breaking into the affairs of this world and the channel of this breakthrough is the people of the Movement, those in the Rule of God. *Haolam Hazeh* — the present age — was getting a shot in the arm. Things on this earth were going to change. The Movement was going to grow, grow so much it would be like the leaven in a woman's dough and like a mustard bush that becomes a tree. Nothing could stop it.

But earth, this planet, was not to be the end of all things, the final scene of ultimate victory over all evil, significant as earth is and its changing under God for the better. There is a world to come, a world that is all supernatural and will be the scene of complete personal victory, a world even the prophets barely saw, a world beyond history and things of this planet. Jesus appears to connect this future world with his own personal appearance at the end of the Kingdom Age on Earth, as we shall see.

No doubt, someone will ask me about several expressions such as the "appearance of the Kingdom of God" or some such phrase which is equated with the personal appearance of Jesus at the end of this age. In the appendix at the end of this book you will find my explanation for this odd use of the Kingdom of God, one agreed upon by both Flusser and me after some years of study.

Flusser has also made what I believe to be a valuable suggestion about the story of the sending of the apostles and the conversation between them and Jesus we have just been reviewing.

He suggests that after Jesus' words about the privilege of "seeing" and "hearing" things that many prophets and saints would have liked to see and hear that Jesus said the following, which now appears in a distant context, Luke 8:10:

> "To you it has been given to know the secrets of God (see the manuscript evidence) but others receive in parables, 'that seeing they may not see, and hearing they may not understand.'"

As Flusser noticed, this is the same theme involving the privilege of the disciples who have entered into the Age of fulfillment. The followers of Jesus have been let into their privileged position while others are still just getting the truth in parables.

Now, as all students of Jewish literature agree, Jesus and the rabbis used parables to make clear some point they wished to make. Why, then, does it seem that Jesus is deliberately using parables with the intention of hiding his message?

And indeed, that is the way this verse is used in Luke 8:10 when Jesus is asked to explain the Parable of the Sower (Luke 8:4-10). Put in that context it seems that Jesus is explaining something that is not to be understood by any but his disciples.

However, if you take this saying and put it at, say, Luke 10:25, immediately after Jesus speaks of the blessing the disciples have received, in contrast to the prophets and saints, it means only that the apostles have experienced something others who have only heard Jesus' message in parables have not yet experienced.

As we have seen often now, Jesus in this saying is using what I have called "Scripture talk," that is, hinting broadly at some verse in the *Tenach* to make a point. In this saying he refers to Isaiah's difficulty in getting the message of the Lord over to the people of his time. God tells Isaiah to shout at the stubborn people of Jerusalem and say

> "Hear and hear, but don't understand!
> See and see, but don't perceive anything!"

Then the Lord says to Isaiah,

> "Make the heart of this people fat
> and their ears heavy
> and shut their eyes,
> Lest they see with their eyes

> and hear with their ears
> and understand with their hearts,
> And turn and be healed" (Isaiah 6:9-10).

By hinting at this Isaiah passage Jesus is saying only that you have to talk to many people with illustrative words and stories to get them to understand at least something. His disciples are in a much better position. They have gotten beyond the message brought in words and illustrations. They have seen the power of the Lord as they healed and cast out evil spirits.

It is no wonder that the scene we are studying in Luke 10 ends with one of the rare prayers of Jesus recorded for us in verse 21.

> "I thank you, Father, Lord of heaven and earth, that you have hidden these things (God's secrets, *razim* in Hebrew) from the wise and understanding and revealed them to babes. Yea, Father, for such was well pleasing in your sight."

Jesus had reason to thank his Father. The Kingdom of God was breaking through.

Hundreds of books written on the life of Jesus have portrayed Peter's confession that Jesus was the Messiah as not only a late episode in his career but also as the first time the apostles finally came to believe in the Messiahship of Jesus. A right understanding of this moment in Jesus' life will correct this mistake. The story of the transfiguration which follows Peter's confession underlines — as does the confession of Peter — the fully supernatural nature of Jesus' Messiahship.

26 WHAT DID PETER SAY?

Matthew, Mark and Luke all soon follow the story of the feeding of the five thousand by a story we call Peter's great confession (Matthew 16:13-20).

It is clearly an important story but is often misunderstood.

The ordinary reader easily gets the impression that only at this late date in Jesus' leading of his disciples do they *finally* conclude that he is the Messiah and Hope of Israel. That this is a mistaken interpretation is evident from story after story we have looked at in this book.

At twelve years of age Jesus already knows of his Messiahship. Satan and demons call him the Son of God, which is a good biblical way of calling him the Messiah. He himself denominates himself the Son of Man, the most supernatural title of Messiah found in the Old Testament. He is Lord of the Sabbath, Forgiver of sins like his Father, King of the Kingdom of Heaven, Shepherd and Leader of a group of men who have power over death, leprosy, disease and unholy spirits. When the disciples call him Lord they are using a title which is equivalent to Messiah.

Peter does not in this story discover that Jesus is Messiah; he produces a motto, a logo, a propositional statement which acts as a summary of the essential commitment each person who comes to accept Jesus as Lord and King will make in the years to come, just as the saying of the *Shema* acts as the statement of faith in rabbinic Judaism.

As the story begins, however, we hardly expect such an epochal statement.

Jesus asks, according to our Greek text, "Who do men say that I am?" Perhaps the Hebrew undertext was more, "What are people saying about me?" for it is not easy to express in Hebrew the sophistication of the Greek suggestion of indirect discourse.

The disciples answer that some have come to the conclusion that John the Baptist has perhaps risen from the dead, for by the time of this story Herod Antipas had murdered John. Jesus may be John, risen from the dead.

"Others," they report, "say you are Elijah." The hope that Elijah must first come before the Messiah is still a part of Jewish tradition and is based on Malachi 4:5:

> Behold I will send you Elijah the prophet
> Before the coming of the great and dreadful day of the Lord.

To this day Jewish families place an empty chair beside the table at Passover "for Elijah."

Still others had suggested, runs the response of the Apostles, that "one of the ancient prophets had risen." Flusser believes that behind this reading may have been a more specific reference to the belief that grew up from the words of Moses, quoted in Deuteronomy 18:15:

> "The Lord your God will raise up for you a prophet like me from your midst, from your brothers. You are to hear him (that is, obey him)."

It seems to be clear that the original meaning of this expression "to raise up" meant that God would someday bring forward a prophet to take the place of Moses. Jews took the prophecy to be one of many promises of the coming Messiah but also often thought of the expression "raise up" as suggesting that God would *resurrect* either Moses or someone like him to be that prophet.

Evidently some people were saying that Jesus was himself the prophet like Moses, the Messiah so long expected. Perhaps some even combined the figures of Elijah and John the Baptist and through the prophecy of Moses had concluded that the combined figure had risen from the dead and was now the expected Messiah.

Jesus, ever the teaching rabbi who asks challenging questions, then asks,

> "And what would *you* say about me? (Matthew 16:15).

Peter does not hesitate. According to Luke he says, "You are the Messiah of God."

This is a literal translation of the Greek. But if we put it back into the Hebrew version from which we would expect the Greek to descend we find the words "You are *Mashiach Elohim*" or You are *Mashiach El*," or, more properly "*Meshiah Elohim*" or "*Meshiah El*."

Now for various reasons "*Meshiach Elohim*" sounds extremely strange in Hebrew. As in I Samuel 26:9 and in many other places David calls Saul, the first king of Israel, "*Meshiach Adonai*" and in Psalm 2:2 we read:

> The kings of the earth have set themselves . . .
> Against the Lord and against his anointed.

Here, in Hebrew, the word "anointed" is "Mashiach." "The Lord" is in Hebrew, "Adonai." But to speak of *Meshiah Elohim* breaks Hebrew biblical tradition.

Almost certainly we are to translate back to Hebrew to get: "You are *Meshiach El!*"

Now to anyone who has studied the Dead Sea Scrolls which were found some years ago at Qumran, the little *tel* at the northwest corner of the Dead Sea, you cannot but think of a multitude of similar Hebrew phrases found constantly in the Qumran scrolls. The Qumran writers had a habit of picking up rare biblical clauses in construct (two nouns placed together in which one acts as a kind of adjective) and turning them into the special cultic "lingo" that they used in talking of their liturgies or commenting on various books of Old Testament prophecy.

One of these phrases was the combination of some noun plus *el*, God. In the poetry of the Psalms we have several of these:

Ps. 19:2 The heavens are telling *kevod el*, the glory of God.
Ps. 73:17 . . . *mikdshei el*, temples of God
Ps. 74:8 . . . *kol moadei el*, all the synagogues of God (literally, all the places God meets us)
Ps. 82.1 . . . *beadat el*, in God's congregation
Ps. 107:11 . . . *imrei el*, words of God

What the people of Qumran did was to take these occasional combinations and add dozens of new "*el*" forms in which the word *el* came as the second noun of the construct phrase. They had

torat el, God's law
chokei el, God's laws
brit el, God's covenant
razei el, the secrets of God
mikdash el, God's temple

atsat el, God's community
goral el, God's lot

and a great many others.

We might quite easily translate these as "the divine law," "the divine laws," "the divine covenant," "the divine secrets," *etc.*

We know of other instances in which Jesus picked up phrases which the Qumran people had apparently made public property in his day, and in the book of Acts we find the apostles using popular Qumranic phrases.

I am therefore suggesting that Peter said,

> "You are *Meshiach El.*"

We might translate this to English as

> "You are the Divine Messiah,"
> "You are God's Messiah,"

or even

> "You are the God-Messiah"

as we might speak of the Bible as "the God-Book" in a less-than-academic way of speaking.

When we recognize that the phrase *Meshiah El* emphasizes in some way the deity side or divine involvement of the term Messiah and that, as we have already seen, in the very use of the word *Mashiach* there is a boldness any first century Jew would feel sensitive to, we can, I think feel the innovation and courage it took for Peter to say Jesus was God's Messiah.

Neither Jesus nor his disciples had used the title Messiah before, choosing instead the sophistication of terms like Son of David, Son of Man or Lord, just as the *Tenach* spoke of the Coming One as David, or the Branch or the Root of Jesse, *etc.*

Now Peter, who for some reason unknown to us must have been called "Rock" in his youth, Peter the outspoken, Peter the bold, steps out on the ice and says the fitting word. What others had long thought appropriate — even no doubt Jesus himself — but dared not use too easily, Peter declares.

It is no wonder that Jesus responds to Peter's confession by saying,

> "Blessed are you, Simon Bar Jonah (Jonah here means John), for flesh and blood has not revealed this to you but my Father who is in heaven" (Matthew 16:17).

As Flusser noted some years ago the moment we put the word "reveal" back into Hebrew we have a verb *(galah)* which can mean either "reveal" or simply "tell." Jesus is perhaps only saying to Peter, "My Father has given you these words," and does not mean that some strong vision of overwhelming, supernatural strength has been granted to Peter. In any case, Jesus is obviously happy indeed that Peter has used exactly the right words to describe Jesus and his mission.

I hope I am making myself clear now. The account of Peter's Great Confession, as Christians call it traditionally is *not at all* a story coming late in Jesus' life career signifying that finally, finally, finally the obtuse disciples had come to the conclusion that Jesus was after all the promised Messiah of Israel, something they had not known or fancied up till now, at least for certain.

The meaning of the story is quite otherwise: the disciples had boldly and openly followed him who the Prophets had promised, calling him Lord and bowing at his feet (the disciples rebuked any who prostrated themselves before them — Jesus accepted such homage!) but only now were they encouraged to speak of Jesus as not only Lord but Messiah, the Hope of Israel and the Gentiles.

How many who have written "lives of Jesus" have erred at this point! No doubt their supposition that Jesus was only recognized as Messiah towards the end of his life has helped to create the legend that Jesus may not have supposed he was the Messiah. *Nothing could be farther from the truth.*

Jesus is simply showing his excitement at Peter's bold choice of the exact words which encapsulate all that Israel has hoped for in the One who was to come. At last, at long last, the terms Jesus would not use until now become fully right, fully acceptable, fully appropriate.

And Jesus, masterful teacher that he is, does not himself say he is God's Messiah but pulls it out of his disciples themselves. By quoting Scripture Jesus had said it himself in Nazareth sometime earlier. Now, one of his *talmidim* who had not been with him in Nazareth but had lived with him and heard him teach for many months, had said it explicitly and quite on his own.

Jesus must have smiled broadly when he responded to Peter as he added,

"Your name is Stone (Greek, *petros*), but ("and" in Hebrew is often "but") on this Boulder *(petra)* I am going to build my *Edah* and the gates of hell will not be able to resist it." We are translating back to

Hebrew and *ekklesia* (Church) is surely *edah*, which in this case must mean a "witnessing community." The gates of hell, *shaarei sheol*, is found one time in the Old Testament (Isaiah 38:10).

Jesus is comparing his community, which he now begins to call his *Edah* to a house. He adds,

> "I will give you the keys of the Kingdom of Heaven, and whatever you bind on earth shall be bound in heaven, and whatever you loose on earth shall be loosed in heaven" (Matthew 16:19).

Here he appears to equate the Kingdom of Heaven with his *Edah*, for he continues the illustration by suggesting the house will have keys, yet now calls it the Kingdom of Heaven.

It is interesting that Jesus seems to have used the Greek *petros* and *petra* even as he spoke Hebrew, *petros* meaning a stone or hand-sized rock but *petra* a large building-foundation rock or boulder. It is quite clear that he meant a contrast between the two kinds of rocks:

> "Peter, you are a rock, yet a small one, but your words are a big rock and they are going to be the foundation for my Movement from now on."

From this time on the Jewish followers of Jesus will usually find themselves saying their Lord is Jesus the Christ, the Messiah, the Hope of Israel and the Prince of life. In fact as thousands of Greek-speaking Gentiles come into the Movement after the Resurrection they will elide "Jesus" with the title *Christos* (literally, Messiah, Anointed) and his name eventually will be Jesus Christ *Iesous Christos*, or, sometimes, *Christos Iesous*, Christ Jesus.

The rabbis constantly talked of "binding" and "loosing" and meant by this "forbidding" and "allowing." Jesus is using their phrase and meaning by it that the order in his Kingdom would be the responsibility of his Kingdom leaders. Whatever they decided God would stand behind.

I am crowding very great and wonderful stories together rather quickly but all of them proclaim one big thing: Jesus is staying close to twelve men he obviously intends to train until they are ready to stand on their own — when he is gone.

There remains one last principal account before Jesus starts on his last journey to Jerusalem with his disciples, apostles and the pilgrims who will be going to the Feast of Passover. It is the story known as the Transfiguration (due to Mark who speaks of Jesus as having been "transfigured" before his apostles on a high mountain).

Luke says that "about eight days" after Jesus had heard Peter declare him "The Anointed of God" Jesus took Peter, James and John to a mountain to pray. While in their prayer meeting the face of Jesus "changed" and his clothes became "white like lightning" (Luke 9:28-33).

Peter and his companions watched in amazement as two men appeared, "who were Moses and Elijah," and they talked with Jesus about his "exodus" (perhaps the Hebrew *tseito*) which was to occur in Jerusalem. The apostles were troubled with sleepiness but kept watching until Moses and Elijah started to leave Jesus, at which time Peter said to Jesus, "Lord, we feel wonderful here (*tov lanu po* has this meaning in Hebrew), so let's make three booths, one for you, one for Moses and one for Elijah." Luke adds, "not knowing what he was saying."

While he was still talking a cloud appeared and covered them. They were afraid.

Then a voice came out of the clouds and said,

> "This is my Son, my Chosen, listen to him " (v. 34-35).

Matthew adds that the apostles were very frightened and fell on their faces. Then Jesus came and "touched them" and said,

> "Rise, and don't be afraid " (Matthew 17:7).

He was alone.

Luke adds that they kept quiet and during those days told no one of what they had seen. But the story has come down to us because they obviously shared it with the others at some later date. The words of the *bat kol*, like the "voice from heaven" often mentioned by the rabbis, were a combination of three famous *Tenach* phrases in prophecies about the One who should come: "my Son" (from Psalm 2:7: "You are my son . . .") "my Chosen" (Isaiah 42:1) and "him shall you hear" (from Deuteronomy 18:15 where Moses promises God will raise up a prophet like Moses).

Even he whom Jesus called *Abba* confirmed Jesus' Messiahship in the rich words of messianic Scripture.

Looking down on the Sea of Galilee from the southwestern hills we can see Jesus cross the sea with the twelve, feed the 5,000, heal the demonized man living in the cemetery and cross again to heal the daughter of Yair (Jairus) in Capernaum.

27 TWELVE MEN IN A BOAT

I have just left my typing and gone for another walk across the rise of Poria. My thoughts are about those last days of Jesus around the Sea of Galilee. I keep thinking about that boat they found down there in Ginosar and about the possibility that it might just have been this wooden craft which took Jesus and the twelve apostles for their last eventful trips around the Kinneret.

Also in my mind was the desire to take another look from Poria at two sites proposed for what we call the story of the Transfiguration of Jesus, that time when the apostles accompanied him up "a high mountain" and his face became as bright as shining brass and his clothes as white as no cleaner could make them, as Mark says.

From our hill we can see to the west the top of Mount Tabor and on a clear day Mount Hermon, forty miles to the north. Pilgrims today go to both of them if possible, just so they can be sure they have visited the true mountain on which Jesus was transfigured.

And of course it does not really matter. What matters is what occurred on that "high mountain."

Nor does it matter very greatly in what sequence some of the last stories about Jesus in Galilee happened.

It is just quite a thrill to see in the far distance from where I am writing that busy northern shore around Capernaum and to think of the happy boat in which Jesus and twelve Jewish laymen — fishermen and businessmen — and perhaps a crew of four or five made their final trips.

I can see these chosen Kingdom leaders get into a boat and head to the east across the sea, to the shores of Gadara, mostly heathen country. From Poria we can see in the distance the white and rusty bluffs directly east of us. For some reason the twelve land and half way up the cliffs they encounter a wild man living among the tombs. He is demonized and Jesus does not hesitate to rebuke the spirits controlling him. He is healed and the people from the nearest village come out to see the man sitting "clothed and in his right mind" (Luke 8:26-39).

But they are pig raisers and they are unhappy about what happened to two thousand head of their pigs when Jesus freed the man from his demons. The spirits had asked to be sent into the swine if they were to be expelled from the man they were destroying. Jesus had allowed them to enter the pigs and to the amazement of everyone the animals had rushed pell mell down the steep slope into the sea, where they had drowned. These non-Jews did not hesitate to ask Jesus and his company to leave their coasts, for their livelihood had been sorely hurt.

I can see Jesus and the sturdy boat with its passengers crossing back to the western shore and finally to Capernaum where people joyfully welcome him. Then it is that Jairus (*Yair* in Hebrew), the ruler of the synagogue, who is perhaps, like all the leaders in the synagogue, a friend of Jesus, comes to Jesus to ask him to heal his twelve-year old daughter who was so sick she was about to die.

Jesus starts for Yair's house while the people flock around him, brushing against him and trying to get as close as possible to him. Then it is that a woman who has had "an issue of blood and been more hurt by doctors than helped" pushes through the crowd, saying to herself, "If only I can touch the phylacteries at the bottom of his skirt I will surely be healed." She manages to touch the hem of his garment and feels healing power pulsing through her body. Jesus turns to his companions and says, "Who touched me? I felt power going out of me."

The woman comes trembling before Jesus and confesses that it was she who touched him. "Your faith has brought you healing," he says to her, faith in Hebrew meaning more persistence and faithfulness than confidence.

Meantime word comes that Yair's daughter has died. Jesus arrives at the home, pulls the parents into the room where the dead girl is lying, takes the girl's hand in his and calls her back to life. He tells them to give her something to eat. The parents are beside themselves with joy (Luke 8:40-56).

I can see also that last voyage the Gospels tell us about, when the twelve and Jesus cross the sea eastward to a spot that is just south of Bethsaida, which is itself just east of the entrance of the Jordan to the Kinneret. The people in Capernaum have seen Jesus and the apostles leaving and they run along the shore as fast as they can, cross the Jordan and late in the afternoon come tired and weary to the uninhabited plain where Jesus seems to be resting with his leaders.

The disciples are a little annoyed. "Send the people away so they can go to the villages round about and find food, for this place is totally deserted" (Luke 9:12).

Jesus says, "How about feeding them yourselves?" Talk about a teasing sense of humor!

Their faces fall. They are dead serious.

Jesus has that twinkle in his eye.

They protest, "We have only five patties of bread and a couple of fish. That is, unless we go to buy food for all these people!"

There were about five thousand people!

Jesus tells his apostles to have the people sit in groups of fifty. He takes the five patties of bread and holds them up as he blesses his Father, breaks the loaves and hands piece after piece to his disciples. Luke says that everyone ate and was filled and of the food that was left over the apostles picked up twelve baskets full!

By joining two passages in Luke and two parables in Matthew and by retranslation of the Greek text to Hebrew we discover an early story about Jesus which reveals his rejection of the disciples' desire for retaliation and his own pain at the thought that he must act as judge already between those who accept him and those who do not. Jesus heals a blind man in Jericho and forewarns his followers that he will be rejected in Jerusalem and brought to death.

28 JERUSALEM PASSOVER

I can look down from the ruins on the top of Poria and see the south end of the Sea of Galilee as if it were an architect's model. From the south shore the wide, flat Jordan valley, bordered on either side by the mountains of Jordan and Israel, spreads out for miles and miles and at night you can see tens of thousands of lights speckling and twinkling from the Arab communities on the east of the valley and the Jewish colonies on the west. It is a beautiful sight.

Bethshan is a half hour's drive going south and it stands at the place where the Valley of Jezreel falls lazily into the Jordan valley from the west. Looking from Bethshan you can look up the Jezreel a long ways and almost see the clump of trees at Ein Harod, which is the spring where Gideon's men drank before being separated to conquer the Amalekites and Midianites.

To the south of Ein Harod lived the Samaritans and to the north was lower Galilee with its hundreds of Jewish villages. The pilgrims going to the feasts in Jerusalem often gathered some miles south of Bethshan and crossed the Jordan to follow the alluvial plain called Perea (the same as Poria, meaning in Hebrew "fruitful") as far as Jericho. There they recrossed the Jordan and took the Roman road west up the mountains of Judea and Jerusalem.

Somewhere south of Bethshan is the probable place where Jesus sent two disciples one evening to ask the elders of a Samaritan village if he and his apostles would be welcome to spend the night. Normally, even in this period the Samaritans would have obeyed the customs of the land and given lodging to Jews or anyone needing it.

This time the inhabitants of the Samaritan village refused. No way. "You are headed for Jerusalem," they said. The Samaritans had their own temple of worship, a rival to that in Jerusalem (Luke 9:51ff).

It was an embarrassing situation and Jesus' companions were angry. They remembered how Elijah had made his last trip south to Jericho so long ago along nearly this same route. They also remembered that just before he started on his journey he had called down fire from heaven to burn up some of Ahab's policemen (compare II Kings 1:10, 12 and 2:1-5).

"Lord," said Peter and John, "shall we call down fire from heaven and destroy them, as Elijah did?"

I sometimes wonder if Peter and John were holding their tongue in their cheek when they asked Jesus this question. Were they joking? Probably not, for Jesus seems to have taken them very seriously.

"You do not know what kind of spirit you have!" he exclaimed. "The Son of Man has not come to destroy men but to save them."

How different was Jesus from many of the people who have called themselves by his name in the past and until now! For him Elijah may have been a very great prophet but what Elijah would do in the rough, undisciplined age he lived in the Son of Man could never do, no matter how many enemies he might have.

We can be grateful for this episode in the Gospels. It makes any Christian who thinks he can take up the sword in the name of Jesus a false follower.

However the episode seems just to have been one of our "incidents" which we have learned once stood at the beginning of a longer story in which Jesus used the incident to teach.

The *REORGANIZED SCROLL* Luke and Matthew had before them clearly showed an incident (which we have just seen), a teaching section and two parables in quite separate places not related to the incident. Let me rebuild this story by adding, first, Jesus' words in Luke 12:49-51: "I have come to cast fire on the earth," Jesus says, "and how can I wish this if it has already begun?"

Here I have to remark that when we put this sentence back into Hebrew we see that Jesus is deeply unhappy about his role of separating people on the basis of being the King of the New Kingdom. His next sentence is parallel in meaning to the first: "I have a baptism to baptize, and how distressed I am till it be completed!"

Now the way I have just translated these two sentences of Jesus is not at all the way they are usually rendered. Here is the way one well-known translation has it:

"I came to cast fire upon the earth;
and would that it were already kindled!

I have a baptism to be baptized with;
and how I am constrained until it is accomplished."

Obviously the sentences are parallel, and therefore should be saying essentially the same thing.

But in such a translation they do not say the same thing and commentators have often been baffled to explain them. Does Jesus *want* to bring judgment on the world, for that is the meaning of casting fire on the earth? On the other hand is Jesus saying he does *not want* to go through some baptism of unknown nature? We would expect fire and baptism to be parallel and the second phrase in each saying to agree that Jesus *wants* something or *does not want* something.

It was Flusser who recognized that Jesus is not talking about "being baptized" but is using the figure of baptism as equivalent to "casting fire" on earth. Both are figures of judgment in Jewish sources. By putting our Greek source back into Hebrew *(yesh li tevila litbol)* he saw that the subject was not Jesus' personal baptism (though the Greek translator could easily understand the Hebrew that way because *litbol* can be translated either "to baptize" or "to be baptized").

In this way the two first phrases in each saying are equivalent:

"I have come to cast fire on the earth . . ."
"I have a baptism (of fire) to bring (on others) . . ."

If we put the second part of the first saying into Hebrew, its parallel relationship with the second part of the first saying also becomes clear:

"and how can I want it if it is already kindled?"
"and how am I constrained until it be accomplished!"

We can now put the two sayings together to emphasize their parallelisms:

"I have come to cast fire on the earth —
and how can I be pleased if it is already kindled?"

"I have a baptism of fire to bring on people —
and how distressed I feel till it be completed!"

The rejection of hospitality by the Samaritans leads him to talk about his role as Separator of people, those that follow him and those that do not. As Messiah his role as prophesied will be eventually to judge. Jesus sees that role already begun:

> "Do you think that I have come to give peace on earth? No, I tell you, but rather division. From now on five in one house will be divided , three against two and two against three.
>
> "Father will be divided against son, and son against father, mother against daughter and daughter against mother" (Luke 12:52, 53).

It is here that we must put the parables of the dragnet and of the tares, now found only in Matthew and quite unconnected by him to this narrative.

> "A man sowed seed in his field, and while he was sleeping an enemy came and sowed tares (weeds which look like wheat) among the wheat. When the plants grew and produced grain the tares also appeared.
>
> "So the man's servants said to him, 'Lord, didn't we sow good grain in your field? Where are these tares coming from?'
>
> "The man said, 'An enemy has done this!'
>
> "Then the servants said to him, 'Do you want us to go and gather up these tares?' But he said, 'No. You might pull up the wheat with the tares. Leave them both till the harvest. In the time of harvest I will say to those harvesting, Gather first the tares and bind them into bundles to burn them, and gather the grain into my barn'" (Matthew 13:24-30).

The second parable (of the Dragnet) is like the first. The separation now going on will one day be complete. It is

> "... like a net thrown into the sea which catches fish of many kinds. When it is full (the fishermen) bring it to the shore and sit down to separate the good fish into baskets and the bad they throw away."
>
> "It will be like this at the end of the age. The angels will go out and gather the evil from the good and throw them into the fiery furnace. There will be weeping and gnashing of teeth" (Matthew 13:47-50).

Very similar to the application of the Parable of the Dragnet is that of the Tares, at least in the end, but there Jesus says it will be the Son of Man who will send out his angels to punish the evildoers.

Where did Jesus and his close companions spend that night? Perhaps as they must often have done, and as many of the pilgrims must have done: by sleeping under their cloaks. In any case it must have been the next morning that they crossed the Jordan into Perea and began the long walk to Jericho.

They would have come two days later to Jericho.

On the way into Jericho a blind man started shouting, "Jesus, Son of David, Jesus, Son of David!" He had heard that Jesus "of Nazareth" was approaching and in his blindness all he could do to get attention was to shout

"Jesus, Son of David,
Jesus, Son of David."

People in front of the walking pilgrims tried to quiet the blind man. His voice was loud and raucous, and more than annoying.

Jesus found him and came up to him. "What do you want?" Jesus asked.

"Lord, to see!"

Jesus said, simply, "See!"

And the man saw (Luke 18:35-42).

I am reminded of my good friend, Arthur Blessit, who carries a cross in many parts of the world. He uses this heavy, ninety-pound cross with a wheel under its tail-piece to attract attention and tell of his faith to anyone who will call to him and talk to him.

I met him first in Jerusalem several years ago. He had brought his wife and five children and I helped him fix up a temporary apartment while he carried his cross around Israel.

At my suggestion he started in Bethlehem, swung by Jerusalem to the east, and went down to Jericho. My son and his wife Samira joined him there and as he preached to people on the streets Samira translated to Arabic, which is her native language. Just north of Jericho Arthur met a blind man sitting on a culvert. He talked to him and prayed for him. He kept hoping the Lord would open this poor man's eyes, but in this case he did not.

Arthur had good reason to hope the blind man would see. Some months before this he had been walking through the busy city of Abidjan in the Ivory Coast. As he proceeded through the streets he stopped to pray for a blind man, then went on up the street carrying his cross.

Suddenly he looked back and saw a commotion some fifty meters behind him. The black man he had prayed for was shouting at the top of his lungs while hundreds of people gathered.

"I can see, I can see, I can see!" he was shouting.

Some American friends of Arthur's who happened to be present saw Arthur was in danger. People came running up the street towards Arthur. The friends shouted to Arthur and hurried him into the shelter of a nearby house. Who knows what the crowd might have done to him otherwise?

I must add that Arthur had a marvelous time in Israel. Israelis, driving their cars at a speedy clip down the highway in the Jordan valley would see this odd sight of a man carrying a wooden cross and would often turn around and catch up to talk to him.

"You are bringing us peace," some of them said. Many of them insisted on giving him food and cans of soft drinks and he would sometimes have so much he could not carry it all. When he arrived at the south end of the Sea of Galilee the commander of the Israeli troops in the Golan Heights came down in his jeep and took him for a tour of the Heights.

According to Luke it was just before Jesus and his apostles arrived in Jericho that he said to them (and I here combine words from two other similar accounts):

> "See now, we are on our way to Jerusalem and all the scriptures given by the prophets about the Son of Man will be fulfilled."
>
> "He will be rejected by the elders and the high priests and the scribes and will be turned over to the Gentiles to be scourged and spit upon, but on the third day he will rise again" (Luke 9:43-45; 18:31-34).

Luke says that the disciples did not understand what he was talking about. They would soon know.

The Roman road still exists and in 1986 was partially paved by the Israel road authorities. The Romans built a road which is a marvel of engineering, mounting as it does in degrees from more than a thousand feet below sea level to the top of the Mount of Olives at 2,500 feet above sea level.

Jesus and the pilgrims with him probably took two days to make the trip on foot. At a point near Bethany his disciples picked up a donkey apparently belonging to an acquaintance of Jesus and as the Galileans came up to the top of the Mount of Olives some of them put their coats on the donkey and placed Jesus on him. Others then spread their garments in front of him on the rocky path as the donkey continued down the slope towards the famous city.

Herod's fabulous Temple with its bright, limestone walls and courts, stood glimmering in the sun as the crowd pressed around shouting,

"Blessed is he that comes in the name of the Lord," a benediction taken from one of the Psalms sung each year as the Galilean pilgrims arrived.

Without doubt, Jesus' many followers meant a great deal more than just the normal words of welcome the pilgrims expected. They came with their Lord and thus "in the name of the Lord!"

The donkey ride down to the Kidron and then up towards the gates of the Temple, where Jesus must have dismounted and continued into the Temple by foot, is sometimes called in Christian tradition the Triumphal Entry. King David and all ancient kings of Israel seem to have travelled processionally by donkey. There was a prophecy in one of the Prophets where it was written:

> Rejoice greatly, O daughter of Zion!
> Shout, O daughter of Jerusalem!
> Behold, your King is coming to you,
> He is just and having salvation,
> Lowly and riding on a donkey,
> A colt, the foal of a donkey (Zechariah 9:9).

The throng of pilgrims from Galilee — a great many of them no doubt followers of this Son of David — must have felt they were seeing this ancient prophecy fulfilled before their eyes. Luke writes,

> As they were drawing near and beginning to descend the steep slope of the Mount of Olives the whole multitude of the disciples began to rejoice and praise God with a loud voice for all the mighty works they had seen, saying, "Blessed be the king who comes in the name of the Lord!" (Luke 19:37, 38).

This excitement and noisy praise of him whom the believers called their Lord annoyed the Pharisees in the crowd, says Luke, and they said to Jesus, "Rabbi, rebuke your disciples."

Jesus' answer showed eloquently his approval of this remarkable scene,

> "I tell you, if these were silent, the very stones would cry out" (Luke 17:39, 40).

The entire episode is, of course, a parable acted out on the rugged terrain of Jerusalem. The enormous stones Herod had quarried to widen the great courts so that thousands of Jews could gather at the three yearly feasts are still here and it comes as no surprise to hear that both in ancient times and today Herod's Temple was and is in its ruins one of the seven wonders of the world. To any modern disciple of Jesus the great stone steps, which led into the Temple from the south and have been partially restored by Israeli archaeologists recently, present the exciting probability that up these very steps Jesus and his followers ascended.

The Temple was the central shrine of Jewish history, of biblical history. The Psalmists called Jerusalem "the city of the great king" and Jesus himself said on one occasion, "It is impossible that a prophet not die in Jerusalem." The people of his Kingdom-Movement were there to celebrate his entry to the Holy City, and he was indeed David's Son, a Prophet and King, though minus soldiers, staves and swords.

As his followers crowded around him he made his way up the great stairs through the Hulda Gates and stood confronting the tables of the money changers. Luke says his first act was to "usher out all those who were making business," as he shouted,

> "It is written, my house shall be called a house of prayer. You have made it a den of thieves!" (Luke 19:45, 46).

From Isaiah 56:7 Jesus takes the phrase "my house shall be called a house of prayer" and the expression "den of robbers" he picks up from Jeremiah 7:11.

They had indeed commercialized the Holy House. Like all temples in the East, or most of them, popularity and populace have quickly turned them into places of commerce in one form or another. Jerusalem could hardly be an exception — it is not today, as any western tourist knows!

Jesus spends a popular week in Jerusalem in the Temple courts. He is tested with "Catch 22" questions by the Sadducaic Temple authorities and the first such encounter involves the woman caught in adultery, a story apparently dropped from Luke's account involuntarily by an early copyist and inserted at the end of the seventh chapter of John's Gospel.

29 OPPOSITION!

It has long seemed a puzzle to me why so many scholars and students of the Gospels think it strange that the opposition to Jesus should have grown until it ended in his crucifixion. "What," they say, "could a man of such peaceful qualities and charm have done to stir up even a small number of his fellow countrymen and cause them to turn him over to the Romans to murder him?"

Flusser, whose origins are European, tells me that in contrast to the Jews he knew when growing up in Czechoslovakia, his hundreds of Israeli students through the years never find it hard to believe that in the time of the Second Temple there were Jews capable of killing other Jews for all the usual reasons. "We are a people like any people," they say. "Haven't we had our terrorists and our murderers in modern times? It is not at all difficult to believe some Jews could have instigated the death of Jesus if they were sufficiently jealous of him or saw him as some kind of threat."

And that really is the point.

Jesus was clearly seen by the Temple authorities, who were largely Sadducees, as threatening their hegemony. Under the Romans the Jews were completely subjugated. At every turn in every street in Jerusalem and all across the country Roman soldiers on patrol or just on their way to a military camp could be seen and heard, the clack, clack, clack of their sandal tacks ever driving the local populace into the shadows and corners. No ordinary Jew dared strike up a quarrel with such rulers. The Pharisees, who have a rather bad press in the Gospels due usually to the last editing of our Greek materials (it is quite easy to separate the many added references to the Pharisees in our texts — Luke has the fewest, Mark more, and Matthew many more) had much less influence over the Temple than the richer and less spiritual Sadducaic priests and their families.

Politically the Temple was, after all, the center of what Jewish power was left to the nation. The priests held court as the larger Sanhedrin (70 or 72 members) or the smaller Sanhedrin (23 members) and judged cases involving other Jews. They were usually forbidden to carry out capital punishment and of course did not sit in litigation on offences of Jews against Romans. This limited legal status was nonetheless backed up by the Temple police who had authority under the Romans to handle ordinary and religious disputes between Jews.

When Jesus swept into the Temple courts with his crowd of Galilean followers — known as provincials due to their clothes and their speech — the Sadducees in charge of the Temple and its courts were clearly alarmed. We must suppose that they had known about Jesus and his Movement for a long time. Some days after his cleansing of the Temple courts they were to arrest him and bring him before Pilate, there to charge:

> "We found this man perverting our nation, and forbidding to give tribute to Caesar, and saying that he is Messiah a king" (Luke 23:2).

The charge was simple enough and was meant to alert the authorities that in Jesus another messianic pretender had appeared and if allowed to continue to incite Jews "from Galilee to Jerusalem" the Romans would have a rebellion on their hands.

Christian tradition has it that the Triumphal Entry occurred on Sunday — "Palm" Sunday — exactly a week before the Sunday of the Resurrection. This calculation may be wrong but the fright Jesus gave the Temple rulers made encounters with them the theme of the week.

It was a week of "testing" in which the "scribes and chief priests" approached Jesus as he was teaching the people in the Temple Courts and attempted to catch him, as it were, off guard. Hoping in every way to discredit him they posed "catch-22" kinds of questions: whatever you answer will make you an idiot, a heretic or a criminal. The answers Jesus gave are not only clever but often a bit humorous and fit for the proverbial wisdom of Solomon.

When Jesus is asked whether it is lawful for Jews to give tribute to Caesar he asks for a Roman coin and then questions his interlocutors, "Whose image is this?" Told that it is that of Caesar his answer is: "Render to Caesar the things that are Caesar's and to God the things that are God's."

When questioned by some who are labelled in the account

Sadducees and who disagree with the Pharisees that there is a general resurrection Jesus is told of a woman who on earth had seven husbands, one after another as each husband died. "In the resurrection whose wife will the woman be?" was the test question. Jesus answered:

> "The sons of this age marry and are given in marriage but those counted worthy to attain to that age and to the resurrection from the dead neither marry nor are given in marriage . . . they are like the angels and as sons of the resurrection are sons of God" (Matthew 22:30).

Fascinatingly enough, it now appears that the very first of these testing questions came the next morning after Jesus had ushered the money-changers out of the Temple courts, though in reading the Gospels of Matthew, Mark and Luke we would not know this. What appears to me certain is that this first testing episode was inadvertently dropped by a scribe as he was copying part of the 19th chapter of Luke.

Let me explain, especially for any who like philological riddles we sometimes find in the Bible.

In the Gospel of John there is a story of conflict between "the chief priests and Pharisees" (7:40-52) and Jesus which ends with the priests saying to one of their number,

> "Are you from Galilee too? Search and you will see that no prophet is to arise from Galilee."

Immediately after that we read,

> They went each to his own house, but Jesus went to the Mount of Olives. Early in the morning he came again to the Temple. All the people came to him and he sat down and taught them.

Then follows the famous story of the woman caught in adultery. It ends with Jesus saying to the woman,

> "Neither do I condemn you. Go, and do not sin again" (John 8:11).

Immediately after this we read in John's Gospel:

> Again Jesus spoke to them, saying, "I am the light of the world. He who follows me will not walk in darkness, but will have the light of life" (John 8:12).

Now for many years it has been recognized by scholars that the story of the woman has somehow been placed awkwardly at the end of the seventh chapter of John. Even in antiquity it was recognized by the copyists that this story was not originally a part of John's Gospel, for two early manuscripts place it just before Luke 21:37. We read in John 7:53,

> And every day he was teaching in the Temple, but at night he went out and lodged on the mount called Olivet.

You will then find the story printed in italics at the bottom of whatever page John 7:53 appears in any given modern translation.

Several years ago I became interested in this story and carefully checked to see what kind of words the Greek text displayed. The result was that the vocabulary was clearly that used by Luke in his Gospel — John's story of the woman caught in adultery must have come from Luke!

Well, then I went looking in Luke for some likely place at which the story might originally have appeared. I did not have to look long.

At the point (Luke 19:46) where Luke completes the story of the cleansing of the Temple and where Jesus says to the money-changers,

> "It is written, 'My house shall be a house of prayer, but you have made it a den of robbers,'"

we read (v. 47),

> And he was teaching daily in the Temple.

"Maybe," I said to myself, "this story has dropped out from its original position between Luke 19:46 and 47. Let me see what happens when I put the passage as it appears today in John in between these Lukan verses."

The rest, at least for me, is history. I even had a friend who enjoys literary puzzles check to see if he too might find, as I said, "in Luke a likely place the passage in John might have slipped out of" and after a few minutes search he said, "How about Luke 19 between verses 46 and 47?"

What seems certain is that the eye of some ancient copyist inadvertently skipped a whole column of the text he was copying. The way this could happen we can illustrate by imagining the series of columns as they appeared in the text he was copying: I give three as they must have appeared in part:

your visitation."
And he entered the
temple and began
to usher out those
who were selling,
saying to them,
"It is written,
'My house shall
be a house
of prayer' but you
have made it a
'den of robbers.'"

They went each
to his own house,
but Jesus went
to the Mount of
Olives. Early in
the morning he
came again to
the Temple. All
the people came
to him and he
sat down and
taught them . . . etc.

And he was teaching
daily in the Temple.
The chief priests
and the scribes
and the principal
men of the people
sought to destroy
him, but they did
not find anything
they could do,
for all the people
hung upon his words . . .

The copyist apparently skipped the middle column, which contained the text we now know from John 7:53-8:11, and went on to copy the third column.

No doubt the copyist discovered his mistake as he continued to copy first Luke and then John's Gospel. What to do? Find as convenient a place in John to insert the skipped column! We can be glad that he copied the text so carefully that it stands awkwardly in the Gospel of John but still fits perfectly when reinserted into the right spot in Luke. The fact that Mark, in copying Luke, shows that he saw this passage but dropped it to put in some special stories of his own not found in Luke has interest to many of us, perhaps, but I cannot discuss such details at this point.

What is important, I believe, is to see that the story of the woman caught in adultery occurred the next morning after Jesus caused alarm to the Temple authorities by acting as if he had a right in the Temple courts they thought belonged in their authority. They were, as we say, "laying for Jesus."

They came bringing a young woman, who they said, had been caught in the act of adultery.

> "Rabbi, this woman has been caught in the act of adultery. Now in the Law Moses commanded us to stone such. What do you say about her? (John 8:4, 5).

It was true that the Torah stated that a betrothed woman caught in adultery should be stoned. She was considered legally the wife of the man to whom she was betrothed. The commandment reads:

> If there is a betrothed virgin, and a man meets her in the city and lies with her, you shall bring them both out to the gate of that city, and you shall stone them to death with stones, the young woman because she did not

cry for help though she was in the city, and the man because he violated his neighbor's wife. In this way you shall purge the evil from the midst of you (Deuteronomy 22:23, 24).

Of course this "catch-22" test of Jesus was intended to make him side with the Mosaic Law against the Roman prohibition of execution by Jews or to side with Roman law against Mosaic Law. The story continues:

Jesus bent down and wrote with his finger on the ground, and as they continued to ask him, he stood up and said to them, "Let him who is without sin among you be the first to throw a stone at her."

And once more he bent down and wrote with his finger on the ground. But when they heard it, they went away, one by one, beginning with the eldest, and Jesus was left alone with the woman standing before him.

Jesus looked up and said to her, "Woman, where are they? Has no one condemned you?

She said, "No one, Lord."

And Jesus said, "Neither do I condemn you. Go, and do not sin any more."

I taught for a semester at Ben Gurion University in Beersheba several years ago and was told by the professor whose place I took that I could teach anything I wanted in the Gospels. At the beginning of the course I made a little survey of the knowledge the students had of the life of Jesus. They knew almost nothing but in spite of this ignorance, several knew of the woman caught in adultery. Apparently the story is one of those rare accounts that is so impressive that it has spilled over from one culture to another.

I was amused one day many years ago when our son Danny, then about eleven years old, came home from his sixth-grade class in the Israeli school he went to in Jerusalem.

"Daddy," he said, "you know what our teacher taught us today?" My answer was no, of course.

"Well, she told us about a famous rabbi who once had brought to him a woman caught in a bad sin and all the people who brought her asked if he would rule that she should be stoned. The rabbi did not say anything. He just bent over and wrote in the sand. Then the rabbi looked at all the people who had brought the woman and said, 'Whoever has not done wrong let him throw the first stone.'"

I was not sure if Danny knew this story was from the New Testament so I asked him if he knew the source.

"Of course," he said.

"Well, what did you say to your teacher? Did you say you knew the story was from the New Testament?"

"Of course not," he said, "do you think I would want to embarrass the lady?" And, naturally, it would have been an embarrassment because of the accepted view in Israeli schools that as a rule one does not refer to the New Testament for reasons of propriety in Jewish circles.

What amused me, of course, was my young son's awareness of the religio-social situation in which we lived.

According to a recent issue of the *JERUSALEM POST* the Israeli department of education has banned the use of the New Testament as a source for use in Israel schools. Some school teachers say they will not obey the new directive.

Recorded in all our first three Gospels is a conversation Jesus had with the chief priests related to John the Baptist. It turns out that this rather short text is only the beginning of a much longer story which has parts in early sections of Luke and contains a parable found only in Matthew. The restored story underlines Jesus' appreciation of John as his forerunner and the obstinacy of the Temple sectarians in refusing to enter Jesus' Kingdom of God.

30 ANOTHER HIDDEN STORY

Not all the opposition to Jesus in the last week took the form of catch-22 testing. At least one confrontation seems almost academic, or at least leisurely. Luke 20:1-8 tells a story that for a long time I thought was complete in itself.

> One day, as he was teaching the people in the Temple and preaching the gospel, the chief priests and the scribes with the elders came up and said to him, "Tell us by what authority you do these things, or who it is that gave you this authority."
>
> He answered them, "I'll also ask you a question. Tell me, Was the baptism of John from heaven or from men?"

Once again, the good rabbinic way of carrying on a conversation — I reply to a question from my debating partner by asking a question myself.

> And they discussed it with one another, saying, "If we say, 'From heaven,' he will say, 'Why did you not believe him?'
>
> "But if we say, 'From men,' all the people will stone us! For they are convinced that John was a prophet."
>
> So they answered that they did not know whence it was.
>
> Then Jesus said to them, "Neither will I tell you by what authority I do these things."

To my great surprise I one day discovered that if I put this story in front of several passages having to do with one of Jesus' discussions about John the Baptist I had a beautiful introduction to material which had needed a proper setting, and thus a certain problem of story-chronology found its solution.

In chapter eleven of Matthew and chapter seven of Luke we have the record of at least two different discussions about John in the words of Jesus, one when John was apparently still alive and one when he seems to have died. (Compare the words that separate Matthew 11:11 from 11:16 and those that separate Luke 7:28 from 7:31.) I mentioned earlier the words of Matthew 11:1-15 and Luke 7:18-28 and Jesus' prophetic description of the Kingdom of God "breaking out" and expanding as hundreds joined his Movement. But where does one put the words of the second discussion?

Moreover, in Luke 5:33-38 (and parallels) we hear Jesus discussing John with some unidentified people who ask why the disciples of Jesus do not fast "as John's disciples do," to which Jesus responds that one day his disciples will fast when he, the bridegroom leaves them. Now for various reasons I judge this passage must not have originally appeared in this early part of the biography of Jesus, one of which is that Jesus is hinting prophetically that he will be taken away from his disciples — we have much evidence that Jesus predicted the future of his own death only in the last weeks of his life. Besides this there is a change of style in the Greek text between Luke 5:32 and 5:33 which indicates a splicing together of distant texts. Suffice it to say that some of these considerations have always troubled interpreters of the life of Jesus, and, incidentally, have caused scholars like Bultmann to suppose we cannot get back actually to the words of Jesus at all.

To make a very long story short, having struggled with these problems literally for years, it suddenly occurred to me one day that the setting in Luke 20 provided the very "incident" needed to rebuild one of these marvelous stories still hidden in our Gospels.

Let's start again with the first words of Luke 20.

> "Tell us, by what authority you do this or who gave you this authority."

Jesus counters with a question of his own:

> "I will also ask you something. Tell me, the baptism of John — was it from Heaven or from men?"

They think about that for a while:

> "If we say, from Heaven, he will say, why didn't you believe in him. But if we say, from men, all the people will stone us!"

So they decide to say, "We don't know." Jesus then says, "And I am not telling you by what authority I do these things."

The story seems to stand on its own. But it turns out that it is just the opening "incident" of a longer story.

We now turn to Luke 5:33-38, fifteen chapters earlier but by theme and word style another story about John the Baptizer which fits precisely here:

> They then said to him, "John's disciples fast often and make prayers ... but your disciples eat and drink."

Implied is the criticism that Jesus and his followers are not as traditionally "religious" as those who follow John and therefore do not deserve to be followed and acclaimed. Jesus answers with a rhetorical question emphasizing the freedom and joy characterizing his Movement:

> "Can the friends of the bridegroom fast while the bridegroom is still with them?"

He then adds: (Matthew 9:15-17).

> "Behold, the days are coming when the bridegroom will be taken away from them. Then — in those days — they will fast."

> "No one puts a patch made of new cloth on an old garment, for the new would tear the old. And no one puts new wine into old wineskins, for the new wine would rip open the old wineskins and all the wine be lost."

Jesus' Kingdom of Heaven is radically and totally new. The time will come when his followers will mourn the loss of him but the fact is that the traditional custom of saying long prayers and torturing the flesh by severe fasting is largely inappropriate to the New Kingdom. As Paul would later write, "The Kingdom of God is not food and drink but salvation (literally, righteousness) and peace and joy in the Holy Spirit" (Romans 14:17).

Now comes Luke 7:31-35 (compare Matthew 11:16-19). Notice how unbelievably it follows the above passage:

> "With what shall I compare this generation, and to what is it like? It is like children sitting in the market place calling to one another and saying, 'We played the pipe for you and you would not dance. We made funeral dirges for you and you would not mourn!'

> "For John came neither eating bread nor drinking wine and they said, 'He has a demon.' The Son of Man has come both eating and drinking, and they have said, 'See this glutton and winebibber, this friend of tax collectors and sinners!'"

Jesus ends with a Hebrew-style proverb which is clear in retranslation to Hebrew but is a little hard to put into English:

> "You can tell if a remark is really witty by the kind of people who say it!"

Nor is this all the reconstruction. We look for two good parables to bring the final punch to all Jesus is saying. And they are there — two parables each featuring two sons, one of which is in opposition to his father, but repents, and the other who claims to love and obey his father, but is disobedient.

One parable stands today in Matthew 21:28-32, while the other is found in Luke 15:11-32 and is familiar to readers of the New Testament as "the Prodigal Son." First let's look at the Matthew passage:

> "What do you think? A man had two sons and . . . to the first he said, 'Son, go work today in my vineyard.'
>
> "The son answered and said, 'I will not,'" but afterward he repented and went.
>
> "Then he came to the second and said the same thing, and this son said, 'I'll go, sir,' but he did not go.
>
> "Which of the two did what the father wanted him to do?" They said to him, "The first."

Jesus answers, "Amen! I tell you that tax collectors and harlots go into the Kingdom of God before you do! John came to you showing the way to salvation but you did not believe in him; the tax collectors and harlots did believe in him, but even when you saw this you were not moved to repent and accept his message!"

The second parable is so famous I will not repeat it in full. It also in an illustration about "two sons."

It is the story of a young man and his older brother, who is the father's right hand man.

The younger man is feeling his oats, as we say. He asks his father for his portion of the family inheritance, takes it and goes away and spends it in wild living. At last he is without money and ends up feeding hogs for a farmer — Jesus makes his situation the ultimate in degradation. At last he decides his best alternative is to go home, ask his father to treat him as one of his slaves, and give him at least something decent to eat.

This the son does and Jesus describes the joy of the father as he runs to welcome his son, kills the fatted calf and lays on a feast never before seen in the family.

Fine. But the older son watches all this with utter jealousy and scorn. He complains to his father that the father has never made such a feast for *him*! The father tries to placate his older son by telling him, "Look, you are always with me and everything I have is yours, but your brother was dead and is now alive, was lost and is found, so it is right we should make merry."

The story closes without our knowing whether the older son ever got over his pique.

Still, the older son sounds very much like some of the very religious Pharisees. We read interestingly that a few weeks after the death and resurrection of Jesus "a great many of the priests" came into the new Kingdom and were "obedient to the faith" (Acts 6:7). In this period the Pharisees were the fundamentalists and spiritual-minded of Jewry, the Sadducees the liberals and doubters.

It is not so hard to understand the subsequent repentance of many Pharisees. There were many good men among them. It is also not hard to believe that the Sadducaic rulers of the Temple felt even more fear and hatred for Jesus and his Galileans after his rebuke of them concerning himself and John. For them Jesus was — as we say in Hebrew — a bone in the throat!

Once again, perhaps in a lull in the controversies of the week, Jesus almost playfully propounds a Scripture riddle based on a messianic Psalm. How can the Messiah be both the "Lord" of David and his son? He is again underlining his supernatural character.

31 RIDDLE FOR THE SCRIBES

One extremely short episode is given by Luke as having occurred during Jesus' last week in Jerusalem. It concerns a riddle put to some of the scribes by Jesus and has to do with the first verse in Psalm 110 — accepted by all the rabbis as a messianic passage.

> The Lord said to my Lord, "Sit at my right hand until I make your enemies your footstool."

Just as with the officials who asked Jesus what right he had to teach in the courts of the Temple there is a kind of leisurely and unhurried atmosphere surrounding this short story which must have characterized many hours of Jesus' teaching. The so-called scribes *(sopherim)* had in the time of Jeremiah and afterwards been secretaries to kings and others, being equipped to read and write, but by the first century they seem to have lived in Jerusalem mainly and acted as consultants whose expertise was the knowledge of the Scriptures and the oral law. They sometimes gathered pupils in private quarters or in the porticos of the Temple and posed for discussion endless points of the *Tenach*. They were the people to whom Jesus could most naturally throw out the kind of riddle we are looking at here (Luke 20:41-44).

"How can people say," said Jesus to them, "that the Messiah is the son of David? David himself says in the Book of Psalms,

> 'The Lord said to my Lord,
> Sit at my right hand
> until I make your enemies your footstool.'

If David calls him Lord, how can he be his son?"

No one answers Jesus. There seems to have been no further continuation of the episode of any kind. What did Jesus mean by this conundrum?

It is interesting that Jesus does not say the Bible calls the Messiah the Son of David, that is, not in so many words. In Ezekiel the prophet speaks of "David" as equivalent to the future messianic king and there are other such references in the Old Testament, but the expression "Son of David" is apparently not found *per se.* It is a popular usage, so usage, so Jesus can ask, "Why do *they* say (that is, people generally) the Messiah is David's son?"

It is also clear that Psalm 110 was an accepted prophecy of the coming Messiah, otherwise Jesus' riddle would have had no point. Jesus will quote a phrase from the same Psalm in his answer to the chief priests later when he is interrogated by them on being asked outright if he is the Messiah or not.

> "From now on the Son of Man will be seated at the right hand of the Power" (Luke 22:69).

Unquestionably he is there identifying himself with David's Lord in Psalm 110.

It looks as if Jesus was, as it were, simply turning the conversation from the kinds of test questions he had been answering with a little more lightness and cleverness than the questions themselves to a Scripture riddle that would intrigue the professional scribes and get them thinking about who he was: more than a man, more than the Son of David, the "God-Messiah" Peter had confessed.

Interpreters of this passage sometimes suggest that Jesus was disavowing the title Son of David to claim only that he was David's divine Lord, or that our Gospel writers were picturing Jesus as refusing to be called David's Son. But Jesus is not refusing to be called the Son of David. He accepted this title from the blind beggar he healed in Jericho (Luke 18:38) and later New Testament writers do not hesitate to call him the Son of David.

I find delightful the fact that this man of Galilee who obviously was completely serious about the Kingdom of God and his own role as leader of this Kingdom could hold his hands out and smile at his detractors and offer a playful, somewhat teasing, riddle to these equally serious men to stop for a minute their heresy-hunting with just the outward possibility that they might discover something — or someone — very important.

We know that Jesus prophesied several times during the period he was in Jerusalem for the last Passover. One of the prophecies was apparently given before the throngs at the temple and spoke of the coming destruction of Jerusalem and the Temple. The earliest form of part of this prophecy is found in Luke 21:5-36. However, to restore the flow of the prophecy we must remove verses 5-7, 21-24 and 34-36 and join them together, after which we can join other passages not in the context to complete the prophecy.

32 DESTRUCTION

I find it painful to write about Jesus' prediction of the destruction of the Temple and Jerusalem. Sometime ago Israeli archeologists excavated in the neighborhood of the Dome of the Rock, the mosque which now sits in the center of the Temple area, and found what became known as "the Burnt House," a house destroyed by the Roman legions in 70 A.D. Scientists that they were, and hardened by years of exploration, these Israelis stood in awe and wept visibly as they thought of their ancient ancestors who had died in the house so long ago. Who does not weep with them?

Jesus not only saw the coming conflagration and disaster of his people but deeply felt it, as we know from a number of his sayings we shall yet mention. However, we must first "do a little digging" of our own to get a right look at what Jesus said about that catastrophe which indelibly left its mark on all subsequent Jewish history and liturgy.

Why?

Because the central prophecy Jesus made about the coming destruction of Jerusalem and the Temple has been mixed by early editors with two other important prophecies, and because of this mixing Christian and Jewish interpreters both have often been unable to clarify what he actually said.

For me the conclusion I reached in 1962 that Luke often preserves the earliest texts available to us was the key that provided the conviction that in the matter of Jesus' prediction of the disaster of 70 A.D. we can, with the right kind of literary analysis, know quite precisely what he said.

I do not want to go into all the details of researching the materials of this prediction but let me start by using our familiar search for

1. an incident
2. a teaching (in this case a prophecy)
3. two parables.

The incident is quite clear in Luke 21:1-4: Jesus and his followers have entered the "Women's Court," which was Israel's public worship area facing the court of the priests some fifteen steps above it. In full view from the Women's Court was the great bronze altar, and towering behind it the Temple itself. In the eastern corners stood large collection boxes put there to receive the money offerings of the worshippers.

Jesus and his *talmidim* and perhaps others who have been listening to his teaching in some portico on the outside watch as rich and poor deposit their coins.

> And he saw a poor widow put in two copper coins. And he said, "Amen! I tell you this poor widow has put in more than all of them, for they have given of their abundance but she has out of her poverty put in all the living that she had."

With this remark of Jesus the group seems to have moved casually around to stand by the fifteen "steps of ascension" and gaze upward at the lovely, white-stone Temple itself.

> And as some spoke of the Temple, how it was adorned with noble stones and offerings, he said, "Behold, the days are coming when not one of these stones shall be left on another unless it has already fallen down" (Luke 21:5, 6).

No one in the crowd seems to take offense. We know from the historian Josephus that from time to time others in this period had prophesied that the Temple would be destroyed at some future time. They ask him,

> "Rabbi, when will this be, and what will be the sign when this is about to take place?" (Luke 21:7).

So far, so good. The incident and accompanying conversation form the expected setting. What happens now to our text is, however, confusing. Jesus answers with a warning not to be led astray by anyone who may come "in his name" and say that he is the returned Lord. This has all the earmarks of a prophecy about the return of Jesus after his resurrection and ascension!

As we continue reading in Luke 21:10-19 we hear Jesus talking about how the disciples will be persecuted and "delivered to synagogues" and "brought before kings and governors." What is all this about?

Quite simply we have three prophecies originally given on three separate occasions, each one with a theme of its own. One shows Jesus predicting the destruction. The second displays his words on some other occasion when he is promising to appear as the Son of Man "with power and great glory." The third shows him telling the disciples what is going to happen to them after he leaves them.

Let us call these prophecies Prophecy A, Prophecy B and Prophecy C. We have found the setting of Prophecy A but no settings are given for the other two prophecies (we shall later find a setting for Prophecy B but in a quite different place in Luke).

Prophecy A can be recovered by putting together

Luke 21:1-7
Luke 21:20-24 and
Luke 21:29-32.

Prophecy B can be recovered by putting together

Luke 21:8-11
Luke 21:25-28 and
Luke 21:34-36.

Prophecy C can be recovered by printing as a separate column

Luke 21:12-17.

As we shall see later this does not mean that we have all of any one of these prophecies which have been mixed together at this point. It only means that when we separate these seven sections of Luke 21:1-36 we recover three continuous sections of Prophecy A and three continuous sections of Prophecy B.

We have already looked at the first section of Prophecy A (Luke 21:1-7).

We now add the second section (Luke 21:20-24):

> "When you see Jerusalem surrounded by armies, then know that its desolation has come near. Then let those who are in Judea flee to the mountains and let those in the city depart, and let not those who are out in the country enter it, for these are days of vengeance, to fulfill all that is written.
>
> "Alas for those who are with child and for those who give suck in those days! For great distress shall be upon the earth and wrath upon this

> people. They will fall by the edge of the sword and be led captive among all nations, and Jerusalem will be trodden down by the Gentiles until the times of the Gentiles are completed."

Finally comes the third section (Luke 21:29-32):

> "Look at the fig tree. As soon as it comes out in leaf you ... know that summer is near. So also, when you see these things taking place, you know that it (compare Mark and Matthew and my Appendix) is near.
>
> "Amen. I tell you this generation will not pass away till all has taken place."

And, of course, following our usual procedure in recovering an earlier, hidden and longer story, we look now for two parables.

Nor are we disappointed. They are there, though not attached to our story in Luke.

The first is the parable called that of the Barren Fig Tree (Luke 13:6-9). The second is the parable we call that of the Wicked Husbandmen (Luke 20:9-18; Matthew 21:33-44).

See how they complete the original story!

> "A man had a fig tree planted in his vineyard, and he came looking for fruit in it and found none. And he said to the vinedresser, 'Lo, these three years I have come looking for fruit on this fig tree and I did not find any. Cut it down. Why should it use up the ground?'
>
> "And he answered him, 'Let it alone, sir, this year also, till I dig around it and put on some manure, and if it bears fruit next year, well and good, but if not, you cut it down.'"

Jesus means of course that the vineyard is Israel (compare Isaiah 5:1ff). Occasional fig trees were often planted in a vineyard and they clearly represent here the leaders of Israel, standing in dignity above the vineyard. The God of Israel, owner of the vineyard, is going to give the leaders a bit more opportunity to "straighten up and fly right," as we say. Looked at historically the meaning probably is that they will be given almost forty years before the final catastrophe occurs.

The next parable is more telling and more tragic:

> "A man planted a vineyard and let it out to tenants and went into another country for a long time. When the season of fruit came he sent a servant to them to get some of the fruit of the vineyard, but the tenants beat him and sent him away empty-handed. And he sent another servant, whom they also beat and sent away empty-handed. And he sent still a third — this one they wounded and cast out of the vineyard.

"Then the lord of the vineyard said, 'What shall I do. I will send my beloved son. Perhaps they will respect him.

"But when the tenants saw him they said to themselves, 'This is the heir. Let us kill him and the inheritance will be ours,' And they cast him out of the vineyard and killed him."

At this point in the story Jesus says to his hearers,

"What is the owner going to do to them?"

The people listening say,

"He will put those wretches to a miserable death, and let out the vineyard to other tenants who will give him the fruits in their seasons."

We now add Matthew 21:43:

"Just so, I tell you, the Kingdom of God will be taken away from you and given to a people bringing forth the fruits thereof."

Read in English this passage is not easily understood — most interpreters suppose that Jesus is saying that up till now the leaders of this nation of Israel have been "in possession" of the Kingdom of God, by this meaning the "Kingdom of Israel." What I am arguing all through this book is that for Jesus the Kingdom of God is not the possession of anyone but God himself, and it is just as little the possession of Israel as a state or government. *The Kingdom of God is limited to the people Jesus is leading as King* and is a spiritual movement without political or military overtones.

What he is saying is something quite different. He is saying that his people make up the Kingdom, the flock, the Movement. They, his followers, have lived and grown within the body-politic and institutions of Israel, but now, with the leaders of Israel about to reject him finally and cause his death, the result will be that the people and power of his Movement will move out of the national milieu they have lived in and become a larger body willing to do what God wishes.

This is not a replacement of the spiritual hegemony which was ancient Israel. This is a new Israel springing from the ancient, prophetic remnant in Israel who were faithful to God's word and are now expanding like the mustard tree or the woman's leaven out of the very heart of the nation of Israel as it was in pre-70 A.D.

As so often after telling a parable Jesus drives the lesson home. Referring to the famous *Hallel* of Psalm 118 he says,

"What is this that is written?

> 'The very stone which the builders rejected
> has become the head of the corner!'
>
> "Every one who falls on that stone will be broken to pieces. Yet on whomsoever *it* falls it will crush him completely " (Matthew 21:42-44).

He is of course saying he is the rejected cornerstone. But his rejection, he says, will only issue in final recognition that he is indeed the head of the corner. Like truth itself acceptance or rejection of him will either leave joy in surrender or judgment in resistance.

At the Passover meal Jesus has several conversations with his apostles. He identifies his betrayer and praises his disciples for their faithfulness to him. He also promises that they will share with him in the leadership of his Movement beyond his present suffering and death. Jesus is arrested and brought before the Temple authorities. In a remarkable confrontation with them he leads them to confess his messiahship quite against their will and finally is brought before Pilate and Herod.

33 THE LAST PASSOVER

There are two levels of looking at Jesus' last earthly days with his disciples, at his opponents who ruled the Temple, and at the common people "who heard him gladly."

The first is the drama in which Jesus sits and talks with his apostles at the last passover meal, then is arrested on the slopes of the Mount of Olives where he and his disciples are camping, afterwards appears before the chief priests, then Pilate, then Herod and then Pilate again, and is finally led out beyond the walls of Jerusalem to be crucified by the Roman soldiers.

The second level asks questions like: what was Jesus thinking during all this drama? What purpose did he see in the animosity of the priests and the cruel mocking of Herod's soldiers? Why does he calmly continue to instruct his disciples about the future in the very face of his knowledge of coming death? Why is he so certain that he will rise from the dead in three days?

The first level and its physical drama occupies two chapters in the Gospel of Luke (in John's Gospel about eight!) and the story is like all Hebrew narrative, short and gripping. I do not want to duplicate all the detail we find in chapters 22 and 23 of Luke but simply to emphasize several important points which may escape the average person reading these chapters.

From the campsite on the western slope of the Mount of Olives Jesus sends Peter and John to prepare the Passover supper. They will meet a man carrying a water pitcher and they are to follow him until they come to an upper room and there make preparations. Since it would have been rare to see a man, instead of a woman, carrying a pitcher of water it is often supposed that the man was from a colony of Essenes who are known to have occupied part of the southwestern hill (today wrongly called Mount Zion) of the city of Jerusalem.

The Essenes maintained a calendar quite different from that of the Pharisees and most other Jews. They divided the year into 28-day months, so that Passover always came on Tuesday evening in the Passover week. Since it is normally assumed that Jesus was crucified on Friday at the time of the slaying of the Passover lambs it is possible that Jesus and his disciples observed the actual Passover meal on Tuesday night, in accordance with Essene practice. This would leave some two days for the arrest on Passover night, the interrogation by the chief priests and the appearances before Pilate and Herod, an arrangement which would make it easier to give sufficient time to what seems to be a crowded schedule of these events as portrayed in Luke and the other Synoptic Gospels (John appears to place the Passover meal a night before the traditional Thursday night).

According to Luke Jesus blessed the wine and then the bread and passed these to the twelve apostles sitting at the table with him. Of the bread he said, as he broke it, "This is my body," and it is clear that he was underlining the certainty of his coming death, just as he underlined it when he mentioned Judas Iscariot, one of the twelve:

> "Behold the hand of him who betrays me is with me on the table. For the Son of Man goes as it has been determined, but woe to that man by whom he is betrayed" (Luke 22:21, 22).

All through these accounts there appear Hebraic idioms and phrases, one of which is the expression Jesus uses when he speaks of his death as "the Son of Man goes." Jesus had not hidden his coming demise from the apostles or the larger band of disciples and it is easy to understand that as the apostles nervously considered what would happen to the Movement with Jesus gone they could argue about "who was to be the greatest," which really meant who was to take over the leadership.

Jesus answered this last without naming anyone of the apostles but with the statement that just as he was the host at the Passover meal and therefore doing the serving so the leaders of the future would be those who served best. They no doubt were comforted with the words that followed:

> "You are the people who have continued with me in my trials. As my Father has promised me a kingdom (literally, covenanted me a kingdom) so I promise you that you will eat and drink in my kingdom and sit on thrones judging the twelve tribes of Israel" (Luke 22:28-30).

The trials Jesus mentions appear to be the opposition and tests he had been going through during the past few days. For the first time Jesus speaks of being given a kingdom, that is, rule, or specific responsibility he can call his own, and this surely means his rule or leadership over the Kingdom of God, the Movement he heads. He will later once refer to himself as King.

He will also share this rule, this leadership, with these *shelichim* and they will in turn — figuratively of course — sit as judges of the twelve tribes of Israel. Here he is using the imagery of Psalm 122:3-5

> Jerusalem, built as a city
> which is bound firmly together,
> to which the tribes go up,
> the tribes of the Lord,
> as was decreed for Israel,
> to give thanks to the name of the Lord.
> There thrones for judgment were set,
> the thrones of the house of David.

Scripture talk!

As in other matters, Jesus' promise to the apostles to sit as judges over the twelve tribes of Israel has often been understood literally by many interpreters. They suppose the Kingdom of God is yet "to be set up" by Jesus in the millennial reign. Here is the way one commentator puts it:

> Our Lord's prediction discloses how the promise of Isaiah 1:26 will be fulfilled when the kingdom is set up. The kingdom will be administered over Israel through the apostles, according to the ancient theocratic judgeship (Judges 2:8).

In one point this interpretation is right. The Hebrew meaning of judge and judgment is more "deliverer' and "deliverance" than the legal figure we call a judge today or the courtroom in which advocates present formal pleas to a judge or jury. The "thrones of judgment" set up in Jerusalem, to which the twelve tribes of Israel go up are symbols, even in the Psalm, of a leadership that is fair and redemptive.

What is needed by Christian interpreters is a little closer understanding of Jesus himself and his concept of "rule." He is talking to the future leaders of his Movement. His Father has already given him the supreme leadership of this growing *Edah. He will not lose it when death comes* but will again sit at table after his resurrection and the apostles will share the leadership in which they "judge the twelve tribes of

Israel," not of course the literal tribes (ten had already disappeared in any case!) but his Kingdom people who form a new Israel.

Once again, Jesus is not denying that there is an ethnic and political Israel whose role in history would always be formative and creative as a result of the written word of God. God's search from the days of Abraham for a people willing to do his will had issued in great and holy traditions and if these had been distorted until the Prophets had to speak of God's turning to a remnant again and again it did not mean that God had failed or that there was no meaning to an Israel that would shortly be deprived of its last religious center, the Temple.

With the apostle Paul, who wrote later, Jesus would readily have agreed:

> "I have great sorrow and unceasing anguish in my heart, for I could almost wish that I myself were accursed and cut off from the Messiah for the sake of my brothers, my kinsmen by race."
>
> "They are Israelites, and to them belong the sonship, the glory, the covenants, the giving of the Law, the worship, and the promises. To them belong the patriarchs, and of their race, so far as the flesh is concerned, is our Messiah " (Romans 9:2-5).

It is only that Jesus sees that his role is to be a "light to the nations" (Isaiah 49:6) as well as the servant of God "to raise up the tribes of Jacob." This vision of a mission to be "a light to the *goyim*, the Gentiles" became the motto of the Jewish believers in Jesus later as they worked mightily to bring the Gentiles into the early Jesus-synagogues.

The Israel of the time of Jesus formed the cocoon in which the Kingdom Movement was nurtured and out of which that witnessing *Edah* stepped forth to "bring obedience to the nations."

For what it is worth that is the way I see the modern state and people of Israel. True, it was born as a refuge for Jews trampled and hunted, but it is more: it has largely succeeded in preserving and recreating much that is good in Israel's history. This is important for Christians. The very revival of the Hebrew language and the tools to understand it historically means that at least a foundation for the right understanding of Jesus has been brought into existence, and this at the very time Christian scholars in Christendom have largely cut the umbilical cord between first century Judaism and Christianity.

This is all very personal with me. I am quite sure that if I had not had the privilege of living as an evangelical pastor for more than forty years in Palestine and Israel I could not have written this book. As Flusser has often said to me, "Lindsey, you cannot work and do your research in the life of Jesus in any other place than Israel!" I believe that. I also believe the same is true of a small but growing body of young Christian scholars who live and work and interact in their studies with Israeli professors who have the expertise to help them.

I am not sure modern Jews and Israelis will agree with me enough to work out the practical applications of what I am saying — the establishment of institutions specifically aimed at helping to train the burgeoning masses of new Christians from especially the third world — but I hope so.

From the Passover meal the band of disciples and Jesus walk down into the Tyropean valley ("Cheesemaker's" valley), the gravelled way crunching beneath their feet. No voices are heard. Climbing again to cross the real Mount Zion they pass in darkness the southern steps of the Temple and descend into the Kidron valley. The brook is flowing gently and they step on stones to keep their sandaled feet from getting wet. Their feet next take them up the slope of the Mount of Olives to the campsite.

Jesus takes the disciples to a quiet area, leaves them with the words, "Pray that you do not fall if you are tempted" and moves away from them "about a stone's throw." They are dejected, and in their depression lie on the ground (not "sleep," as our translations say) only to hear him calling out (Luke 22:42-68),

> "Father, remove this cup from me if it is possible."

Yet as he continues to cry he also says,

> "But not what I want. Your will be done."

He returns and it is not long before the Temple police arrive and Judas plants a kiss of betrayal on his face.

> Then Jesus says to the chief priests and captains of the Temple and the elders ... "Have you come out as against a robber, with swords and clubs?"
>
> "When I was with you day after day in the Temple you did not lay hands on me. But this is your hour — and the power of darkness."

The police take Jesus away, Peter following at a distance. At the house of the chief priest Jesus is held all night and it is here that the

Temple patrol, no doubt bored and trying to stay awake, play their little game of blindfolding Jesus and ask him,

> "Prophesy! Who struck you?"

When challenged by a young woman Peter denies that he knows Jesus, and hears the cock crowing, just as Jesus said he would. He is overcome by his failure.

In the morning a group of chief priests and scribes seat Jesus before them. It is not a trial but an interrogation. Now comes a Greek text that translates to Hebrew word by word:

> "If you are the Messiah tell us!"

How will Jesus answer this one? He is facing a hostile crowd.

> "If I tell you, you will not believe,
> and if I ask you, you will not answer."

That is, if Jesus tries to carry on a conversation like those we have seen him engaging in not long before in the Temple courts he will not be able to do so. Normally he could have asked a question of his own in answer to theirs. But no, Jesus is obliged to turn to the method of "Scripture conversation."

> "But from now the Son of Man shall be seated at the right hand of Power (that is, God, *Hagevura*, an evasive term for God)" (Luke 22:69).

The ears of these clever men perk up. They know that the expression Son of Man is equal to the name Messiah. They also know that "seated at the right hand" suggests David's Lord in Psalm 110. As we have seen before the rabbis connected Psalm 110 with Psalm 2 where God says to the anointed king,

> "You are my son, this day have I brought you forth."

Without quite realizing what they are doing, and rather proud of themselves for figuring out Jesus' Scriptural conundrum, they say,

> "So you are the Son of God!" (Luke 22:70, 71).

They had arraigned Jesus. Now he has them in the palm of his hand. In saying he is the Son of God they are saying he is the Messiah. He replies,

> "Now it is *you* who are saying that I am (the Messiah)!"

That angers them, of course, and they take him away to Pilate, the Roman procurator.

"You are the King of the Jews?"

Pilate asks, half as a statement, half as a question. Jesus' answer has often been understood as in agreement with Pilate's version but when he speaks he simply says,

"That is what you say" (Luke 23:3).

In actuality Jesus never claimed to be the King of the Jews, firstly because in Hebrew you used the name Israel or Israelite or son of Israel for the Greek or Aramaic term "Jews." Secondly, because Jews generally did not accept him as their king. He was only the king of a large and growing band of followers.

Herod Agrippa was visiting in town and Pilate decided to send Jesus to see him. Jesus had once called him "that fox" but he did not answer the questions the cunning king asked him. Herod dressed him up and made fun of "this Jewish king" and sent him back to Pilate.

The prophecy of the suffering servant in Isaiah 52:13 — 53:12 clearly forms the backdrop for Jesus' thinking as he faces humiliation and death. As we read these words in Isaiah we learn more about Jesus' understanding of his sacrifice than the straightforward reporting of the Gospels can tell us.

34 LIVING ON SCRIPTURE

As we have noticed it was the habit of Jesus to hint at passages of Old Testament Scripture more than to quote them at length. If we ask what Jesus was thinking about at any given point in our records it is more than likely that we will receive our answer from some Scripture he refers to, even if this reference is minimal.

Sometimes scholars suggest that the Old Testament quotations in the Gospels were mainly the product of the "later community which wrote about Jesus." There are, indeed some references to prophecies in the *Tenach* which are obviously added by our writers but these are usually lengthy. Jesus' use of written texts is normally of a quite different type. He often refers obliquely to some text, hearing which his audience is expected to fill in what he means to say. Often enough as we look at the Greek text we miss some almost hidden reference and this failure is only exaggerated when the Greek passage is translated to English.

But on the last night at the Passover meal Jesus says to his disciples:

> "When I sent you out with no purse or bag or sandals, did you lack anything?"
>
> They said, "Nothing."
>
> He said to them, "But now, let him who has a purse take it, and likewise a bag. And let him who has no sword sell his mantle and buy one. For I tell you that this Scripture must find its fulfillment in me: 'And he was reckoned with transgressors" (Luke 22:35-37).

The phrase Jesus quotes is from a famous passage in Isaiah (52:13-53:12). His point seems to be that since the prophecy concerns a description of the Messiah in which he is thought to be a transgressor or criminal it is only appropriate that there should be a sword or two in the possession of his band so that when arrested or apprehended the symbols of rebellion will put Jesus, as it were, in the company of rebels.

The disciples show him a couple of swords they happen to have and comment,

> "Look, Lord, here are two swords."

His answer is,

> "It is enough" (Luke 22:38).

Of course, he must have smiled lightly, for the swords are only tokens. In the face of death he can somehow laugh.

There are perhaps only one or two other expressions in the many words of Jesus recorded for us which hint at what must have been long hours of meditation on passages such as those we recall when we mention Isaiah 53. The sparsity of such references only emphasizes that high intellectual sophistication by which he lived on those Scriptures which spoke so clearly to him.

Anguish and suffering were prophesied:

> As many were astonished at him —
> his appearance was so marred, beyond human semblance,
> and his form beyond that of the sons of men —

Rejection would meet him:

> He was despised and rejected by men,
> a man of sorrows and acquainted with grief . . .

Yet his suffering would be with dignity:

> He was oppressed and afflicted,
> yet he opened not his mouth,
> and like a sheep that before its shearers is dumb
> so he opened not his mouth.

The end would be death:

> They made his grave with the wicked
> and in death the rich,
> although he had done no violence
> and there was no deceit in his mouth.

Yet the death would not be meaningless:

> We esteemed him stricken,
> smitten by God and afflicted.

But he was wounded for our transgressions.
he was bruised for our iniquities.
Upon him lay the chastisement that made us whole,
and with his stripes we are healed.

Nor would it be permanent!:

When he makes himself an offering for sin,
he shall see his offspring,
he shall prolong his days.

The beauty of these words in Hebrew is almost beyond description. It is no wonder that Jews in ancient times read them with great pathos. Up to a thousand years ago the rabbinic commentaries applied the words to the Messiah and only with Rashi was there a first attempt made to apply them to Israel as a suffering nation. The passage is not read in the synagogue today, but no one can be certain why this is so.

Putting together three short prophetic utterances of Jesus we hear him again prophesying of the disaster soon to come on Jerusalem and the "house" — the time-honored name of the Temple in Jewish tradition. Jesus' last words on the cross are taken from a Psalm and are still used in the Orthodox Jewish burial service.

35 BEYOND THE WALLS

Under the pressure of "the chief priests and the rulers of the people" (apparently Sadducees) Pilate freed a popular Jewish rebel instead of freeing Jesus.

Jesus was led away, carrying his cross. To the women who followed in the crowd Jesus called out (Luke 23:26-31),

> "Daughters of Jerusalem, don't weep for me, but weep for your children. Behold, the days are coming when people will say, 'Blessed are the barren and the wombs that never bore, and the breasts that never gave suck!'
>
> "Then they will begin to say to the mountains, 'Fall on us' and to the hills, 'cover us.'
>
> "For if they do this to the green tree what will they do to the dry?"

I am indebted to my friend David Bivin, director of the Jerusalem School for the Study of the Synoptic Gospels, for pointing out to me that Jesus is referring in his usual way to a Scripture, in this case Ezekiel 20:47ff:

> "Behold, I will kindle a fire in you and it shall devour every green tree in you and every dry tree."

Ezekiel 21:4 explains this symbolism, saying that the Almighty promises he "will cut off from you both righteous and wicked."

The green tree, says David, represents the righteous, the dry tree the wicked. The Hebrew behind doing "to the green tree' or "to the dry tree" has been literally translated by many translators as "do in the green tree" or "do in the dry" but in Hebrew *laasot be* . . . means "to do to" someone or something.

Jesus is saying that if he as *hatsadik* (the Righteous One, a messianic title) is being treated as a criminal and taken to crucifixion how shall the non-righteous be treated? Much worse, of course.

Matthew and Luke both preserve a further passage which must earlier have followed Jesus' warning to the daughters of Jerusalem:

> "O Jerusalem, Jerusalem, you who kill the prophets and stone those who are sent to you! How often would would I have gathered your children together as a hen gathers her brood under her wings, but you did not want it.
>
> "Behold, your house is left to you desolate! And I tell you, you will not see me until you say, 'Blessed be the one who comes in the name of the Lord" (Matthew 23:37-39).

To this we must add, from Luke 19:41-44:

> "Would that even today you knew the things that make for peace! But they are hidden from your eyes.
>
> "The days are coming when your enemies will cast up a bank about you and surround you, and hem you in from every side, and dash you to the ground, you and your children within you, and they will not leave one stone upon another among you, because you did not know the time of your visitation."

In the person of the Prophet from Nazareth God had visited his people to redeem and heal but most of his people had been unable to grasp what this visit meant.

Luke writes with great economy:

> And when they came to the place which is called The Skull, there the Roman soldiers crucified him (Luke 23:33).

Two criminals were nailed on crosses next to him, one on the right and one on the left.

> And Jesus said, "Father, forgive them, for they do not know what they are doing."

Jesus knew. The pagan soldiers of Rome could not know.

In his anguish one of the criminals shouted at Jesus:

> "Aren't you the Messiah? Save us and yourself!"

The other asked Jesus to remember him when he came in his "kingly power." Jesus answered him,

> "Amen! I tell you, today you will be with me in *gan eden* (Paradise, literally, the Garden of Eden, a common name for the world to come among Hebrew speakers).

Both Matthew and Luke record that when death came Jesus called out in a loud voice and Luke writes that his words were:

> "Father, into your hands I commend my spirit" (Luke 23:34-46).

This phrase is from Psalm 31:5 and it is used until today in Jewish burial services.

Jesus' resurrection from the tomb was seen by none but the Father but the faithful women found the stone rolled away and Simon Peter first met him to talk with him, while others saw him and heard him, including the apostles in the upper room. The two disciples who met him on the road to Emmaus found he could still tease.

36 RELAX — HE IS RISEN!

Once when my good friend and colleague Flusser came back to Israel after a visit to the United States he told me of an experience he had as he nervously stood before the customs counter wondering whether he would be required to open his luggage. He had nothing of special value with him but he said that he obviously showed his nervousness to the customs officials.

Finally one of the officials held up his hand in a friendly gesture and said, "Mister, don't be worried, just relax!"

Flusser had evidently never heard this American phrase, but as he meditated on its meaning, he decided that these words were characteristic of Jesus.

"That is exactly what Jesus is all about," he said to me. "Jesus says to people, 'Relax!'"

And if you think about it a bit that is indeed the tone of the events and words of Jesus at the first Easter.

Because it was just before the Sabbath when Jesus died and his body was laid in the unusually large tomb of Joseph of Arimathea ("with the rich in his death"), ointments and spices had not accompanied the burial. Some of the women who had followed from Galilee nevertheless prepared spices and came early on Sunday morning to anoint the body. It was they who first discovered that the stone before the tomb door was rolled away and the tomb itself empty.

Some names have been preserved for us: Mary Magdalene (of Magdala, the little village just south of Ginosar) Joanna, and Mary, the mother of James. With other women who had gone with them they saw two men "dressed in dazzling apparel" who said to them,

> "Why are you looking for the living among the dead? Remember how he told you while he was still in Galilee that 'the Son of Man must be delivered into the hands of sinful men and be crucified, yet on the third day ride again?" (Luke 24:5-7).

Of course they ran as quickly as they could to tell the apostles (Judas had committed suicide so there remained only eleven). To the apostles

> these words seemed an idle tale, and they did not believe them (Luke 24:11).

It would take more proof for these sturdy, sensible men of Galilee.

And it was soon forthcoming.

One of our best sources about the appearances of Jesus after his resurrection is in a casual reference in the first letter of Paul to early Greek Christians in Corinth.

> I handed on to you as of first importance something I also received, that the Messiah died for our sins as the Scriptures said, that he was buried, that he was raised on the third day as the Scriptures said, and that he appeared to Cephas, then to the twelve.
>
> Then he appeared to more than five hundred brothers at one time, most of whom are still alive — though some have died. Then he appeared to James, then to all the apostles.
>
> Last of all, as to one untimely born, he appeared also to me (I Cor. 15:3-8).

The Gospels tell of only some of these appearances. Their writers do not seem to be concerned with proving that Jesus came alive — the facts seem to have been common knowledge and it is rather remarkable that even Jesus' enemies in ancient times did not trouble greatly to prove he had not been resurrected. Perhaps this was partly because Jews and non-Jews believed in many kinds of miracles. Philosophical skepticism about such things is in any case a pseudo-scientific development only a couple of hundred years old.

If Paul can write nearly thirty years after the event that most of the five hundred brothers who saw Jesus on one occasion are "still alive" it may indicate why the Jewish Christians had little interest in gathering evidence to prove to people like ourselves far down in history that Jesus rose from the dead. No one really denied it.

Even the accounts of appearances of Jesus are "relaxed." One that I find ever so fascinating is that about the two disciples who met Jesus on the road to Emmaus (perhaps Motsa today, just west of Jerusalem a few miles (Luke 24:13-35). These two men were

> talking with each other about all the things that had happened when... Jesus himself drew near and went along with them, but they did not recognize him.

> And he said to them, "What is this conversation you are having with each other . . .?
>
> And they just stood still, and looked sad.
>
> Then one of them, named Cleopas, answered him, "Are you the only visitor to Jerusalem who does not know the things that have happened there in these days?"

Jesus, so typically, leads them on to keep them talking.

> "What things?" he said to them.
>
> "Concerning Jesus of Nazareth, who was a prophet mighty in deed and word before God and all the people, and how our chief priests and rulers gave him over to be condemned to death, and crucified him.
>
> "But we had hoped that he was the one to redeem Israel. Yes, and besides all this, it is now the third day since this happened.
>
> "Moreover some women from our group amazed us. They were at the tomb early in the morning and did not find his body, and they came back and said that they had even seen a vision of angels, who said that he was alive.
>
> "Some of those with us also went to the tomb and found it just as the women had said, but they did not see him."

With this, finally, Jesus took on his real role:

> "O foolish men so slow of heart to believe all that the Prophets have spoken!
>
> "Did not the Messiah have to suffer these things and then to enter into his glory?" (Luke 24:14-26).

At this point he "began with Moses and all the Prophets and explained in all the Scriptures the things about himself."

What were all these Scriptures? No doubt they must have included Isaiah 53, but we cannot know fully. It would have been exciting to people of today if at least a written record of his discussion had been preserved for us.

But the story is not over:

> They came to the village to which they were going and he appeared to be going on further, but they urged him and said, "Stay with us for it is almost evening and the day is nearly over," so he went in to stay with them.

> Now while he was sitting at the table with them he took the bread and blessed (God) and broke it, and gave it to them.
>
> Then their eyes were opened and they recognized him. But he vanished out of their sight (Luke 24:28-31).

The story complements all those we have been seeing in this book. It is the same gently teasing, almost playful Jesus. He may be back in a different body which appears and disappears and walks through walls but he can be recognized and he acts just as he did when in his unresurrected body!

It is the same when Cleopas and his friend rush back to Jerusalem that evening and find "the eleven" gathered together in their upper room with others. On hearing the two from Emmaus they confirm their testimony and say,

> "The Lord has risen indeed, and has appeared to Simon!"

Then Jesus appears — as the group sits startled and frightened.

In essence he says, "Relax!"

> "Why are you troubled and why these questionings rising up in your hearts? Look at my hands and my feet, that it is I myself. Handle me and see. No ghost has flesh and bones like these I have!"
>
> And while they still disbelieved for joy, and marveled, he said to them, "Do you have something to eat here?"
>
> They gave him a piece of broiled fish, and he took it and ate before them. (Luke 24:34-43).

Flusser was right.
Jesus says, "Relax."

Scattered throughout Matthew and Luke are sayings of Jesus which do not fit easily into the contexts assigned to them. These sayings demand for their setting a time when Jesus could forewarn and foretell of a period when his followers would need the Holy Spirit for guidance and patience in tribulation. When we assume these prophetic instructions were given to the disciples during the 40-day period after the Passover we find they make especially good sense.

37 LOCATING LOST WORDS

Matthew and Luke end their Gospel stories with recounting various incidents in which Jesus appeared to the women or to the apostles but also with words reflecting Jesus' instructions to some one hundred and twenty disciples about what was to be their next step. Luke concludes his narrative with these words:

> And he said to them, "Thus it is written, that *hamashiach* (the Messiah) should suffer and on the third day rise from the dead, and that repentance and forgiveness of sins should be preached in his name to all the Gentiles, beginning from Jerusalem."
>
> "You are witnesses of these things. And behold, I send the promise of my Father upon you — but stay in the city until you are clothed with power from on high."
>
> Then he led them out as far as Bethany, and lifting up his hands he blessed them. While he blessed them, he was carried up into heaven.
>
> And they returned to Jerusalem with great joy and were continually in the Temple blessing God. (Luke 24:46-52)

It is on the same theme that Luke begins his book we call the Acts of the Apostles, which deals with the way Jesus bid farewell to his disciples, of their filling with the Holy Spirit on Shavuoth, the Feast of Weeks or Pentecost, and the subsequent miracles and travels of the Apostles, Saul or Paul being one of the chief figures in the book.

Addressing the book to someone by the name of Theophilus, he mentions his earlier book, no doubt his Gospel.

> In the first book . . . I have dealt with all that Jesus began to do and teach until the day when he was taken up, after he had given commandment through the Holy Spirit to the apostles whom he had chosen (Acts 1:2).

Now the words translated "given commandment" *(enteilamenos)* can correctly be translated "giving instructions." This piece of information seems to be slightly expanded in the next verse (Acts 1:3):

> To them (the apostles) he presented himself alive after his suffering by many proofs, appearing to them during forty days, and speaking of the Kingdom of God.

Since there are fifty days between the feasts of Passover and Pentecost we assume that Jesus' ascension into the heavens occurred forty days after his resurrection, that is, ten days before the special event in which the Holy Spirit descended in power on the one hundred and twenty in what may have been one of the rooms in the Temple — the story is found in the second chapter of the Acts.

The question is: what kind of instructions did Jesus give as he appeared and reappeared to his leaders during those forty days? What does Luke mean when he says Jesus talked to them about the Kingdom of God during that period? And have we any record of what he said?

It is generally assumed that we know next to nothing.

But that may be an error.

The truth is that we possess a large number of sayings of Jesus, some long and some short, which appear not to have been said at the points they now appear in our first three Gospels. In these sayings Jesus talks about the persecutions his believers are going to go through and says they will be arrested and forced to witness before Jewish kings and Gentile rulers but that they are not to be afraid, for the Holy Spirit (about whom he gives almost no instruction until the Spirit is mentioned in the end of his ministry) will give them words of testimony they will find surprising and powerful.

For example, we talked earlier about the three prophecies which appear in Luke 21 mixed together and how it is that to understand this entire passage we have to separate Prophecy A from Prophecy B and Prophecy C from both of them. We noticed that Prophecy A and B each have three short sections while Prophecy C has only one. Prophecy C has to do with what was to happen to the disciples when Jesus was no longer with them (Luke 21:12-17):

> "But before all this they will lay their hands on you and persecute you, delivering you up to the synagogues and prisons, and you will be brought before kings and governors for my name's sake. This will be a time for

> you to bear testimony. Settle it therefore in your minds not to meditate beforehand how to answer, for I will give you a mouth and wisdom which none of your adversaries will be able to withstand or contradict. You will be delivered up even by parents and brothers and kinsmen and friends, and some of you they will put to death. You will be hated by all for my name's sake."

From all the evidence we take it that Jesus did not begin to prophesy often until his last days as he planned to go to Jerusalem. Our sources say that he prophesied of his death and resurrection on the way, as it were, to Jerusalem. Luke tells us that Jesus next prophesied of the destruction of the Temple in the Temple courts. A less public prophecy is that in which he tells Peter at the Passover meal that he will yet in this same night deny him. We are able to locate more or less that context in which each of these prophecies occurred.

However, we are not told explicitly where Prophecy C or the other sayings I have mentioned were given. A good guess seems to be that they were said by Jesus *after his resurrection during the forty days.*

This would explain, for example, why the Holy Spirit is mentioned so prominently in just these sayings. Jesus clearly knew he was to "go back to the Father" and this meant that he would be obliged to lead and guide his followers no longer physically but through the Holy Spirit. Such a change would of course be necessary if the Kingdom was to grow and expand not only in Jerusalem but also in Judea, Samaria and "the uttermost parts of the world" (Acts 1:8).

It would also explain why he emphasizes the persecutions the disciples would encounter. As long as Jesus was with his followers physically they might have faced some personal rejection but certainly nothing that could be named persecution. Jesus warns that even "some of you they will put to death" (the promise that "not a hair of your head will perish" (Luke 21:18) must be related to those who were warned to flee when Jerusalem was about to be destroyed).

It would also explain why "testifying" and "testimony" are mentioned by Jesus. As long as Jesus was with them the disciples were not given an order to testify about Jesus, so far as we know. After he was no longer with them one of their big tasks would be to talk about him and all the things he did and said. This is why we may suppose that the Greek *ecclesia* was originally in Hebrew *Edah*, the witnessing body.

It would explain another thing that Jesus mentioned in these sayings: he carefully warns his disciples not to deny him in any fashion and these words concern the danger to the disciples of any cover-up about their identity as followers of Jesus. No cover-up was needed or possible while Jesus was with them. Afterwards, yes.

It is easy to understand how Jesus' instruction to his disciples after the resurrection originally got separated from their first context. In the stage when the author of our REORGANIZED SCROLL placed the teachings and conversations of Jesus into "complexes" of sayings or possibly into just one long series of sayings in his scroll he of course had separated the sayings from the narrative incidents which preceded them. And this meant that our writers no longer always knew to what incident or story to connect them.

In any case the editor of the first RECREATED STORY did not hesitate to put three prophecies together — our Prophecies A, B, and C. After all, the style of Old Testament prophecy characterized each and perhaps he thought he was as able to restore a more original prophecy of Jesus as anyone.

On the other hand the author of our Greek Matthew seems to have felt he could find an original context for the material we might call the "Future of the Disciples" (Luke 21:12-17) when he attached it to the instructions Jesus gave on sending out the Twelve to heal and cast out demons (Matthew 10:16ff). He therefore left out almost all of Prophecy C when he copied Mark's version of this Prophecy (which Mark had in turn taken from Luke 21 — see Matthew 24:9 and Mark's parallel, Mark 13:9-13 and Luke 21:12-17), for he had given the same basic sayings in his tenth chapter.

Indeed, Matthew gives in 10:1-15 the basic words of Jesus when sending out the Twelve, as we saw before, but without any change of place gathers many of our almost lost post-resurrection instructions to the apostles (Matthew 10:16-18):

> "Behold, I send you out as sheep in the midst of wolves. So be wise as serpents and innocent as doves.
>
> "Beware of men, for they will deliver you up to councils and flog you in their synagogues and you will be dragged before governors and kings for my sake, to bear testimony before them and the Gentiles."

At this point the instructions are almost the same as those we found in Prophecy C in Luke. However, in Matthew 10:23 we read:

> "When they persecute you in one town, flee to the next . . . I tell you, you will not have gone through all the cities of Israel before the Son of Man comes."

Despite the fact that Matthew is gathering together material from more than one original area the famous Albert Schweizer made this verse the key to his interpretation of Jesus' plans for "the establishment of the Kingdom of God." Since the disciples came back before "the Son of Man came" — whatever Schweizer thought this meant — Jesus concluded his prophecy had been untrue and he turned to the idea of death as the alternative.

Schweizer's highly questionable theory points up the importance of a right analysis of our Gospel materials. The simplest solution of this question is that Matthew himself felt the similarity between the instructions Jesus gave to the Twelve when he sent them to heal the sick in Galilee and his instructions after his resurrection and copied down the second set of sayings immediately after the first. It is surely after the resurrection that Jesus is saying,

> "A disciple is not above his teacher, nor a servant above his master. It is enough for the disciple to be like his teacher, and the servant like his master. If they have called the master of the house Beelzebul, how much more will they malign those of his household."

He is also saying,

> "So have no fear of them, for nothing is covered that will not be revealed or hidden that will not be known. What I tell you in the dark, utter in the light, and what you hear whispered proclaim upon the housetop.
>
> "And do not fear those who kill the body but cannot do any more (see Luke's parallel). Rather, fear him who can kill and then has the power to cast into hell (Matthew 10:24-28).

I have turned to Luke's parallel to these sayings in Luke 12:4-10 to present them here, for Matthew's version clearly shows a less Hebraic text at this point than does that of Luke. Matthew's text, as in some other materials in Matthew, shows a Greek rather than a Hebrew understanding of some matters (the same tendency towards Greecism sometimes shows up in Luke when it does not do so in Matthew), so that Matthew writes,

> "Do not fear those who kill the body but cannot kill the *nephesh* (soul). Fear him rather who can destroy both soul and body in hell "(Matthew 10:28).

The Greek word used by Matthew is *psyche* which is the normal Greek translation of the Hebrew *nephesh* but *nephesh* never has the meaning of "immortal soul" as does *psyche* in later Greek. Matthew gives a text that uses *psyche* as equivalent to "immortal soul" and it therefore cannot come from Hebrew understanding. On the other hand Luke's parallel show us a text that does not have this problem, that is, shows no tendency to Greecism.

From Luke we see that Jesus wanted to comfort his followers even as he warned them:

> "Are not five sparrows sold for two pennies? Yet not one of them is forgotten before God. Why even the hairs of your head are all numbered!
>
> "Fear not, you are of more value than many sparrows" (Luke 12:6-7).

Both Matthew and Luke read in their *REORGANIZED SCROLL* just after this word of comfort that the disciples must be careful to acknowledge their association with Jesus, even when there is danger in such acknowledgement.

> "I tell you, everyone who acknowledges me before men, the Son of Man also will acknowledge before the angels of God, but he who denies me before men will be denied before the angels of God " (Luke 12:8, 9).

On the other hand the point of the next saying appears not to be a warning to the disciples but a promise to them that if they live by the direction and power of the Holy Spirit *they* will themselves be blessed but *the one who criticizes* the Spirit as he works through them is in imminent danger:

> "Everyone who speaks a word against the Son of man will be forgiven but he who criticizes the Holy Spirit will not be forgiven" (Luke 12:10).

You can criticize the Son of God all you please — and, strangely, some do.

But if you criticize and curse these followers of Jesus who are trying to do his will you are actually criticizing the Holy Spirit and you will bear the consequences.

A great many Christians who take the Bible seriously get deeply concerned about what they call the "sin against the Holy Spirit for which there is no forgiveness." Almost any pastor finds from time to time that some man or woman will come to him asking whether this or that wrong thing he or she has done may have been to "commit the unpardonable sin." As a rule such a pastor finds himself explaining that the "sin against the Holy Spirit" is to attribute to the devil the work of the Holy Spirit.

This may well be true but Jesus seems to be giving a word of comfort to his servants who will find themselves severely criticized in the very act of working in the Spirit's power. They are to know that as long as they operate in the power of the Spirit, criticism of them will be severely punished by God himself. They are in a ministry of divine power that shares the effective presence and protection of the Almighty.

One of the themes of these sayings is the importance of having a right view of Jesus' authority. In both Matthew and Luke we have the following statement of Jesus:

> "All things are given to me by my Father and no one knows the son like the father or the father like the son, and to whomsoever he wishes he will reveal him" (Matthew 11:27, Luke 10:22).

As we have seen this saying of Jesus loses none of its power when we render the Greek into Hebrew:

> All things are given to me by my Father, and no one knows a son like a father or a father like a son, and to whomsoever he wishes he will reveal him."

Jesus is the special Son of his Father but his original way of speaking of himself and his Father seems not to have been in a non-Hebraic usage such as "The Son" or "The Father."

It is because Jesus is this special Son that he has the right to introduce people to the God of Abraham, Isaac and Jacob and can choose apostles and leaders about whom he can say,

> "He that receives you receives me and whoever receives me receives him who sent me" (Matthew 10:40).

Similarly encouraging to those he will send are the words,

> "He who receives a prophet in the name of a prophet will receive the pay of a prophet and he who receives a righteous man in the name of a righteous man will receive the pay of a righteous man" (Matthew 10:41).

Perhaps after this saying Jesus said,

> "Amen. I tell you whatever you (plural) bind on earth will be bound in heaven and whatever you (plural) will loose on earth will be loosed in heaven" (Matthew 18:18).

These are like the words of authority that Jesus gave to Peter. They derive from the rabbinic idiom by which something is declared permitted or forbidden. Here again are words of comfort for these who will shortly be having to make decisions only Jesus had been making until recently. "Heaven," that is God himself, will stand behind whatever decisions they have to make.

Just as comforting are Jesus' words of promise concerning things the disciples will pray about:

> "I tell you (plural) that if two of you shall agree on earth about any thing they wish to ask it will be done for them by my Father who is in heaven, for wherever two or three gather in my name there am I in the midst of them" (Matthew 18:19-20).

Jesus does not hesitate to tell his followers that their responsibility matches the call to what we might call the redemption and salvation of the present order. Probably we are obliged to put together the words presented in Matthew with those of Luke at this point in the fashion we have found it necessary earlier. From Matthew 5:13-16 and Luke 14:34,35 we may collect the following words:

> "You are the light of this world (that is, this age). A city set on a hill cannot be hid. Nor do men light a lamp and put it under a bushel, but on a stand, and it gives light to all in the house.
>
> "Just so, your light is to shine before men, that they may see your good works and give glory to your Father who is in heaven. Salt is good but if it has lost its taste how shall its saltness be restored? It is fit neither for the soil nor for the compost pile. Men throw it away and trample it under foot.

As we have seen again and again Jesus is not saying that the people of his Movement are identical with any kind of culture or society. On the contrary they are not to lose their identity, for they *give light* to each culture or society. If they are not careful they may get so concerned with themselves and their organizations within the Kingdom of God that they can actually settle back into a corner and hide their influence under a ceramic vessel, where the lamp will not only not give light but die because of lack of oxygen — as so often Jesus' illustrations are hyperbolic and this one probably brought a smile to the faces of his disciples.

Salt, too, was brought in those days from the area of the Dead Sea and was rarely simply sodium chloride, so that it indeed could "lose its savor." Salt was used to preserve dried fish, olives and certain vegetables but here it no doubt means it has its greatest value in giving flavor to food. The people of God's Kingdom would in the present age modify and bless a world still far from God and greatly in need.

From Matthew 5:11, 12 and Luke 6:22, 23 we see that the *REORGANIZED SCROLL* tended often to put sayings together on the basis of some word or idea. Where the word "persecuted" appeared in the eighth beatitude in Matthew (5:10) the author of this scroll combined a further saying about persecution, but this time, in contrast to the beatitude, you (plural) is used:

> "Blest are you when men revile you and persecute you and cast your name out as evil (a Hebraism preserved by Luke but not by Matthew and meaning to give a bad name to someone) because of the Son of Man."

Normally none would enjoy being made fun of and laughed at, but Jesus calls his people to treat those that despise them as sources of joy if this is because they are associated with him. They are laughing at you. Turn it all around, and laugh yourself.

> "Rejoice and be glad, for your reward is great in heaven, for in the same way men used to persecute the prophets who were before you" (Matthew 5:12; Luke 6:23).

You have joined the great prophets. They had lots of troubles and so will you! You just have to laugh when Jesus says it!

But many have proved it works!

Smile and the world smiles with you, weep and you weep alone! Victory lies in the lap of the persecuted, not the persecutor.

When Anatoly Sharansky managed to come out of the Russian jail he had been in so many years he is reported to have said,

> "Actually I was the free one. My jailers were the ones in bondage. They had to guard me but I did not have to guard them!"

Nor is Jesus just glorifying suffering. Look at his words of warning about how to know if you are dealing at any given time with someone likely to cause you harm. He is probably talking about the circumstances under which they are to give their testimony:

> "Don't give what is holy to dogs and don't throw your pearls to the pigs, lest they trample them under their feet and turn and rend you. (Matthew 7:6)

"By their fruits you know them. Men do not gather grapes from thornbushes or figs from thistles.

The rule is to be

"... as cautious as serpents and innocent as doves" (Matthew 10:16).

"I tell you," says Jesus,

"on the day of judgment men will render account for every careless word they utter, for by your words you will be justified and by your words you will be condemned" (Matthew 12:36).

As the disciples are to watch their words they are also to flee any tendency to do wrong. Using again his words of hyperbole, Jesus says,

"If your hand causes you to fall cut it off and throw it away from you. It is better for you to come into life maimed or lame than with two hands to be thrown into eternal fire.

"And if your eye trips you up dig it out and throw it away from you. It is better for you to come into life with one eye than with two eyes to be thrown into Gehenna" (Matthew 18:8, 9).

Jesus also gives instructions about how to deal with a brother who "sins against you." First,

"go and tell him his fault, between you and him alone. If he listens to you you have gained your brother.

"But if he does not listen, take one or two others along with you, that every word may be confirmed at the mouth of two or three witnesses.

"If he still refuses to listen to them, tell it to the *Edah* (the Church), and if he refuses to listen even to the church he is to be to you like a Gentile or a tax collector" (Matthew 18:15-17).

Yes, but what if this brother repents of what he did that was wrong towards you and asks your forgiveness? Do you just keep forgiving him or is there a cut-off place where you stop forgiving even if the man says he is sorry and repents.

Peter asked that.

"Lord how often shall my brother sin against me and I forgive him? Seven times?

"Jesus said to him, "I do not say to you seven times but seventy times seven!" (Matthew 18:21, 22).

In all these instructions we hear the voice of Scripture. Punishment of an evil thing was meted out only after the testimony of "two or three witnesses" (Deuteronomy 17:6) and if Cain would be avenged seven times Lamech would be avenged "seventy times seven" (Genesis 4:24).

We all live in glass bubbles, our good and bad sides exposed to the public. Particularly is this true of those who would serve the Lord and "be his witnesses." So utter humility is the only attitude to have.

> "Will any one of you who has a servant plowing or keeping sheep, say to him when he has come in from the field, 'Come now and sit down to the table?' No, he will rather say to him, 'Prepare supper for me and gird yourself and serve me till I eat and drink, and afterward you shall eat and drink?'
>
> "Does he thank the servant because he did what was commanded? You too, when you have done all that is commanded you, say, 'We are unworthy servants. We have only done what it was our duty to do" (Luke 17:7-10).

Nor must anyone feel proprietary about living within the special blessings of the Kingdom of God. On the contrary there is to be "weeping and gnashing of teeth" when it is discovered that the Kingdom of Heaven is full of people good members of the Kingdom would not have dreamed would be there.

> "I tell you, many will come from the east and the west and sit at table with Abraham, Isaac, and Jacob in the Kingdom of Heaven " (Matthew 8:11).

It is here we may probably put the parable of the laborers in the field. Jesus said,

> "The Kingdom of Heaven is like a householder who went out early in the morning to hire laborers for his vineyard. After agreeing with the laborers for a dinar a day, he sent them into his vineyard.
>
> "And going out about the third hour (nine a.m.) he saw others standing idle in the market place. He said to them also, 'You go into the vineyard too, and whatever is right I will give you.' So they went.
>
> "He went out again about the sixth hour and the ninth hour and did the same. And about the eleventh hour he went out and found others standing, and he said to them, 'Why are you standing here idle all day?' They said to him, 'Because no man has hired us.' He said to them, 'You go into the vineyard too.'
>
> "And when the evening came, the owner of the vineyard said to his steward, 'Call the laborers and pay them their wages, beginning with the last up to the first.'

"And when those hired about the eleventh hour came they each received a dinar. When the first came they thought they would receive more, but each of them received a dinar.

"On receiving it they grumbled at the householder, and said, 'These last worked only one hour and you have made them equal to us who have borne the burden of the day and the scorching heat.'

"But to one of them he replied, 'Friend, I am doing you no wrong. Did you not agree with me for a dinar? Take what belongs to you and go. I am choosing to give this last person the same amount I gave to you. Am I not allowed to do what I choose with what belongs to me? Or is your eye evil because my eye is good (to have an evil eye in Hebrew means to be stingy and mean, while to have a good eye is to be generous)?" (Matthew 20:1-15).

How easy it is for those who share the grace of God and who have served him for many years to begin to think of themselves and their children as "those who deserve" whatever good things have issued from their hard work in the Kingdom. Those of us who live in the Middle East constantly witness groups of religious people claiming special privileges, material and otherwise, while at the same time erecting cultural, ethnic and even racist walls around their little establishment.

As I understand it Jesus long ago warned against this failure to share. No doubt he has been breaking up little fiefdoms set up in his name ever since he uttered these words. In fact, isn't this the meaning of the multitudes of new churches and movements which have always denied the right of the large traditional churches and groups to control them?

You want to see how a religious group throws up a wall around itself, puts its light under the empty ceramic jar and slowly dies?

Look around you.

And then look inside you. All of us like to be proprietary.

Although the sequence of Jesus' prophecy and instructions concerning the future ministry of the apostles is not easily determined, the prophecy of his future return in power and glory finds a setting in a meeting between Jesus and his disciples just prior to his ascension on the Mount of Olives. The prophecy itself is made up of a number of passages which are quickly assembled. Of particular importance is Jesus' refusal to give specific signs of his future appearance until the day in which he is to be revealed. He promises to take into his beatific supernatural those watching for his return.

38 IF YOU'RE ON THE ROOF

To tell the truth I dreaded trying to write that chapter we just finished. For some months I worked collecting these sayings and even if I believe we now have a viable explanation for the scattered nature of their appearance it is not easy to put them into a reasonable order. We can perhaps take comfort in the fact that many other units fit like a glove to a hand and make it possible to recover many hidden stories.

Happily this is the situation we face when we come to Jesus' last prophecy, that fascinating lecture on what the New Testament calls the "appearing of our Lord Jesus the Messiah." In fact, once we have determined the extent and content of Prophecy B in Luke 21 we have only to place the words of Luke 17:22-27 before Prophecy B and we have substantially — apart from certain parables and applications — the body of the prophecy.

Here again we find our pattern,

Incident
Teaching
Parables

The suggestion needed for the location of the incident is the final day or hours just before his ascension. We find such a suggestion in Luke 24:50:

> Then he led them out in the direction of Bethany . . . blessed them . . . and parted from them.

and in Acts 1:12, where we hear that the Apostles returned from the Mount called Olivet to Jerusalem and the upper room in which they seem to have been living during the forty days which followed the last Passover.

As usual, our prophecy has been separated from the original incident and we are obliged to rebuild it from the materials left to us. These have been beautifully preserved, even if we have to put them together. In Luke 17:22 Jesus is apparently speaking on the Mount of Olives,

> "The days are coming when you will wish you could see one of the days of the Son of Man, but you will not see it. And some will say to you, 'Lo, there!' or 'Lo, here!'
>
> "Don't go, don't follow them. For as the lightning flashes and lights up the sky from one side to the other, so it will be with the Son of Man in his day."

At this point a little editorial note pokes its head into Jesus' words and it would be wise to mark it as such when translating the passage:

> "(But first he must suffer many things and be rejected by this generation.)"

This is not the only such note (compare Luke 9:21, 22) which either Luke or an earlier editor has inserted into the body of our material from time to time. And, of course, there is no reason an editor should not have made this addition once he placed the sentence before the account of death and resurrection.

Jesus continues (Luke 17:22-30),

> "As it was in the days of Noah so it will be in the days of the Son of Man — they ate, they drank, they married, they were given in marriage, until the days when Noah entered the ark and the flood came and destroyed them all."

This is Jesus' first parabolic illustration in this text. The partner illustration follows immediately:

> "In the same way in the days of Lot they ate, they drank, they bought, they sold, they planted, and they built, but on the day when Lot went out from Sodom fire and brimstone rained from heaven and destroyed them all. This is the way it will be on the day when the Son of Man is revealed." (Luke 17:22-30).

Students of this theme of the Lord's "revealing" often miss an important point here: Jesus says that there is little or no preliminary sign of his coming. The sign that the flood was coming in the days of Noah was no more than Noah's entering the ark. The sign that Sodom was about to be overthrown in hissing steam and brimstone was only that Lot and his family started walking away from Sodom. Apart from these acts the people went right on eating and drinking and marrying and being given in marriage till the day itself.

But the mind of man is curious. We like fortune telling. Evangelists and date-setters are always nearby trying to satisfy us with lurid descriptions of the famines and earthquakes occurring "two months ago" or "just last night" in the South Pacific or in Mexico!

Not Jesus.

It was not that he minded giving signs of the events he prophesied about — *if there were to be signs*. He told his generation in detail about what would happen before the Roman troops came to destroy Jerusalem, told them to get out of the city, and gave them enough signs that it is said that in 70 A.D. the believers fled Jerusalem and took refuge in Pella, a city across the Jordan valley to the east of Bethshan.

Jesus describes the coming of the Son of Man as an event quite different in nature than that of the local, Jerusalem-centered destruction of Jerusalem and the Temple.

> "On that day let him who is on the housetop, with his goods in the house, not come down to take them away. Likewise let him who is in the field not turn back" (Luke 17:31). Don't run.

On the contrary, at the destruction of Jerusalem his followers should run.

> "Let those who are in Judea flee to the mountains and let those who are inside the city depart, and let not those who are out in the country enter it" (Luke 21:21).

The coming of the Son of Man would be completely different. It was to be a totally supernatural event.

If you are on the housetop get ready for the kind of rapture Enoch experienced,

> "I tell you, in that night there will be two in one bed. One will be taken and the other left."

> "There will be two women grinding together. One will be taken and the other left." (Luke 17:34, 35).

If you are out in the field you are not to start running or climbing a tree. Your redemption is at hand. You will be caught up from the field just as you will be caught up from the roof — that is, if you are ready!

> "Remember Lot's wife. Whoever tries to save his life will lose it, but whoever loses his life will preserve it" (Luke 17:32-35).

The illustration has in view the story of the overthrow of Sodom and Gomorrah in the eighteenth chapter of Genesis, and even the words in Greek, when translated back to Hebrew, hint at the expressions in that chapter. Lot's wife seems to have disliked leaving her home in Sodom and kept looking back until it was too late. She became just a pillar of brimstone and rock.

At these words the disciples no doubt were startled and perhaps for a moment or two sat silently as Jesus detailed the way in which the hand of God would reach down out of heaven and rapture this one or that at the coming of the Lord. At last they blurted out,

> "Where, Lord?"

Maybe they did not really want to know exactly where all this was to happen and meant by "where" what we mean sometimes in modern Hebrew by *eipho*, "where" in the sense of "surely not," or "how can that be?"

In any case Jesus answers their "where."

> "Where the dead body is there the eagles will be gathered together" (Luke 17:37).

This was evidently a kind of proverbial expression, for we find it in Job 39:30. It sounds crude to us but probably not to these men who had so often seen the great, black vultures huddled around the body of a dead animal in the open field or on the dusty road leading to their village.

It simply meant that when their Lord would appear his believers would be found in his presence.

We now add to this description of the last days of the Kingdom of God on Earth — can we call it our KGE? — the words of Prophecy B we discovered in Luke 21.

> "Take heed that you are not led astray, for many will come in my name and say, 'I am he!' and, 'The time is at hand!' Don't go after them.
>
> "And when you hear of wars and tumults, don't be terrified, for this must first take place, but the end is not immediate" (Luke 21:7-11).

Just as normal life continues, so do the local traumas and tragedies of this globe. Probably the following words, too, speak of this unceasing pattern of planetary disasters here and there:

> "Nation will rise against nation, kingdom against kingdom. There will be great earthquakes and in various places famines and pestilences,"

yet these do not portend in themselves the coming of the Lord. They are characteristics of God's kingdom age on earth.

But all this regularity in marrying and giving in marriage and even in what we call natural disasters will one day give way to really large interplanetary signs just before he appears:

> "And there will be signs in sun and moon and stars, and upon the earth distress of nations . . . at the roaring of the sea and waves, men fainting with fear and with foreboding of what is coming on the world, for the powers of the heavens will be shaken.
>
> "And then they will see the Son of Man coming in a cloud with power and great glory (Luke 21:25-27).
>
> "Now when these things begin to take place, look up and raise your heads, because your redemption is drawing near" (Luke 21:25-28).

How long after the frightening signs in such cosmic elaboration will it be before the Lord comes? A day? A week? A few hours? Minutes? Jesus does not say, but it is clear he sees even these last-minute signs as in no way contradicting his warning that the Coming will be sudden:

> "Now take heed to yourselves lest your hearts be weighed down with dissipation and drunkenness and cares of this life, and that day come upon you suddenly like a snare. For it will come upon all who dwell upon the face of the earth.
>
> "Watch at all times, praying that you will have the strength to escape all these things that will take place, and to stand before the Son of Man" (Luke 21:34-36).

It would seem that the words of Luke 12:35-48 came originally at this place:

> "Let your loins be girded and your lamps burning, and be like men who are waiting for their master to come home from the marriage feast, so that they may open to him at once when he comes and knocks.
>
> "Blest are those servants whom the master finds awake when he comes. Amen! I tell you he will gird himself and have them sit at table and he will serve them.
>
> "If he comes in the second watch, or in the third and finds them so, blessed are those servants.

"Know this, that if the householder had known at what hour the thief was coming he would have been awake and would not have left his house to be burglarized.

"You also must be ready, for the Son of Man is coming at an hour you do not expect."

Jesus further underlines the need for expectancy:

"Who then is the faithful and wise servant whom his master has set over his household, to give them their food at the proper time? Blest is that servant whom his master when he comes will find so doing. Amen! I tell you he will set him over all his possessions.

"But if that wicked servant says to himself, 'My master is delayed,' and begins to beat his fellow servants, and eats and drinks with the drunken, the master of that servant will come on a day when he does not know, and will punish him, and put him where the hypocrites are."

It has been noticed that sometimes the second of Jesus' parables involves women instead of men. Apparently Jesus matched this parable of men waiting for the return of their master with the parable of the waiting virgins:

"It will be like ten maidens who took their lamps and went to meet the bridegroom. Five of them were foolish, and five were wise, for when the foolish took their lamps, they took no oil with them, but the wise took flasks of oil with their lamps.

"As the bridegroom was delayed they all slumbered and slept.

"But at midnight there was a cry, 'Behold the bridegroom is coming. Come out to meet him.' Then all those maidens rose up and trimmed their lamps.

"And the foolish said to the wise, 'Give us some of your oil, for our lamps are going out.' But the wise replied, 'There may not be enough for both us and you. Go to the dealers and buy for yourselves.'

"And while they went to buy, the bridegroom came, and those that were ready went in with him to the marriage feast, and the door was shut.

"Afterward the other maidens came also and said, 'Lord, lord, open to us.' But he replied, 'I tell you I do not know you!'

"Watch therefore, for you (plural) do not know either the day or the hour" (Matthew 25:1-13).

From the beginning of this book I have been trying to say that Jesus is in every way a shock for a great many modern people. He heals without prayer and casts out demons with a simple command. He talks of himself in words of ancient Scripture that God himself used long ago. He accepts the highest accolade Israel could give: "the Messiah of God." He quietly forms a movement which he says will expand from Israel and become an enormous force in history, fulfilling as it grows the visions of the Prophets for a golden age.

And, finally, he says that earth's history will come to a close when in his Father's time he himself will appear in great honor and power to bring joyfully into "the world to come" those who have loved him and kept his commandments.

There is simply no way to look at the words of Jesus and not come up with this solemn, shocking picture.

Nor when we study this picture is there any way we can avoid directly confronting this Man of Galilee. He is either that one he says he is, as echoed by a billion followers today, or he is the most successful "con" man in history. If he is the former — as I must confidently affirm after these blessed years of study in Israel — the only thing worthwhile is to fall on this Stone rejected by the builders, and be broken, or fall beneath the Stone as it descends in judgment, and be crushed.

But why should anyone make the second choice?

It is often supposed that when the disciples asked Jesus whether "at this time" he would return the Kingdom to Israel they were wondering if he would set up immediately a political kingdom such as that David the king had ruled over. As we have seen Jesus does not use the expression "Kingdom of God" (evidently meant here by "kingdom") as other than the spiritual one he heads. We must understand the disciples' question in the light of Matthew 21:43 where Jesus prophesies that the Kingdom of God—his Movement—would be taken away from its homeland. The book of Acts tells us that is what happened to the early Church.

39 LEAD ON, KING JESUS!

I should have liked to write somewhere before this last chapter about Jesus' prophecy of his future judgment of the Gentiles (wrongly understood as the Judgment of the Nations in the sense of England, Germany or the U.S.A.) found in Matthew 25:31-46. As in all his prophecies Jesus speaks with great authority and foreknowledge and the passage shows the usual power and passion of Hebrew prophetic poetry.

But I am sorry to say that although it is clear Jesus must have uttered these words of prophecy in some connection with his prophecy of Return, I have been unable to find just how that connection appeared originally. Perhaps at some future time this matter will be clearer.

What seems of no doubt to me, however, is the relationship of that last great prophecy we have just studied to the question of the disciples in Acts 1:6ff, in which they ask,

> "Lord, will you at this time restore the Kingdom to Israel?"

to which Jesus replies,

> "It is not for you to know times and seasons which the Father has fixed in his own authority, but you shall receive power when the Holy Spirit has come upon you, and you shall be my witnesses in Jerusalem and in all Judea and Samaria and to the end of the earth."

About Jesus' answer students of this passage have been in general agreement: Jesus is prophesying that in a short time there would come a powerful anointing of the Spirit of God on the whole band of followers somewhat like that when Saul joined the band of prophets and spoke in words of prophecy, or the ancient prophets were "moved by the Spirit" (compare I Samuel 10:1-13; also Numbers 11:24-30).

And, just as Jesus predicted, the Holy Spirit fell on the disciples in the upper room and the entire story is told in the early verses of the second chapter of the Acts. We will come shortly to make a few remarks about this event but for now let me comment on the question of the disciples:

> "Lord, will you at this time restore the Kingdom to Israel?"

I have been saying all along that Jesus meant by "the Kingdom of God" essentially that with him had come a new divine rule and penetration into the affairs of men. Through his leadership miraculous and divine intervention was occurring, people were being healed and delivered from Satanic power, and by accepting him as their guide and Messiah were being brought into his Movement, which Jesus called the Kingdom of God.

We saw that Jesus foresaw and forewarned the Temple authorities that "the Kingdom of God" would be taken away from them and given to a people "who would bring forth the fruits thereof" and that a right understanding of this prediction involves seeing that the people, the Movement, of Jesus, would one day be withdrawn from the body politic of Israel. We have excellent evidence that Jesus consistently used this phrase in just this way and there is no reason to think that the disciples, or for that matter, the Temple priests, supposed Jesus meant anything else.

We also noticed that Jesus at the last Passover spoke of his Father's having given him a kingdom or rule and that he would be sharing this rule with his chosen apostles, apparently after his resurrection.

It is simply impossible to suppose that the apostles were thinking by their question that Jesus might at sometime restore some kind of Davidic political rule. The idea that this is what they meant has become so much a part of modern Christian thinking that all of us automatically suppose that that is what the apostles meant.

I am saying that when the apostles spoke of whether "at this time" Jesus was going to "restore the Kingdom to Israel" they were asking Jesus whether he was planning to bring the Kingdom back some time in the future, after it had been separated from Israel. Would Jesus set up again his Movement among the people of Israel?

We must remember that these Jewish followers of Jesus had up till now known no other form of the Kingdom movement except that fully associated with the land and reality of Israel. They had moved around the country with Jesus leading and ministering, and had even had a taste of a two-by-two mission when Jesus had sent them out to heal. Obviously they felt an attachment, even a sentimental attachment, to this way of living in which Jesus woke them up in the morning and walked before them day by day.

It is also clear that as yet the Kingdom movement had not been removed from the land of Israel. The phrase "at this time" cannot therefore be a reference to the time in which the disciples are asking the question.

If I am right the only meaning to the phrase "at this time" must be in pointing out the time in the future when Jesus would return, when he would come and "every eye see him."

In other words, just after Jesus' powerful description and prophecy of his future appearing at the end of the age the disciples asked,

> "Lord, will you *at this time* (at the Appearing) restore the Kingdom to Israel"? (Acts 1:6).

In this book we have become accustomed to having to put passages together as they must have stood in the earlier story of Jesus, both that in Hebrew and the Greek copy of the same. That is what we apparently have to do with the passages before us. We must put together Jesus' words in

Luke 17 and 21
Luke 12:35-48
Matthew 25:1-13, and then *add* these words from Acts 1:6-8.

Did the disciples suppose that at the coming of Jesus at the end of the age Israel would still exist even after, perhaps, the desolation Jesus had said to the people in the Temple would come? Would such a future nation of Israel receive back into it Jesus' Kingdom of God? Could the Kingdom Movement be reintroduced in some form to the nation in its land again?

We really do not have enough information to answer these questions.

But I sometimes wonder if we are not seeing even in the State of Israel today the reintroduction of the Kingdom Jesus leads through the Holy Spirit. I personally know hundreds of people in this State who either secretly or openly claim Jesus of Nazareth as Messiah. If this is true the question of the disciples would illustrate just what Jesus said in answering it:

> "It is not for you to know the times and seasons which the Father has fixed by his own authority" (Acts 1:7).

The Father may right now be restoring the Kingdom to Israel!

However that may be Jesus certainly pressed his disciples for the moment in one direction: to wait in Jerusalem until they would be endued with power from on high.

> "You will receive power when the Holy Spirit has come upon you, and you shall be my witnesses in Jerusalem and in all Judea and Samaria and to the end of the earth" (Acts 1:8).

When Jesus earlier sent out the twelve he commissioned them only to "go the lost sheep of the house of Israel" (Matthew 10:5, 6). Now he sends them to the entire world. They must move beyond the borders of Israel — go, go, go in his name.

We read that with these words, as they were looking on,

> he was lifted up and a cloud took him out of their sight" (Acts 1:9).

We call this the Ascension.

Two men stand by the disciples. They are dressed in white robes and they say,

> "Men of Galilee, why do you stand looking into heaven? This Jesus, who was taken up from you into heaven, will come in the same way as you saw him go into heaven" (Acts 1:11).

The disciples keep standing there awhile, but at last they move silently down the mountain towards Jerusalem.

Ten days later they are in the Temple.

> And suddenly a sound came from heaven like the rush of a mighty wind, and it filled all the house where they were sitting. (Some interpreters understand "the house" as the Temple.) (Acts 2:2).

Tongues of fire stood upon the heads of all the people in the crowd.

> And they were all filled with the Holy Spirit, and began to speak in other tongues (tongues they did not naturally know) as the Spirit gave them utterance (Acts 2:4).

There were Jews from all over the known world in Jerusalem just at that time, for it was the Feast of Shavuoth, or Pentecost. They heard all the commotion, came running together and were amazed and bewildered at the sound of each of these Galilean Jews speaking languages they did not know themselves but which the hearers understood.

> "Are not all these who are speaking Galileans? How is it that we are hearing each of us in his own native tongue?" (Acts 2:7, 8).

Ancient prophecy has been characterized as "ecstatic," out of oneself. The prophet is removed, as it were, from the usual interconnection between mind and matter and speaks with the words of a supernatural spirit. Visions and utterances predicting some future happening flow from the mouth of the seer and in Hebrew prophecy there is exhortation that the hearers will be obedient to God's warnings and instructions involving the future.

Prophets like Joel many centuries before the period of the second Temple had spoken of a time when the God of Israel would "pour out his spirit on all flesh," on sons and daughters, on old men and young men and "even on menservants and maidservants" (Joel 2:28, 29).

God would not limit his prophetic gifts to a select body of professional prophets but would spread out his heavenly knowledge and spiritual gifts to all kinds of human beings, regardless of class, gender or position. It was a thrilling thing to think about.

For a great many years since the days of the great Prophets Israel had, admittedly, heard the voice of the Lord directly through prophets only rarely. There is a story which comes from the age of the Maccabees, some one hundred and fifty years before the time of Jesus, which tells about the deliverance of the city of Jerusalem from the hands of pagan soldiers from the north. The story tells of the finding of a great stone which was judged to have once been a part of the temple compound of Solomon. However, no one knew exactly where the stone once lay in the holy area, so, after much consideration, those who found it rolled it to a place above the Kidron on the east of the city and laid it gently in an exposed spot, because, as they said, "we must wait for a prophet to come and tell us where to put the stone."

The rabbinic sources take it for granted that prophecy had ceased after the period of the Old Testament writing prophets, although sometimes the hope was expressed that God would someday bring back both prophets and prophecy again when Messiah should come. The book of Acts is witness to the fact that among Jesus' followers prophecy and direct answers to prayer became the rule in the company of the early Jewish believers in Jesus.

That is a story in itself. Peter and the other leaders go out laying hands on people and healing them. Demons are cast out. One apostle is moved supernaturally and bodily from one physical place to another miles away. Prison doors are twice opened miraculously. Paul is bitten by a poisonous snake but shakes it off and survives.

The letters of Paul, written later, are full of references to signs and wonders which accompanied his message of salvation in the name of Jesus as he went from synagogue to synagogue in Asia Minor. Thousands of Gentiles already attracted to the moral character of the Jewish community and the Greek Scriptures became followers of Jesus and began to build Jesus-synagogues of their own.

No matter what has happened through the years to separate Jews and Christians no one can argue against one simple fact:

Christianity is a Jewish faith.

It is also a faith that rediscovers Jesus and His Kingdom of Heaven again and again. Its followers by the millions seek somehow to hear the words of Jesus as summarized apparently by some early Greek believer in filling out the torn ending of the Gospel of Mark:

> Go into all the world and preach
> the Gospel to every creature.
>
> He who believes and is baptized
> will be saved but he who does
> not believe will be condemned.
>
> And these signs will follow those who believe:
> In my name they will cast out demons
> They will speak in new tongues . . .
> They will lay their hands on the sick
> and they will recover.
>
> Mark 16:15-18

40 SUMMING UP

Someone has said that a book always needs a final summing up, a last chapter which gives the author a chance to clear up some point or other or to emphasize something he may already have said. He may also find it good to add a few words on some important subject he did not manage to mention.

Let me briefly put down here some points of emphasis.

I have said very little about the Pharisees. This is partly because the relationship of the Pharisees to Jesus is not easy to determine.

On the one hand the Pharisees show friendship to Jesus at least once, when they warn him of the evil intentions of Herod towards him (Luke 13:31), and Jesus suggests at least once to his hearers that the things taught by the Pharisees should be heeded even if their religious ways were somehow hypocritical and not to be emulated (Matthew 23:3).

On the other hand the author of the First Reconstruction seems to have caused Luke to identify opponents of Jesus as Pharisees when Mark and Matthew do not so identify them (*cf.* Luke 5:17 with Mark 2:1 and Matthew 9:1; *cf.* also Luke 6:7 with Markan-Matthaean parallels). Later Mark and Matthew tend to make the same kind of identifications at points Luke does not do so!

The expression "scribes and Pharisees" (in Mark it is often Pharisees and scribes) surely becomes in this way stereotypic — probably the original usage is by Jesus in Matthew 23:3.

Thus the proliferation of the term Pharisees is much more editorial than theological. Apparently the First Reconstructor began this editorial use of the term and it was picked up by Luke himself and in their own way by Mark and Matthew.

What is important here is that in working over Greek texts considerably removed from the culture of Jews and Jesus our Greek writers have uncritically and with no special malice towards existing cults simply added the term Pharisees as a kind of foil or literary plumbline — if Jesus at that time had opponents they must have been Pharisees, or so they supposed.

This same tendency to stereotyping an expression occurs in Matthew's recording of Jesus' strong words to the Pharisees. Here Matthew adds to the name Pharisees "hypocrites" again and again (Matthew 23:12-29, *cf.* with Luke 11:39-47) while no such continuous use occurs in the Lukan parallel, itself an indication that the source of Matthew and Luke had no "hypocrites" in such a section.

It is thus my conviction that this kind of simple literary editorializing by later Greek writers in no essential way detracts from the remarkably authentic core of the units and stories in our Synoptic Gospels. Our writers have on occasion picked up a stereotypic expression and applied it themselves to some text or another but it is usually easy enough to detect these additions and get back to the earlier form of the text.

I am sorry, too, that I was unable to discuss the units which evidently once formed a complete story about Jesus' preaching of "the Word of God."

We know this in connection with the Parable of the Sower, one of the most influential parables known to Christian students and preachers.

Probably this story started with the story of Jesus' mother and brothers coming to visit Jesus and finding him surrounded by many people (Luke 8:19-21). Someone said to Jesus,

> "Your mother and brothers are on the outside trying to see you."

Making a point, Jesus said,

> "My mother and brothers are those who hear the word of God and do it."

It may be at just this point that a woman shouted from the crowd:

> "Blessed is the womb that bore you
> and the breasts that suckled you " (Luke 23:29).

Jesus responds:

> "Yea, rather, blessed are those who hear the word of God and keep it (Luke 11:27, 28).

If we then attach Jesus' story of the Sower going forth to sow (Luke 8:5-8), dropping out the verses (9, 10) Flusser suggests belong in Luke 10 and add the interpretation of the Parable (Luke 8:11-15) we come easily to a second parable, the House Built on the Rock (Luke 6:47-49;

Matthew 7:24-27) as the probable completion of the original story.

> "Everyone who hears these words of mine
> and does them will be like a wise man who
> built his house upon a rock. . . .

As we have seen all through this book it is altogether like Jesus to equate his own words with those of his Father. Here his own words are the Word of God itself.

Other deficiencies will be found in my book, of course, and none is as aware of them as I.

Let me, however, emphasize just here some of the reasons I have felt I must write what I have written.

The first is that to my knowledge almost no modern author of a work on the Life of Jesus has insisted that our Gospel texts must first be translated from the Greek to Hebrew before they can be fully understood.

It is almost universally said that Jesus spoke and taught in Aramaic. Along with a few others, I am saying that both the external and internal evidence is that Jesus taught in Hebrew. For a simple statement of the external evidence I suggest the book by Roy Blizzard and David Bivin, *The Difficult Sayings of Jesus* (Center for Judaic-Christian Studies, P.O.B. 293040, Dayton, OH, 45429).

For details about how retranslating our Greek texts to Hebrew throws light on Jesus' sayings I refer to the pages which precede. Here are some of the results I would emphasize.

1. The body of our Greek stories in Luke and often in Matthew are almost always Hebrew-Greek, that is, we can understand them best when we translate them back literally to Hebrew. Often enough there are introductory phrases in the given unit which are clearly later — added by our writers or a compiler before them. We can sometimes detect these secondary notes because the Greek is non-Hebraic.

2. For the most part Mark's Gospel resists direct, idiomatic retranslation from Greek to Hebrew. This means that we must look to Luke and the non-Mark-like parts of Matthew to get our earliest text. Luke and Matthew, as sources, are extremely rich and we can have confidence that we possess the greatest part of the original biography of Jesus written by the Matthew of tradition.

3. Quite a number of Greek words and expressions show that their range of meaning is Hebraic. For instance, the word righteousness, as used in Matthew, is definitely Hebraic in use, its meaning more salvation, vindication, and redemption than what is meant in either Greek or English by our word righteousness, which means to us something like strong, personal goodness or correctness. In Hebrew righteousness is an *outgoing*, redemptive concern for those in need.
4. Retranslation of some words of great theological value can greatly help in our understanding. For instance, the Messianic title Son of Man which Jesus clearly adopted from Daniel 7:13 and which may be described as the most deity-laden messianic expression in the Old Testament is often used by Jesus in an oblique reference to himself. It is a barbarism in Greek but points to the concept of the Divine Messiah — one like the Angel of the Lord in the Old Testament who prophesies and speaks in his own name in manifesting God on earth.
5. Retranslation of the phrase Kingdom of God or Kingdom of Heaven immediately makes it necessary to recognize it as a term developed by the Pharisees. As used by them it is a spiritual concept. It is definitely not what many historians have supposed, a term involving the hope of a physical messiah sitting on a throne ruling the world. Jesus means by it the penetration of God's power through him to the plane of earth and he includes only those who have heard him say "Follow me" and have obeyed. The Kingdom is his *messianic movement* and it will one day give way to the "world to come" which is beyond earth and history. A secondary, editorial use of the term is like that in Luke 17:20, 21 where it is equated with the phrase the coming of the Son of Man (*cf.* vs. 22), but in original contexts Jesus always speaks of the Kingdom of God as having come with his advent (see my Appendix).

Some of what I have written is not new but I believe the use of the tool of retranslation often confirms views which would be described today as old and valuable. Most of what is being taken for granted among New Testament scholars today assumes that our synoptic materials cannot give us an accurate picture of Jesus and the things he taught. The evidence collected by myself, Professor Flusser and others who have been working along these lines — mainly in Jerusalem —

suggests a far more conservative picture and gives reason to declare that our materials are as a whole excellent and authentic.

For some who read these lines it may seem a bit strange to find that I understand the relationship of our Gospels to be somewhat different than that usually accepted. However, the conclusions I have reached about this relationship are somewhat alike those proposed by schools of thought which insist that the order of our Gospels is first Matthew, then Luke and, finally, Mark using both Matthew and Luke. This, the Griesbach hypothesis, has come to be accepted by quite a number of scholars despite the fact that it is radically different from the usual hypothesis that Mark wrote first and that his Gospel was used independently as a source by Matthew and Luke. Actually, I see my theory of relationships as inherently nearer the Markan hypothesis than that which asserts any kind of Matthaean priority. I came to the conclusion that Luke did not use Mark but Mark Luke for many reasons. Anyone who is acquainted with the "Proto-Luke" theory which was espoused by strong advocates of Markan Priority will, I think have more sympathy for my view that Luke is used by Mark, but I beg all who are interested in this question to look into the array of evidence I have collected in *A Hebrew Translation of the Gospel of Mark* (Dugith, Baptist House, 1973, Jerusalem).

In the search for the earliest form of the story of Jesus and his words a right theory of the synoptic relationships is sometimes of the greatest importance.

A case in point is the earliest form of the eschatological discourse (sometimes called "the little apocalypse") in the parallels of Matthew 24:1-26, Mark 13 and Luke 21:5-36.

Reams and reams of scholarly papers have been written in an attempt to understand why Jesus seems to mix three themes in his prophecy: a prophecy of the coming destruction of Jerusalem and the Temple, a prophecy of his sudden return and appearance to all of earth's inhabitants and a prophecy which gives details of that which is to happen to his disciples as they go out to witness about him after his departure from them.

The solution has often been sought by carefully exegeting the text of Mark or Matthew. As we have seen earlier it is far easier to separate Luke 21:5-31 into seven separate sections and to note that three of these describe the first theme, three the second theme and one the third theme (*cf.* my book on Mark, pp. 42-44). If we now attach each of the sections to its rightful fellows we can restore as follows:

Destruction of Jerusalem	Second Coming	Disciples' Future
vss. 5-7 20-24 29-32	vss. 8-11 25-28 34-36	vss. 12-18(19)

The explanation of this obviously favorable and justifiable restoration is simple: someone before Luke (probably our First Reconstructor) combined excerpts from three separate prophecies and made of them *one* prophecy. Why this was done is not clear but once we have restored the parts of these prophecies we see that each restoration fits precisely other contexts in which Jesus speaks of the Destruction, the Coming and the Future of the Disciples (see my chapters 32, 37 and 38).

Thus, Jesus gives signs of the coming destruction of Jerusalem but in no way mentions himself as involved personally in the catastrophe.

On the other hand in the second prophecy there are *no signs of his personal return* except those accompanying him as he steps out of heaven so all can see, but he himself is in the center as "the Son of Man" at the Appearance. As we have seen (chapter 38) this absence of warning signs fits Luke 17:22-37 where the Appearance is unheralded even as men and women continue to marry, give in marriage, eat and drink, *etc.*, until the sudden advent of the Son of Man.

Still different are the words of the third prophecy where we need to see them as a part of Jesus' special predictions and instructions to his disciples as they learn to operate in the power of the Holy Spirit after his departure from them. These are but a small portion of the words I have gathered in chapter 37 which I am suggesting were spoken by Jesus to his disciples during the forty days, in which he often appeared to them and "gave them instructions" (Acts 2:1,2).

Some have told me that this last suggestion is one of the most important made in this book. If I am right we have excellent evidence that Jesus carefully prepared his immediate followers at exactly the point in time which was of the greatest importance to them. They were facing a future with a Lord who would be seated above them at his Father's side and available to them no longer visibly but through the Holy Spirit.

Amazingly, the forty-day period is the perfect time to prepare those who had known him on the physical level and were now coming to know him on a different spiritual level — he is no longer with them all the time but comes at intervals to be with them and teach them. How badly they needed this interim period to help them get used to the dispensation of the Holy Spirit! In the goodness of God the forty days of affirmation and preparation formed the bridge to the new way Jesus would continue to lead his believers in the age of the Edah, the Church, the continuing Kingdom of Heaven.

One last illustration of the advantage of seeing Luke as our first Gospel. As is well known Mark (and therefore Matthew) preserves much fewer details of the appearances of Jesus after his resurrection than Luke; indeed, Luke's account of the appearances is unhurried and beautifully rich. Unlike Mark, who speaks of expected resurrection appearances in Galilee but does not display them, Luke locates the appearances around Jerusalem. This makes Luke's picture altogether consistent: Jesus tells his disciples to tarry in Jerusalem and he ascends before them on the Mount of Olives in Jerusalem.

Despite the preference of many scholars for Mark, it is surely clear that Luke's account cannot be derived from Mark and the internal evidence of timing, language and geography is so strong that we cannot but find it in every way remarkably trustworthy.

In closing let me simply list what seem to me the most important conclusions detailed in this book:

1. The earliest story of Jesus was biographical. It was not, as so many have contended, a "Gospel tract" more "preaching" than history.

2. This story was written in Hebrew, as affirmed by Papias and other early Church Fathers.

3. Matthew and Luke retain large numbers of units of material which, although in Greek, give certain evidences that they derive from Hebrew originals.

4. The order of these units is often not that of the earlier Hebrew story but the units themselves are so well preserved that we can often combine them to get remarkable, early, longer stories.

5. Luke is the first of our Gospels but Mark has rewritten much of Luke and Matthew has himself followed Mark's rewritten story.

6. All of our Gospel writers know and use units or stories which descend from a Greek translation of the first story of Jesus in Hebrew.
7. This was known to them by a scroll which displayed parts of earlier stories which had been divided into narrative, instructional or parabolic units. Each writer labored to bring back into a continuous story these units as best he could, particularly Luke and Matthew.
8. So well preserved are these units in Luke and Matthew that we can rebuild many of the original stories and thus draw a more original picture of Jesus.
9. It is clear that we have remarkably good sources for studying the life of Jesus. The emerging picture of Jesus shows a Messiah fully consonant with the Jewish culture of his age and fully conscious of his role as a Heaven-sent, divine figure heading a new dispensation and believers' movement (The Kingdom of God) who is yet to be the Judge of the whole world. This is essentially the view of the early Church and it was obviously derived from the historical knowledge of Jesus we find so well expressed in the Gospels of Luke, Mark and Matthew.
10. Once we recognize that the Hebraic-Greek story of Jesus lost its continuity when some writer reorganized the material into episode, teaching (sayings) and parables it becomes clear that there is no reason to suspect that Jesus did not give a number of the now-scattered sayings on a definite occasion. Such sayings were not aphorisms spoken and recorded as totally separate items but originally appeared as part of one or more discourses. A number of these seem to have been a part of the teaching of Jesus in the post-resurrection forty-day period.

All kinds of problems are solved if this suggestion is true.

I am convinced that it is true and that many other suggestions in this book pave the way towards the painting of a clearer picture of Jesus of Nazareth. I extend my thanks to a great many friends who have helped me through the years to come to the conclusions I have stated and most of all to Him whom we have learned to know as Father of all and, especially, Father of our Lord Jesus.

APPENDIX
OUR RECONSTRUCTING EDITOR

In making a proper analysis of the sources of our Synoptic Gospels I have suggested that it is imperative that we recognize that Luke had two principal sources, the first, which we have called the REORGANIZED SCROLL, and the second, the First Reconstruction, or RECREATED STORY which was a short continued story of the life of Jesus built on the REORGANIZED SCROLL.

The REORGANIZED SCROLL (we may refer to it as RS) was the result of an editor who decided to put together all the narrative incidents he found in the Greek biography, then all the discoursive or teaching sections he found in individual stories, and finally all the parables, many of which were "twin" parables. To do this he was obliged to separate the materials found in a number of longer stories as to whether they could be classified as

1) Incident
2) Teaching, or
3) Parables.

From certain things said in the first four verses of Luke's Gospel it seems clear that early writers on the life of Jesus tried to find ways to restore as far as possible the order of the stories and sayings of Jesus which had characterized the Hebrew biography of Jesus and the Greek translation of this biography. However, they seem no longer to have had either the Hebrew or Greek versions of the original story and were obliged to do the best they could to recover the sequence of the units they found in the REORGANIZED SCROLL. Luke appears to have found the work of an author who had obviously used the RS and chosen from it the units he felt could help him to present a more connected narrative of Jesus' life.

We know this First Reconstruction (FR) or RECREATED STORY only through study of Luke and the fact that Luke preserves parallel texts (the "doublets of Luke") from both RS and FR, and thus gives us a way of comparing the two texts.

From the evidence I have been able to gather there are certain things we can know about the style and contents of these two sources. The first is that as Luke uses RS (and to a certain extent Matthew, who knows RS, does the same) he transmits a "clean" Hebrew-Greek text which as a rule easily translates back to Hebrew, usually retaining Hebrew word order and Hebraisms of many kinds (Matthew follows the same principle when not copying from Mark's Gospel). The second is that FR presented a less Hebraic text and often has what we may call editorial inserts which apparently represent the ideas and understandings of this editor.

The reason the REORGANIZED SCROLL has Greek texts which translate back to Hebrew so easily must be that little or no change was made in copying the Greek materials from the earlier, very literally-translated, Greek text of the Greek biography of Jesus. The editor of RS simply separated the longer stories he found on the basis of our incidents, teachings, and parables. The teaching units he placed together often without even adding any editorial "bridge" to connect them. The same was true of the parables. Occasionally he placed together sayings (which appeared originally in quite different contexts) on the basis of some common word in the newly joined texts: one of these we saw in Matthew 7:21 where "Lord, Lord" appears in a text dealing with people joining the Kingdom of God during Jesus' ministry while next to this, in Matthew 7:22, 23 we find "Lord, Lord" in a text dealing with the judgment at the end of the age.

This latter tendency of the author of RS has led to the idea that RS is essentially a "topical" text. However, it appears that the editor who lifted such teachings sections from distant contexts only joined texts with word associations when he happened to notice these associations. Most of the time he simply joined incident to incident, teaching to teaching, and parables to other parables. He was, in fact, a *reorganizer* who carefully copied his materials and preserved the texts exceedingly well even while categorizing them according to incident, teaching and parable.

The person (our FR) who drew units from RS and made a first reconstruction from it had other purposes. He wanted to "draw up an ordered account of the events which occurred among us," to use Luke's words in Luke 1:1. He chose episodes about John the Baptist and then about Jesus from RS and tried to give them the most original order he could. He seems to have done a very commendable job but very often did not know how a teaching unit needed to be added to an incident unit or two parables added to a teaching unit. This is abundantly clear from the researches of Flusser and myself — it would be impossible for us to succeed in putting together these "hidden" stories in the way I have explained had the editor of the FIRST RECONSTRUCTION understood this matter better.

For our purposes here, however, what we must note is that our First Reconstructor felt it necessary *to add an occasional editorial sentence or make minor verbal changes* now and then in an effort to bind together his chosen units and to given an intelligent sequence to them. As a rule our Reconstructor does not interfere greatly with the texts from RS he chooses, but this is not always true and we can sometimes check for originality the verbal accuracy by retranslation to Hebrew or by comparison of some passage in Luke with a parallel found only in Matthew — Matthew uses RS but in some parallels Luke uses FR even when he apparently has the same unit in RS.

Luke, for instance, seems to have copied the story of Levi, the tax collector, from our Reconstructor (Luke 5:27-32) but the continuation of this story from the REORGANIZED text (Luke 15:4-10).

Luke's version of what we call the sermon on the plain (Luke 6:17-49) has many of the same sayings as Matthew's Sermon on the Mount (Matthew 5, 6, 7) but the verbal differences are serious. The explanation appears to be due to the changes made by the editorial hand of the Reconstructor, whose work was used by Luke but not by Matthew. If we look for the earliest text Matthew is unquestionably closer at this point.

We have already found it necessary to separate the prophetic discourse in Luke 21:5-36 into seven interlarded sections, three of which belong to one prophecy, three to a second, and one to a third. This special treatment of parts of three different prophecies of Jesus appears to be the work of our Reconstructor. Happily he has changed the prophetic texts much less than the sequence of the materials, as we can say with much certainty by retranslating to Hebrew.

However, it appears that a number of our Reconstructor's editorial notes have caused many a theological headache for interpreters of the Gospels. For example, the German scholar, William Wrede, found in studying the Gospel of Mark (which he supposed was a source of both Matthew and Luke) that one of the things Mark mentioned often was an idea which Wrede labelled *Das Messiasgeheimnis*, the Messianic Secret. Wrede wrote a book by this name in 1901 and in it brilliantly argued from many passages that Mark's Gospel was essentially an apology attempting to explain why the Jews of the time of Jesus rejected him as Messiah.

Wrede wrote that Mark imposed on the Gospel stories his belief that Jesus deliberately "hid his Messiahship" and that was the reason Jews could not believe in him.

I think it is possible to prove that in actuality many of the passages Wrede used to prove his thesis are, as so often in Mark, elaborations of some of *the notes of our Reconstructor* which Mark read in Luke, especially in Luke chapters four through nine.

It is clear that the editor of FR interpreted several Gospel stories as suggesting that Jesus *did* hide his Messiahship. He seems to have copied the very first story of a demonized man in the synagogue of Capernaum with accuracy (Luke 4:33-37). In this account Jesus tells the demon to "be quiet and come out of him." And, as a result, the victim is convulsed but delivered. A few verses later (Luke 4:41) the Reconstructor apparently adds an editorial note about healings in the evening:

> And demons came out of many, crying and saying, "You are the Son of God." And he rebuked them and did not allow them to speak because they knew that he was the Messiah.

There are other reasons which would normally be thought to explain why Jesus made the demons in the synagogue be quiet, one being that they were known to be great liars, but the introduction of the word Messiah and the reason given in the Luke 4:41 summary does indeed look as if our Reconstructor had concluded Jesus was beginning to hide his Messiahship.

The same kind of explanation occurs in connection with the story of the leper whom Jesus sends to the priests to get clearance that his leprosy has been cleansed (Luke 5:14). Our editor uses the words "and he *strictly forbade* him to tell anyone" as a part of Jesus' instructions to the leper. In a story farther on a young girl is raised from her deathbed and exactly these words are used by Jesus, "... he *strictly forbade* them to tell anyone the thing that had happened" (Luke 8:56). Similarly, in Luke 9:21 the same words appear again at the end of the declaration of Peter that Jesus is God's Messiah, for there we read that Jesus rebuked his disciples and "*strictly forbade* them to tell anyone this thing."

In all probability our Reconstructor had no intention of starting a doctrine that would trouble twentieth century New Testament scholars to the point that they would deny the essential historicity of Mark or our other Gospels. But, along with two or three other editorial sentences, there is little doubt that our editor of FR made an interpretation which at least explained to him why Jesus caused a demon to keep quiet, a leper to go to the priest, a mother and a father secretly watch their daughter rise from her deathbed, and why there was shock and surprise when Peter confessed Jesus through a kind of holy revelation. We have already noted in Luke 8:10 the use of a saying of Jesus which probably belonged originally near Luke 10:24 and which suggests in Luke's context that Jesus deliberately used parables to keep men from understanding. Such an idea (as Wrede knew) turns the normal reason for using parables on its head. Parables, by nature and usage, are intended to clarify and underline.

Sometimes just one word in Greek will reveal the presence of an editorial note in FR.

For instance, Luke uses the word *pleyn*, "but" or "on the contrary" fifteen times in a special way known only in his Gospel. By looking at this usage in Luke it is easy to detect the hand of our Reconstructor and even something of what he thought. Let us use "BUT" to represent *pleyn*.

In Luke 6:35 we find

> "BUT love your enemies and do good to them"

after Jesus has already earlier in the passage said the same thing.

In Luke 10:11 we find

> "BUT know this, that the Kingdom of God has drawn near,"

after exactly the same thing has been said without *pleyn* just two verses prior to this.

There is no such repetition in Matthew's general parallels to these passages. What is more interesting is that in Luke 11:41 we read,

"BUT give for alms those things that are within"

where the Matthaean parallel has nothing of the kind.

Perhaps the most interesting is this from Luke 18:8:

"BUT when the Son of Man comes, will he find *the* faith on earth?"

Now this strange verse is all the stranger because it comes after Jesus has just said emphatically that God will certainly "vindicate his elect" (Luke 18:7). Moreover this is the only place in our Synoptic Gospels where "the" faith as a phrase appears. We hear in Acts 15:22 that Paul encouraged the believers in places like Antioch to continue in "the" faith and the same expression is used a couple of times in one of Paul's letters to Timothy, but it is un-Hebraic and quite unlike Jesus. The verse is surely added by our Reconstructor and represents some kind of pessimistic view he entertained about things in general, or the future.

The failure to recognize editorial notes of this kind can be seriously misleading. There have probably been thousands of sermons preached about some kind of future apostasy in which the preacher describes in great detail the coming "apostasy at the times of the end." One pastor whom I know told me he once thought this negative verse was very important and portrayed a near apostasy already begun. He said he began to warn his church members about the coming apostasy and insisted on it so long that little by little his whole congregation apostasized — left his church for good!

Now, contrary to what some extreme critics might like to think, these editorial comments and occasional minor changes can usually be corrected with relative ease, partly by using the control of retranslating to Hebrew, partly by comparing the usual Matthaean parallel, and partly on the basis of normal philological analysis. The basic authenticity and accuracy of our materials in Matthew and Luke is excellent and there really is no room for the radical skepticism of many modern students of the Gospels.

Let me close this small excursus about the occasional editorial phrases introduced by our First Reconstructor by referring to the special use he seems to have made of the expression "the Kingdom of God." *For him the expression Kingdom of God could be used as synonymous with the coming of the Son of Man.* A little reflection will show that this is not the usual way in which Jesus talks about the Kingdom of God. For Jesus — many texts show it — the Kingdom of God or Heaven emphasizes the way in which he through "the finger of God" heals and successfully confronts Satan and his demonic powers.

He, as King of the Kingdom of God, gathers more and more subjects for this Kingdom who will become the spearhead of God's healing and delivering power after he no longer is himself physically leading the Movement.

Yet someone has added a quite different meaning of the expression Kingdom of God to several of our Gospel passages, especially and almost completely in Luke. In philological research we call this a secondary usage. It is apparently the usage adopted by our Reconstructor.

We can perhaps see this special meaning given to the Kingdom of God best by comparing the two versions of the parable of the talents (Matthew 25:14-30 and Luke 19:11-27). In Matthew a man who owns slaves goes away and leaves five "talents" of money to one of his slaves, two to another and one to a third servant. When he returns he asks what they have done with the money entrusted to them. By lending the money out the one who received five talents had increased his holdings to ten and the one who received two had doubled his money as well, but the one who received only one talent had gone and had dug a hole in the ground and buried it for safety. The owner commends the first two and says to them "Enter into the joy of your lord," but to the third he says,

> "You knew that I harvest where I did not sow and gather where I have not winnowed. You should have deposited my silver with the bankers and I should then have come and received my interest" (Matthew 25:26, 27).

Now because this parable mentions a man "going away" yet later expected to come back and demand an accounting with his servants it is taken for granted in both Matthew and Luke that it is a story about Jesus' going away in his ascension and coming back at the end of the age. More than a story about the coming of the Son of Man, the parable however seems to be a story illustrating the right use of money. It is probably the twin of the Parable of the unjust steward (Luke 16:1-12), which deals with the same subject, but it is in the Luke version that we see how the Parable is elaborated until it becomes not one but two parables.

In Luke the Parable is introduced by the words,

> . . . He told them another parable, since they were near Jerusalem and they thought that the Kingdom of God was about to appear" (Luke 19:11).

According to Luke (but not Matthew) the man went away to a far land *to receive a kingdom*. As in the Parable in Matthew he gives money to three slaves and tells them to do business with the money he has given them until he returns.

Meantime, however, according to Luke, we hear that there were certain "citizens" of his who hated him and sent a delegation after him saying that they did not want him *to rule over them*.

Later the man returns with his kingdom securely in his possession, calls his servants, and commends two of them because they had increased his money, but punishes the third because he had hidden it "in a cloth."

However, the story is not finished, because he must deal with the "citizens" who had hated him. We then find our editorial *pleyn* appearing,

> "BUT those enemies of mine who did not want me to rule over them bring them out and slaughter them before me" (Luke 19:27).

Obviously it is our Reconstructor who has had a hand in mixing a second theme into a parable which teaches about stewardship of possessions. What is more important for us here is to note that the second theme involves speaking of the Kingdom of God as "appearing."

Now we know that the word "appearing" is used of the personal return of the Son of Man in some of Paul's letters and its idea is at the base of Jesus' words when he says in Luke 21:27 that "they shall see the Son of Man coming in great power and glory." The thought that the Kingdom of God will "appear" is evidently our Reconstructor's way of saying that — as he understands it — Jesus was thought to be about to appear in Jerusalem as the Son of Man in power and glory. No, says our editor, Jesus told this parable to show that he would go away to a far country and only return later — the Kingdom of God was not about to appear at the time of Jesus' last visit to Jerusalem. But the King would get his "Kingdom" and come back, and at that time would punish the people who did not want him to rule over them.

It is probable that because of this edited version (and perhaps because of some of John's visions in the book of Revelation) the coming of the Lord has been depicted by a great many Christian artists as not only a moment of great glory but also as Jesus' personal victory over his enemies — he usually holds a two-edged sword and frowns angrily as he prepares to slaughter them.

Once again, how easily we can err when we do not recognize the editorial comments of an author like our Reconstructor. Nor is this the only place we find our editor using the Kingdom of God as a synonym for the coming of the Son of Man. In Luke 21:31, in a passage which has to do with a context in which Jesus compares the signs of the destruction of Jerusalem to the budding of the fig tree just before summer we read,

> "You too, when you see these things happening, know that the Kingdom of God is near."

In the parallels of Mark and Matthew we have only

> "You too, when you see these things happening, know that *it* is near, even at the doors."

At this point Mark rejects this secondary use of the Kingdom of God, as does Matthew, who simply copies Mark. However, our Reconstructor, as I have already suggested, was responsible for the interlarding of the three prophecies in Luke 21, and now shows us how he is interpreting the fig tree illustration. For him the coming of the Son of Man is expressed by the phrase "the Kingdom of God is near." By putting together parts from two different prophecies he interprets the budding of the fig tree as a sign of the coming of the Son of Man.

Here again allow me to remark that the failure to perceive these rather small editorial changes has resulted in a great deal of misunderstanding on the part of interpreters and ordinary readers of these passages alike. Such readers are hardly to be blamed if they suppose Jesus' words about "this generation" not passing away until all is fulfilled means the "generation" when the Lord returns, not the generation Jesus was speaking to who would see the destruction of Jerusalem. Nevertheless, without a careful analysis of our materials we can easily miss the editorial work imposed on what are otherwise excellent and early texts.

I do not want to mention all the secondary uses of the Kingdom of God which Luke has preserved but one that is of special interest is that found in Luke 17:20, 21. As usually translated it reads,

> Being asked by the Pharisees when the Kingdom of God was coming, he answered them, "The Kingdom of God is not coming with signs to be observed. Nor will they say, 'Lo, here it is!' or 'There!' for behold, the Kingdom of God is in the midst of you."

Almost certainly these two verses are the work of our Reconstructor. This would be clear even from our study of this special use of the Kingdom of God as equal to the expression "the coming of the Son of Man." However, it is the long passage of Luke 17:22-37, which gives us the words of Jesus about his coming and which comes immediately after the quotation above, that is important here.

> He said to his disciples, "The days are coming when you will be very desirous to see one of the days of the Son of Man, but you will not see it.
>
> "And they will say to you, 'Behold here, behold there . . .'"

The key words in the paragraph mentioning the Kingdom of God and the one following, which mentions only the coming of the Son of Man, should be compared (Luke 17:21 with Luke 17:23):

"They will not say 'Behold here or there'"	'Behold there, behold here.'"

What has happened here is that our Reconstructor has given a short summary in Luke 17:21 of the original passage in Luke 17:23ff. We should translate:

> "The Kingdom of God does not come with signs you can see, and they are not going to say, 'Behold here! or there! the Kingdom of God is among you.'"

Or to make it even more explicit as to what our secondary editor is saying:

> "The Son of Man is not coming with signs you can wait for, and people are not going to say, 'Look, the Son of Man is right among you, here he is, there he is.'"

In other words our editor is summarizing and repeating (from Luke 17:23) that Jesus is saying that people at the future time when he will come will *not be going around and saying* that the Son of Man has come and that he is either here or there. Jesus is *not* saying, says our Reconstructor, *that the Kingdom of God is among you* (as we usually think when we read this sentence in our published translations). He is saying only that people will not be able to say the Kingdom of God has come (that the Son of Man has come) and is among you. Why? Because when the Son of Man returns it will be so sudden and certain that every eye shall have seen him and *it will not be necessary to inform anyone* that he "is in the midst of you."

Our translations have so long implied *that Jesus himself* said as a matter of theological information that "the Kingdom of God is among you" and we have so long failed to suppose that the Kingdom of God is an expression here meaning the Son of Man who will come that this text has formed the false basis for all kinds of speculation.

If asked what he knows about the Kingdom of God almost any reader of this passage will answer that he guesses the Kingdom will come some day "like Jesus said it would" but that we can even say today that the Kingdom of God is "among us" or "inside us." What they understand by this phrase is usually that "we have God's Kingdom rule already in our lives."

That is rather a nice idea.

But it is not what this passage means!

Index of Biblical Texts

Old Testament

New Testament

For further information regarding Dr. Lindsey's books, tapes, and articles please send a self-addressed stamped envelope to:

HaKesher, Inc.
9939 S. 71st E. Ave.
Tulsa, OK 74133

To stay informed of the latest research being done by the Jerusalem School, write for their bi-monthly report:

Jesusalem Perspective
P.O. Box 31820
Jerusalem 91317, Israel

For further information regarding the Hebrew Heritage of our Faith, write:

Center for Judaic-Christian Studies
P.O. Box 293040
Dayton, OH 45429